IMMIGRATION AND APOCALYPSE

# Immigration and Apocalypse

## How the Book of Revelation Shaped American Immigration

YII-JAN LIN

Yale
UNIVERSITY PRESS
NEW HAVEN AND LONDON

Published with assistance from the Mary Cady Tew Memorial Fund.

Yale University Press books may be purchased in quantity for educational, business, or
promotional use. For information, please e-mail sales.press@yale.edu (U.S. office) or
sales@yaleup.co.uk (U.K. office).

Set in Electra LT Std type by IDS Infotech, Ltd.
Printed in the United States of America.

Library of Congress Control Number: 2024940435
ISBN 978-0-300-25318-4 (hardcover : alk. paper)

A catalogue record for this book is available from the British Library.

This paper meets the requirements of ANSI/NISO Z39.48-1992
(Permanence of Paper).
10 9 8 7 6 5 4 3 2 1

For my mother, Ching-Lu Lin,

And my father, Bo-In Lin

# CONTENTS

# CONTENTS

# ACKNOWLEDGMENTS

The history I cover in this book extends into the present, and the bones—literal and figurative—of its narratives still lie in the soil across the United States. I felt I could not share these histories unless they were, to paraphrase the Bible, things which I have seen with my eyes, which I have looked at and touched with my hands (1 John 1:1). This would have been impossible without the guides, archivists, and repositories of living memory at each of the sites I visited. I am indebted to Casey Dexter-Lee, my guide at Angel Island State Park, who helped me locate certain poems on the old barracks walls and spent the day with me and my family walking through the buildings and museum; my thanks go also to Edward Tepporn, executive director of the Angel Island Immigration Station Foundation, who met to discuss the project and put me in touch with Casey. I am also grateful to Merlin Garcia, my guide through the quarantine and hospital areas of Ellis Island; Ed Surato at the Whitney Library of the New Haven Museum; Michelle Reynard Georgevich, sexton of the Center Church on the Green of New Haven and my guide through the crypt; the staff at the Mashantucket Pequot Museum and Research Center in Ledyard, Connecticut, and at the Museum of Us in San Diego, California. Special thanks go to Rich Wright, my guide in El Paso and Ciudad Juárez at the border, for bringing to life the history of these two cities.

Numerous colleagues have generously invited me to share and discuss my ideas, and the feedback from them and their communities has been invaluable. I gave the first sketch of the book idea at the International Congress of Ethnic Chinese Biblical Scholars at the Chinese University of Hong Kong in 2014, where I benefited from the feedback of its students and faculty, as well as from Mary Foskett, Timothy Lim, and Gale Yee. I am also grateful to Jacqueline Hidalgo and Phillip Webster, who invited me to speak at Williams College; Olivia Stewart Lester, Michelle Fletcher, and the John's Apocalypse and Cultural Contexts Ancient and Modern section of the Society of Biblical Literature, along with my respondent for that session, Roberto Mata; Kelley Coblentz Bautch, Shayna Sheinfeld, Rodney Alan Caruthers, Gabriele Boccaccini, and the Enoch Seminar; Tat-siong Benny Liew, Caroline Johnson Hodge, and Timothy Joseph, hosts of the Divided Worlds? conference at Holy Cross, and my respondent, Thomas Martin; Garrick Allen, Kelsie Rodenbiker, and the Biblical Interpretation and Theology seminar at the University of Glasgow; Elizabeth Castelli and all the students of the Barnard Religion Salon; Claudia Setzer and the Bible in America section of SBL; Andrew Hui and all those at Yale–National University of Singapore College who hosted me so graciously; and Christine Pae, Boyung Lee, and the scholars in the Antiracist Asian American Feminist Theology project.

I am also grateful to the publishers who allowed for earlier versions of my work to be included here. The material from chapters 3 and 4 appeared in an earlier form as "An Apocalyptic Epidemiology of Foreignness" in *Divided Worlds? Challenges in Classics and New Testament Studies*, edited by Caroline Johnson Hodge, Timothy A. Joseph, and Tat-siong Benny Liew (Atlanta: Society of Biblical Literature Press, 2023), expanded and revised here by permission. Portions of chapters 1 and 2 appeared in an earlier form as "America, the New Jerusalem, and Anti-immigrant Discourse" in *Embodying Antiracist Christianity: Asian American Theological Resources for Antiracism*, edited by Keun-joo Christine Pae and Boyung Lee (London: Palgrave Macmillan, 2024).

I am especially thankful to the American historians who read an early draft of this book as part of a manuscript workshop: David Holland, Chrissy Lau, and Tisa Wenger. Their thoughtful questions and suggestions vastly improved the shape of this book—and any missteps I take are my own. Special thanks go to Chrissy for pointing me toward essential texts, and Tisa as a wonderful resource and advisor to a newcomer in American religious history.

I am surrounded by insightful and inspiring scholars, colleagues, and friends at Yale. Those who helped me bring this book to completion include Laura Nasrallah, mentor and generous reader of chapters; Jacqueline Vayntrub, Donyelle McCray, and Clifton Granby, my writing and conversation partners as the book took shape; Adela Yarbro Collins, who continues as a mentor and endless resource on all things apocalyptic; Timothee Goselin, a constant support in administrative details; Dean Gregory Sterling, who sincerely supports my scholarship in word and deed; and the students with whom I am privileged to share my ideas and from whom I receive resource suggestions, tips on where to eat in San Diego, and memes: Joseph Lee, Jon-Paul Lapeña, Tianruo Jiang, Christopher Atkins, Lizzy Hane, and Hatty Lee.

I am grateful to Heather Gold, my editor at Yale University Press, for her steady guidance of this project from proposal to publication, and also to Elizabeth Sylvia for her ready help along the way. Two anonymous readers read the manuscript carefully and provided insightful and invaluable feedback for improvements. Robin DuBlanc copyedited the manuscript with care and clarity, making my task of reviewing edits easy and smooth.

Many thanks for the research assistance of Kathy Chow in organizing the dates and events of the book for appendix A. Heartfelt thanks go to Anna Cwikla, rapporteur of the manuscript workshop, writing partner, and New Haven Green enthusiast. I am indebted to Susanna Szeto and Joe Leong for a beautiful space in which to think and write, in loving memory of Jonathan. And I could not have persevered without checking in and commiserating with Cuilan Liu.

My parents and sister have, as ever, generously taken on childcare and given me extra time and space to focus, both abroad and at home. Finally, I could not have written this book without the unwavering support of John Noël Dillon: his confidence in my scholarship, wrangling of James and John, and patient, careful listening to probably all of this manuscript read or wrestled with aloud.

A note about the photograph on the cover: I take the use of this photograph seriously. I consulted several colleagues, a few with backgrounds similar to those in the picture, before I decided to use it. I also corresponded with the photographer, Loren Elliott, who gave me the fuller context of the photograph and its subjects. The people in line are migrants from several Central American countries who had been brought across the Rio Grande to Hidalgo, Texas, by human smugglers on the Mexico side of the border. Once on the U.S. side, they searched for the Border Patrol in order to turn themselves in and to seek asylum. The man at the center in red is Jose Luis (last name withheld), from Guatemala, who had crossed with his daughter Joselin, standing in front of him. Joselin and Jose Luis gave the photographer permission both to photograph them and use their names in publishing the photo. I want to thank Joselin and Jose Luis for their generosity.

# Introduction

O beautiful for patriot dream
That sees beyond the years
Thine alabaster cities gleam
Undimmed by human tears!
America! America!
God shed his grace on thee,
Till nobler men keep once again
Thy whiter jubilee!

—*Katharine Lee Bates, "America" (1895)*

I began to think of my own prospects on the other side of Jordan.
Suppose Dennis Kearney, the California sand-lotter, should slip in and
meet me there, would he not be likely to forget his heavenly songs,
and howl once more:
"The Chinese must go!" and organize a heavenly crusade to have me
and others immediately cast out into the other place?

—*Wong Chin Foo, "Why Am I a Heathen?" (1887)*

In the popular sense of the term, *apocalyptic* can aptly describe the experience of immigration, capturing the disaster and catastrophe or fulfillment and rejoicing as one way of life ends and another begins. The term in its literary-historical sense, signifying an ancient genre of Jewish and early Christian literature, seems less applicable. In the study of the ancient world, the label "apocalyptic" is given to texts, such as the book of Revelation (also known as the Apocalypse of John), that describe divine visions or knowledge of other worlds and end times imparted to a seer. This sense of *apocalyptic* seems to have little to do with immigration. But consider this scene from the ancient book of Revelation: "And I saw the dead, great and small, standing before the throne, and books were opened. Also another book was opened, the book of life. And the dead were judged according to their works, as recorded in the books" (20:12).[1] Every traveler who has waited to cross a country's border recognizes this scene. This is where documents must be checked and identities verified before entry, and the wait may seem an eternity.

But the similarities between Revelation's Judgment of the Dead and the procedure at the border between nations are a result of more than just coincidental resemblance, particularly for the United States and its history. Revelation and its apocalyptic vision of the divine city, the New Jerusalem, have served as a central founding myth for America and a powerful metaphor for American identity, belonging, and exclusion. From the beginning, America has been conceptualized as a prophetic destination and as God's shining city, the New Jerusalem.

The heavenly city metaphor has proved politically expedient and effective in promoting the country as exceptional, eternal, and righteous—particularly in portrayals of the United States as a refuge for pilgrims seeking a home. For immigrants arriving at Ellis Island, the Statue of Liberty was supposed to symbolize welcome to "the homeless, tempest-tossed" as she raised her lamp "beside the golden door." These words from Emma Lazarus's oft-quoted poem "The New Colossus," set at the foot of Lady Liberty, help form the positive, nation-of-immigrants narrative of America. The poem also imagines entry into the country as through "the golden door," the apocalyptic Christian symbol of arrival at God's city for God's people. So too, on the other coast of the nation, immigrants entered the country through the Golden Gate, with some stopping first on the heavenly Angel Island.

The national discourse regarding the country's identity and those who make it their home is laced with the imagery and vocabulary of the New Jerusalem. This makes for a compelling portrait of a land of promise destined for greatness, shining with riches, with gates flung wide in welcome. But both popular and biblical apocalyptic narratives contain more than a golden aesthetic and utopian glory; in fact, the term *apocalyptic* today connotes catastrophe first and foremost. Revelation may end with entry into the New Jerusalem—but only for those whose names are written in the Book of Life. The rest are cast into the lake of fire or they lurk in the darkness outside the gleaming walls.

For centuries America has been conceptualized as Revelation's New Jerusalem, and this national metaphor extends also to the ways the country excludes those who are unwanted at the pearly gates. Revelation's text describes the enemies of God as the idolatrous, the criminal, the murderous, the sexually immoral, those marked by disease, the "dogs" outside the city's defensive and enormous walls. So also, American immigration discourse has marked unwanted people groups as essentially heathen, violent, sexually corrupting, both plagued by sickness and a plague themselves, subhuman and bestial, to be kept outside the United States by a great border wall.

The following chapters demonstrate the influence and presence of Revelation's imagery, language, and logic in both the American founding myth and subsequent discourse surrounding immigration. Included in the analysis are political speeches, newspaper articles, political cartoons, sermons, and other media of American public discourse. Analysis focuses on discourse driving popular narratives that often but do not necessarily affect or effect policies and legislation. In some cases discussed in the book, the language of Revelation clearly connects to subsequent immigration policy, but the goal of this book is to show the overall influence of the New Jerusalem metaphor on American immigration ideology and imagination.

Thus, this project might generally be categorized as American interpretation history of the book of Revelation. At a few junctures, however, I present analysis that is not typical historiography but hybrid and interdisciplinary not only in content but in methodology. In sections of the book, particularly chapters 5 and 6, I use the ancient text and its historical context to interpret American immigration dynamics. For example, I read the underlying principles of U.S. immigration and naturalization as parallels to Revelation's Book of Life and Book of Deeds, the heavenly records used to adjudicate entry and citizenship. I do this not because U.S. legislating around entry and citizenship uses the ancient text explicitly but because the foundational concepts of birth, belonging, and oath-taking in America descend genealogically from notions of earthly and heavenly citizenship in the Christian West, whose theology is grounded in Revelation and other biblical texts. As the quintessential text of the heavenly city of God, Revelation has provided themes and concepts of citizenship and political administration through the centuries.

In other instances, as in chapter 7 on walls and borders, I use the U.S. context to interpret the text of Revelation. I do so, for example, in comparing the stadium lighting of the border wall in Tijuana during the 1990s to the radiance of the walls of the New Jerusalem. I thereby interpret the heavenly city's constant light not only as aesthetically pleasing or evidence of God's glorious presence but also as the light of surveillance. This kind of reading veers from the general historiography of the book to take advantage of the productiveness of comparative readings for the benefit of biblical studies, where Revelation has only recently begun to be read in terms of migration.[2]

Thus, in the few sections where I use elements of U.S. immigration to interpret the ancient apocalyptic text, I do so because this expands the understanding of Revelation (and apocalyptic in general) and interprets it as a text of immigration and citizenship—not just in modern interpretation but also in its *ancient* context. Revelation tells the story of migration to a new place, with mechanisms—documentation, gates, and walls—set in place to prevent or aid entry. It details what one must do to enter and be a citizen of the New Jerusalem, and it describes all the horrible climate catastrophes and wars its refugees escape, as well as all the glories waiting for them within its walls. Read in this way, the juxtaposition of U.S. immigration history and Revelation is not as surprising as it may at first seem. Revelation is more than just a text of theology and eschatology—it is also a text shaped by and shaping ideas of peoplehood, migration, entry, and exclusion.

The organization of the book is chrono-thematic, with chapters divided by theme and the contents within each chapter arranged chronologically. I focus on historical flashpoints and critical junctures where the use of Revelation and the New Jerusalem myth are the most apparent in immigration discourse. This book therefore does not offer a comprehensive history of

American immigration, although the analysis runs from European discovery to the time of writing. This book also does not give a comprehensive discussion of apocalypticism in American history but focuses on the presence of Revelation in the country's history of immigration. The speeches, texts, illustrations, and other media I discuss here represent only a wide sampling of the use of Revelation in discussing immigration and the identity of a country. There are many more examples that could be included, and comprehensiveness is impossible, as it always is in such historiography, but I hope readers may use this book to identify further cases of such apocalyptic discourse both in the past and the precarious present.

Additionally, given its focus, this book does not include analysis of the entire text of Revelation but focuses instead on the New Jerusalem, the Judgment of the Dead, the Whore of Babylon, and the infliction of plagues on people marked by the Beast of the Sea. In other words, I highlight and analyze the passages most often used in describing the United States as exceptional and, conversely, most often used against the immigrants that America has wished to exclude, remove, and destroy.

Of course the book of Revelation is not the only biblical text used in conceptualizing the United States or deployed in immigration discourse, nor did it arise ex nihilo from the mind of a late first-century prophet living in the Roman Empire. When relevant to the focus of the book, I discuss other ancient Jewish apocalyptic texts, particularly Daniel and Ezekiel, from which Revelation cribs so much. I also include other biblical texts, such as Exodus, Nehemiah, Matthew, and Romans, as forming the repertoire drawn on by colonizers, politicians, and pundits to justify, inspire, and criminalize.

But Revelation remains a text uniquely important to the American origin myth and to arguments against the inclusion of certain immigrant groups. Within the Christian biblical canon, it is the text that most explicitly portrays Christ as a conqueror who establishes God's kingdom, elements easily reusable for envisioning the establishment of an idealized nation-state. Revelation also contains the most detailed descriptions of the enemies of God: Satan and his angels, the Beast and its worshippers, and the Whore of Babylon. The depictions of their depravity and violence as well as their utter destruction by fire provide a sacred vocabulary for describing an enemy and divine justification for exclusion at the walls of God's city.

A study published in 2022 in the *Journal for the Scientific Study of Religion* found a "strong, positive correlation between believing in supernatural evil and holding restrictive views of immigration," and that "belief in supernatural evil is one of the strongest predictors of stricter immigration attitudes, even compared to other prominent group identifiers, such as political partisanship and religious identity."[3] Throughout this book, speechmakers and writers deploy the language of supernatural evil to create animosity against immigrants. Whether they or their audience personally believe in supernatural evil is unclear—but what is certain is the convenience of using Revelation's narrative and imagery to depict the threat at the gates of God's chosen nation.

Through all the chapters, the New Jerusalem metaphor proves to be a flexible, recyclable, and manipulable myth for American discourses of immigration, citizenship, and exclusion. At times the uses of Revelation's metaphor and language are contradictory, but the nature of apocalyptic literature invites such contradictions, with mysterious imagery and confusing timelines that yield infinite possibilities.

While I do at points include the voices of excluded and exploited immigrants, I focus primarily on the use of Revelation in dominant white nativist discourses and their racialization of peoples categorized as non-white or "white other." I also wish to note that, although I analyze dominant white conceptualizations of race categories, racialization occurs multi-directionally, among, between, and within groups, whether oppressing or oppressed. Much more could be—and has been—said about relational racialization, that is, the continual construction of racial identities among groups, which is relative to and contingent on other racial constructions.[4] An example of this would be the early American categorization of Native peoples as non-white so that because of their indigenous identity, Mexican Americans would later also be racialized as non-white and "brown." These conceptualizations would factor into the arguments of those seeking to be categorized as "white" in order to be eligible for citizenship, such as Takao Ozawa and Bhagat Singh Thind. In this book, I focus primarily on dominant nativist categorization of races and subsequent policies of citizenship.

To aid readers in tracing the events in Revelation and in American immigration history, I offer two appendices at the end of the book. Appendix A gives a timeline of American immigration and citizenship events, laws, and policies, particularly those treated in the book. Appendix B gives a general outline of the narrative structure of the book of Revelation, as far as such a narrative can be delineated.

Finally, I reject in this book the notion that America is "a nation of immigrants." While this phrase may be used in appeals for acceptance and diversity, it is fundamentally wrong about the history of the land. This idea erases the existence of indigenous peoples and their home, and it ignores what Paul Spickard calls "the first fact of the history of American immigration," the genocide of Native peoples.[5] While this book does not focus on indigenous histories per se, I include discussion of the apocalyptic language used to justify the violence and theft of land committed against Native peoples. As stated above, many Mexican peoples are indigenous to the lands now part of the United States, and my discussion of the history of immigration and Mexico deals with the changing American construction of Mexican identity, which shifts from indigenous to possible citizen, then from migrant worker to "illegal."

Furthermore, in discussing immigration and immigrants, I focus on those who desired to come to America or at least saw that destination as their goal. This is not the history of enslaved Black peoples who were stolen, chained, denied their humanity, and treated as property. The dynamics of the apocalyptic discourse I analyze, in its lauding of the New Jerusalem and vitriol against idolatrous invaders, generally does not include a place or metaphorical vocabulary for the enslaved person in America. In matters of citizenship and personhood, however, public discourse did discuss the status of the enslaved within the heavenly metaphor, and I analyze this in chapter 5. And although I do not concentrate on indigenous and enslaved Black history, I want to state that American immigration history is impossible without the two foundations of the country, genocide and slavery, the bodies and blood upon which America the New Jerusalem is built.

# PART ONE

# Conceptualizations

# ONE

# America the New Jerusalem

The fourfold interpretation of Holy Scripture is clearly implicit in the word Jerusalem. In a historical sense, it is the earthly city to which pilgrims travel. Allegorically, it indicates the Church in the world. Tropologically, Jerusalem is the soul of every believer. Anagogically, the word means the Heavenly Jerusalem, the celestial fatherland and kingdom.

—*Guillaume Durand, as quoted in Christopher Columbus,*
Libro de las profecías *(1501–4)*

## Apocalyptic "Discovery"

The history of America as the New Jerusalem starts with the first wave of immigrants to the Americas in the last millennium, beginning with Christopher Columbus's (1451–1506) first voyage in 1492. Long before Columbus made landfall in Guanahani, modern San Salvador, European theologians and cartographers had unconsciously and proleptically created a place for the Americas in the geographic imaginary of the fifteenth century. This theologically charged geography placed the holy city of Jerusalem at the center of the world—not only in recognition of the centrality of Jerusalem in Christian salvation history but also in proclaiming its *future* as the city to be retaken by Christians and the location of Christ's return and millennial reign. This symbolism is expressed with the succinct trigness of the T-O *mappamundi* ("map of the world"), common throughout Europe at the time (figure 1).[1]

Figure 1 is a T-O map of the world from around the year 1500. This map does not, obviously, convey much geographical information; its power lies

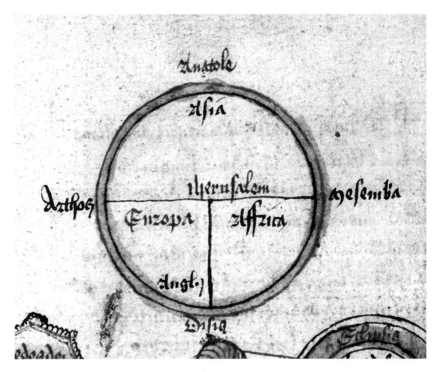

**Fig. 1.** T-O world map, detail from folio 17r, mssHM 64, an astrological and medical compilation, England, end of the fifteenth century. (The Huntington Library, San Marino, California.)

in its symbolic presentation of the world. The map shows an encircling ocean—the O—divided by a T made up of rivers (the horizontal line of the Don and Nile, from left to right) and the Mediterranean Sea (running perpendicularly downward). These waters separate Asia, Europe, and Africa, placing the city of Jerusalem at the physical, geographical, and theological center. Asia forms the top half of the circle, with the rising sun (labeled *Anatole*) the highest point of the map.[2]

With a few simple strokes, this tripartite map neatly encapsulates the key elements of Christian geography and chronology: it marks the East, representing Eden at the creation of the world; Jerusalem, the Israelite center of power, the location of the temple, and the site of the crucifixion and resurrection of Christ—emphasized by the T lines forming the cruciform and the crucified body of Christ—and finally the Jerusalem-yet-to-be,

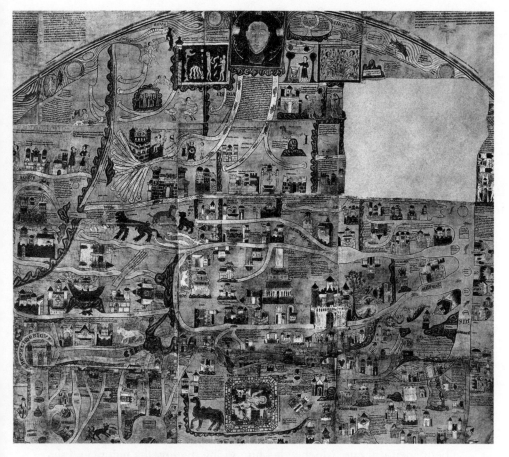

Fig. 2. Upper-half detail of the Ebstorf Map of Kloster Ebstorf, Germany, ca. 1234. (American Geographical Society Library Digital Map Collection, University of Wisconsin-Milwaukee Libraries.)

widely understood as the future site of Christ's return and earthly reign (Rev 20:1–6).[3]

Figure 2 is a round mappamundi from the thirteenth century: the Ebstorf Map of Germany. Although not a tripartite T-O map, it follows a similar symbolic schema and provides far more detail and incorporates the world as Christ's body.[4] At the top of the map, just by Christ's head, lies the walled Garden of Eden with the Tree of knowledge and Adam and Eve. Out of Paradise flow four rivers, as described in Genesis 2. Again, at the center of the map sits Jerusalem, here with the detail added of Christ, described in the map's text as the "conqueror of death" (*victor mortis*), rising from the tomb, centering the world both geographically and theologically. The placement of Paradise at the top of the world and Jerusalem with Christ both crucified and resurrected at the center can be found in the other extant great medieval mappaemundi, such as the Psalter Map (ca. 1262–1300), the Hereford Map (ca. 1290), and the Hanns Rüst Map (ca. 1480).

From 1100 CE onward European mappaemundi commonly place Jerusalem at the center of the world, although belief in its centrality had existed long beforehand, justified by Bible verses such as Ezekiel 5:5: "Thus says the Lord God: This is Jerusalem; I have set her in the center of the nations, with countries all around her." The shift toward consistently centering and focusing on Jerusalem came in the wake of the Crusades and the repeated attempts to conquer, "redeem," and make pilgrimage to the holy city.[5]

Christopher Columbus began his travels within this context, in this geographical and theological vision of the world. While medieval mappaemundi could hardly have helped Columbus determine longitude, latitude, trade winds, and currents, he quite likely used their symbolic orientation to understand his personal role and mission throughout his voyages. Multiple passages of Columbus's travelogues evince the use of both nautical charts and symbolic maps, so it seems that "he sailed with two very different cartographic images in mind: a portolan one, which guided the navigation, and a hermeneutical one, which aided him in interpreting the nature and significance of the new geography he was encountering."[6]

Both literally and hermeneutically, Columbus aimed for two destinations, the same two highlighted on medieval T-O maps: Jerusalem and Paradise. It was his belief, informed by the apocalypticism of abbot and mystic Joachim of Fiore (c. 1135–1202) and the Franciscans, that the end of the world was rapidly approaching, but also that certain prophecies had yet to be fulfilled to usher in the eschaton.[7] Columbus's *Libro de las profecías* ("Book of Prophecies"), written and compiled primarily in 1501–2, between his third and fourth voyages, gathers together biblical quotations, theological writings, and Columbus's own notes regarding the coming apocalypse and the events leading up to it.

In the letter to King Ferdinand and Queen Isabella included at the beginning of the work, Columbus cites the sources he uses to tabulate the number of years until the eschaton: Holy Scripture, St. Augustine, and other church authorities. He concludes: "According to this calculation, only one hundred and fifty years are lacking for the completion of the seven thousand years which would be the end of the world according to the learned opinions that I have cited above. Our Savior said that before the consummation of this world, first must be fulfilled all the things that were written by the prophets." And what must be fulfilled before the consummation of the world? The first paragraph of the *Libro de las profecías* states these events plainly: "Here begins the book, or handbook, of sources, statements, opinions and prophecies on the subject of *the recovery of God's Holy City* and Mount Zion, and on the discovery and *evangelization of the islands of the Indies and of all other peoples and nations.*"[8]

First, Jerusalem must be taken from the infidels and brought under Christian rule; and second, the Christian gospel must reach all peoples on earth. Columbus considered himself the primary instrument of God to bring these two events to fulfillment. He tells the king and queen "that for the execution of the journey to the Indies I was not aided by intelligence, by mathematics or by maps. It was simply the fulfillment of what Isaiah had prophesied." Furthermore, he claims that Joachim of Fiore had predicted Columbus's individual role: "The Abbot Joachim, a Calabrian, said that the restorer of the House of Mt. Zion would come from Spain."[9]

The belief in an eschatological restoration of Jerusalem has its foundations in Hebrew prophecies, and these make up the bulk of the biblical excerpts in Columbus's *Libro de las profecías,* with the book of Isaiah enjoying pride of place. But the Joachimites and Columbus oriented the prophecies of Jerusalem and Zion using the eschatology of the Revelation of John. Thus, while Jerusalem was to be restored, it was not for the sake of Israelite rule but for Christ's millennial reign, foretold in Revelation 20, and this reign would of course be located in the holy city at the center of the world. This prophecy went hand in hand with the spread of Christendom throughout the world because Revelation 7:9 describes a holy multitude at the end times "from every nation, from all tribes and peoples and languages."

In Columbus's mind, the Holy Spirit had inspired his voyage across the ocean so that he could fulfill these two prophecies. By sailing westward, he would reach rich lands in the East. Consequently, he could bring home the wealth needed for a final crusade to take back Jerusalem. At the same time, the gospel would reach the peoples found at the ends of the earth. Columbus in fact credits the Revelation of John and divine vision for his conception that he would find lands by sailing to the west, writing after his third voyage, "Of the new heaven and earth of which Our Father spoke through Saint John in the Apocalypse, after it was spoken through the mouth of Isaiah, he made me messenger and showed me that place."[10]

Because the statements quoted above were written after Columbus's first voyage, he might be accused of explaining prophecies *ex eventu,* that is, retroactively interpreting his discoveries as the fulfillment of an apocalyptic timeline. But documentary evidence shows that Columbus had already created a version of the *Libro de las profecías* by 1481, more than a decade before he made landfall in Guanahani. Additionally, in his diary on December 26, 1492, written while in the Caribbean on his first voyage, he recalls how he had pleaded with the king and queen of Spain to support his apocalyptic mission even before sailing: "I urged Your Highnesses to spend all the profits of this my enterprise on the conquest of Jerusalem."[11]

So in Columbus's imagination, the islands he reached in the Caribbean were no less than the apocalyptic lands that Revelation had "shown him," signaling the fulfillment of his predictions. These lands he also conflates with the terrestrial paradise, the Garden of Eden at the easternmost end of the world—at the highest point of the theological mappaemundi, closest to heaven. Thus on his first voyage, sailing southeast of Cuba, he writes (referring to himself in the third person): "He marveled greatly to see so many and such high islands. . . . And he says that he believes that these islands are those innumerable ones that in the maps of the world are put at the eastern end. And he said that he believed that there were great riches and precious stones and spices in them. . . . Some of them appear to reach the heavens and are formed like points of diamonds."[12]

Thus, via the Revelation of John, Columbus frames his discovery as ultimate and apocalyptic in three ways: these lands are literally, to him and to

Europe, a new earth that nearly touches heaven; they are the Edenic terrestrial paradise, full of riches for a new Jerusalem crusade; and they contain the final peoples to convert before the apocalypse. Ultimately, when Columbus envisioned these lands, he saw recapturing Jerusalem—and the coming down of the heavenly New Jerusalem beyond that—as the final end to his task.[13]

Believing himself to be the recipient of God's revelation, Columbus saw himself as a seer and a prophet, like those of Jewish and early Christian apocalypses. In Revelation and in other ancient apocalyptic texts, such as 2 Enoch, the seer must ascend (whether on a journey to the heavens or up a mountaintop) to receive a vision and secret knowledge. So also Columbus understood his own journeys as an ascension both literally up to Anatole, the most heavenward point of the earth, and eschatologically toward the fulfillment of prophecy and the arrival of believers at the New Jerusalem. His vision conflates—as visions of the end times tend to do—Paradise and Heaven, Old and New Jerusalem, the literal and the figurative, the earthly and the celestial. This complex understanding of Jerusalem is reflected in Columbus's copying into his *Libro de las profecías* the quotation of Guillaume Durand's fourfold interpretation of the city, the epigraph of this chapter. And Columbus's apocalyptic vision of Jerusalem, transatlantic voyages, so-called discoveries, and evangelization continued long after his death in 1506. The conquistador Hernán Cortés (1485–1547) would come to be understood as the Moses of the New World, and twelve Franciscan missionaries who arrived in "New Spain" in 1524 would become the Twelve Apostles of Mexico, ready to usher in a new and final age, the millennial reign of the saints.[14]

What the arrival of these men meant to the Native peoples who watched these immigrants arrive on their shores was devastation and death through disease and warfare, and the destruction of their home by the violent reinterpretation and appropriation of it as a terrestrial paradise. By the start of the seventeenth century, the decimation of Native populations combined with social and parochial conflict depressed the "apocalyptic optimism" of the Franciscans. In its place, a new millenarian understanding was emerging from Native peoples who had adopted the Christian faith and among a new generation of fluid heritage and identities. Occupying a hybrid space, two *criollo* Peruvian friars, first Francisco de la Cruz (1530–78) and then Gonzalo Tenorio (1602–c. 1682), proclaimed apocalyptic visions that reappropriated Revelation for a postcolonial reality, rejecting Spain as the place of God's favor and instead foretelling the Indies as the center of the blessed millennial kingdom.[15]

But whether a passionate belief of the Spanish explorers or of later *criollo* friars, the identification of the New World with the New Jerusalem had been irrevocably established the second Columbus sighted land on October 12, 1492. This event remains the most serendipitous and simultaneously catastrophic in history—the incredible convergence of fervent apocalyptic expectation, passionate crusader dreams, and the realization of prophetic visions in the encounter with mythical lands across the sea. It does not matter that the lands were not the terrestrial paradise in reality: they had appeared on the horizon of European knowledge at a cultural, theological, and political moment awaiting just such an apocalyptic happening. This collision of prophetic imagination and fulfillment, of navigation and hermeneutics, entrenched the understanding that "the New World equals the end of the world," that the New World is the New Jerusalem.[16]

## Pilgrimage to the New Jerusalem

In the early evening of May 21, 2011, two young men sat on a bench on the New Haven town green, a broad sixteen-acre expanse of grass at the center of the city. They had not chosen the location due to its history, but only because it seemed a good, open place for witnessing the eschaton, as predicted by Christian radio evangelist Harold Camping for that particular date and time. But a reporter from the *New Haven Independent* interviewing them wanted to know if they were aware of history of the New Haven Green as an apocalyptic site. The Green is so large, the reporter explained, because "Puritan founders wanted a space large enough to accommodate all 144,000 souls scheduled to be raptured up per prophesies in the Book of Revelation."[17]

The two men had never heard this history, but the story that the New Haven Green had been laid out by Puritan founders to fit 144,000 bodies is a widespread local legend. In my effort to identify the source of this story, I asked a Connecticut state archaeologist, a state historian, a New Haven Green church historian, and a librarian of the New Haven Museum about it, and they all had heard the same story: that John Davenport (1597–1670), the prominent Puritan founder of New Haven, devised the town green to fit the 144,000 mentioned in Revelation 7:3–8 and 14:1–5.[18]

I have found no historical document to confirm this legend, but its existence and wide circulation are understandable. In October 2012, a year and a half after Harold Camping's predicted eschaton did *not* occur, Hurricane Sandy swept through New England and uprooted the century-old Lincoln Oak that once stood in the New Haven Green. In its upended roots were found human skeletal remains, which alarmed townspeople (it also happened to be the day before Halloween) until the bones were determined to be simply part of the many bodies buried on the Green from the founding of the city in 1638 until 1821. The number of people buried in the New Haven Green is estimated to be in the thousands, and while almost all headstones were moved to the Grove Street cemetery, the bodies remain. And to this day, there remain 137 graves with headstones standing in a crypt underneath the Center Church on the Green, the oldest church in New Haven, whose current building was constructed over these graves in order to keep them intact. These bodies beneath the gravestones all face east, symbolizing, according to church historian Harold Peck, "the beginning of a new day, the beginning of eternal life."[19]

So while no historic document explicitly states that the Green was meant to hold 144,000 bodies, whether standing alive together or buried, the site does contain thousands of bodies of people who presumably believed in their resurrection at the end times. More significantly, the layout of the Green and the rest of the city of New Haven is almost certainly a result of apocalyptic urban planning. Davenport and other town leaders laid the city out in a nine-square grid with the Green at the center, surrounded by eight squares allotted to leading households of the town (figure 3). The square symmetry of the layout, the central Green space occupied by the church, and the allotment of the surrounding squares to founding families are themes consistent with biblical layouts of the Israelite encampment of

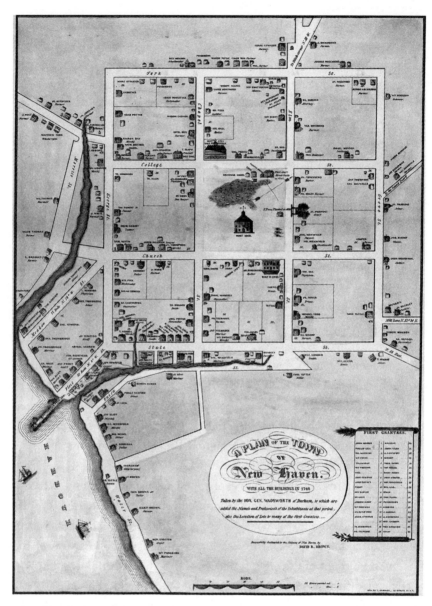

**Fig. 3.** James Wadsworth, *A Plan of the Town of New Haven with All the Buildings in 1748*, New York: C. Currier, ca. 1865. (Beinecke Rare Book and Manuscript Library, Yale University.)

Numbers 2:1–31, the vision of the temple and its city in Ezekiel 40–48, and finally the New Jerusalem in Revelation 21. All three biblical layouts present a square space, with the perimeter squares occupied by or bearing the names of the twelve tribes of Israel, and with a place of worship at the center.[20]

Furthermore, each square of New Haven's nine-square grid measures approximately 52 rods square, or 858 square feet, roughly equal to the 500 square cubits of the temple of Ezekiel's vision (Ez 45:2). In laying out the town plan, Davenport was almost certainly influenced by the heavenly utopian schema and the apocalyptic predictions of fellow Protestant Reform intellectuals. These include Johann Valentin Andreä's (1586–1654) utopian vision in *Christianopolis* and John Drury's (1596–1680) interpretation, outlined in the preface to *Clavis Apocalyptica*, that the New Jerusalem, arriving in 1655, would be manifested through God's church on earth, according to Revelation's description. Andreä, Drury, and Davenport were in turn influenced by the graphic and textual visualizations of Ezekiel's temple and Revelation's New Jerusalem published in the late sixteenth and early seventeenth centuries, such as those designed by Sebastian Castalion (1515–63), Cornelius à Lapide (1567–1637), and Juan Bautista Villalpando (1552–1608).[21]

So whence arose the legend of the Green holding 144,000 chosen souls? Consider the following. Davenport almost certainly laid out New Haven to evoke the heavenly measurements of the New Jerusalem of Revelation, as modeled after and expanding Ezekiel's visionary temple and city preceding it, and Israel's encampment in the wilderness before that.[22] The Green served as the location of the sanctuary, a place where all the congregation of New Haven's faithful would be gathered. These faithful would live as the "tribes" of the surrounding eight squares, having twelve outward-facing sides, symbolizing twelve tribes in all, like the twelve gates of the New Jerusalem: "It has a great, high wall with twelve gates, and at the gates twelve angels, and on the gates are inscribed the names that are the names of the twelve tribes of the Israelites: on the east three gates, on the north three gates, on the south three gates, and on the west three gates" (Rev 21:12–13).

And in Revelation it is stated that from each tribe of Israel there would be marked as faithful twelve thousand: "And I heard the number of those who were sealed, one hundred forty-four thousand, sealed out of every tribe of the people of Israel" (7:4). Likewise, though not literally 144,000, it is possible and probable that Davenport and his fellow churchmen understood those gathering at the Green from the surrounding households of New Haven to symbolize and *be*, in essence, the 144,000.

Davenport's own writings declare that the Congregational assembly he strove to build in New Haven truly embodied (in contrast to Anglican precincts) the New Jerusalem, "measured," as the heavenly city is, by a "golden reed": "But that Members so qualified as Christ requireth, and so confederating, should ordinarily meet together in one Congregation, for the solemn worship of God, and their mutual edification, is the Ordinance of Christ, and according to the measure of the golden Reed, whereby the City and Gates, and the dimensions of the New Jerusalem are measured, Rev. 21.15."[23]

Davenport intended all layers of life in New Haven—from civic and ecclesial governance to doctrinal "purity" to the literal urban structures of everyday life—to comply with the golden measurements of the New Jerusalem. This was, after all, the enterprise John Cotton (1585–1652) promised him when he urged Davenport to sail from his exile in Holland to New England. Cotton, the leading minister of Boston and the Massachusetts Bay Colony, boasted in a letter to Davenport that "the Order of the Churches, and the Common-Wealth, was now so settled in New-England, by common Consent, that it brought into his Mind the New Heaven, and the New Earth, wherein dwells Righteousness [2 Peter 3:13]." Thus motivated, Davenport set out to establish the New Haven colony and "did all that was possible," reports Puritan minister Cotton Mather (1663–1728), "to render the Renowned Church of New Haven, like the New Jerusalem."[24]

The name "New Haven" itself may possibly be derived from "New Heaven," for none of the city's first settlers came from New Haven, England, and "New Heaven" may have been changed for modesty's sake to "New Haven." However the town name came about, it continues the series of "New" names given during the colonization of America—the New World, with New England and New Haven echoing the apocalyptic hopes for the New Jerusalem, the telos longed for by their Puritan settlers. New York, New Jersey, New Hampshire, New Haven, New England: these signify both a remembrance of the past and a desire for a greater, more glorious future.[25]

And just as the New World's "new" names present a mix of longing for both a new creation and a re-creation, so also the New Jerusalem of the ancient text of Revelation builds on the memory of Jerusalem and its temple to present a new, stronger, more awesome city. The city of Revelation is both "the new Jerusalem" and "the New Jerusalem," that is, both something old made new and something wholly new, for the Greek text does not distinguish between descriptor and name. This divine city appears in other ancient Jewish texts (many of which Revelation uses) in similarly ambivalent ways, as a conflation of old and new, on earth and in heaven, in the future or preexistent and presented long ago to Adam and Moses.[26]

Likewise, dominant Puritan discourse of the New Jerusalem ranged from the literal to the allegorical, earthly to heavenly, aspirational to doctrinal, depending on the rhetorical moment and audience. Puritan interpretations of the New Testament agreed, in the main, that the Jews must be converted to Christianity as part of eschatological events. In this, though in scant other ways, they agreed with Columbus before them and envisioned the earthly Jerusalem restored and returned to Israel—a converted, Christian Israel. While this "New Jerusalem" on earth would be in Palestine, Puritan discourse also emphasized a heavenly city. In Increase Mather's (1639–1723) understanding, it literally hovered above the earth: "It will be seated over the Land of *Israel*, which will now again be possessed by the *Israelitish Nation*."[27]

But beyond these understandings of the New Jerusalem, there is without a doubt a conflation of America, and New England in particular, with the New Jerusalem, whether in a spiritual, physical, geographical, or missional sense.[28] Even if Puritan eschatological *doctrine* located the New Jerusalem proper in Palestine, the Puritan leaders of New England made it their *mission* to make their towns and congregations come as close to embodying that heavenly city as possible. Thus Davenport might have been motivated to lay out New Haven in nine holy squares, five hundred cubits each, while also working toward, in his own words, the apocalyptic and millennial "Majesty and glory of the Church," during which the Church enjoys "such a perfection of light, and holiness, and love, as is attainable on this side of heaven."[29]

Similarly, John Cotton in Boston preached that New England congregations had the opportunity to work toward purity and reform so that they might be a part of Christ's millennial kingdom by "rising againe, not into a loose frame, but a state rising into a Church body, and the church body so reformed as may beare witnesse against all Antichristianisme in doctrine, worship and government; This is the first resurrection."[30] For Cotton, if New England was not to be cast into the outer darkness but to enjoy Christ's reign, its inhabitants had to work toward perfection in "doctrine, worship and government," that is, on every level of community life, in ideology, church ritual, and civic conduct.

This eschatological and apocalyptic rhetoric begets and fuels the New England American exceptionalism we find in the writings of Cotton Mather (John Cotton's grandson) two generations later. "Sirs," Mather declares in *Theopolis Americana,* a sermon preached to the Massachusetts General Assembly in 1709: "NEW ENGLAND is a Countrey, that has made a more than ordinary *Profession* of Religion. . . . It is true, I must believe, that *New-England* is not worse than other Places. . . . But, O NEW ENGLAND; There are a *Thousand* Reasons, why thou shouldest be Better than *Other Places*; A more Glorious *Land of Uprightness!*"[31]

Mather claims New England must be "a more glorious land of uprightness" because of its Puritan doctrine, its metaphorical (and in the case of New Haven, perhaps literal) foundation: "There is not a Street of more *Pure* Gold upon the Face of the Earth at this day, for the GOSPEL generally Preached in the true *Purity* of it, than the *Churches* of NEW ENGLAND." If New England continues in such purity, Mather preaches, then "there will be fulfilled unto us, that Word; Isa. 1.26. *Thou shalt be called, The City of Righteousness, The Faithful City.* A CITY of such a GOLDEN STREET, will be a *Strong City*; God will *appoint Salvation for Walls and bulwarks* unto it; while not but a *Righteous Nation, which keeps the Truth,* inhabits it. O NEW-ENGLAND, Keep such a STREET; and *Sweep* it, where it wants to be better. Than, there *will be no breaking in or going out.*"[32] Here Mather takes the "city of righteousness" from Isaiah 1:26 and combines it with the details of the New Jerusalem of Revelation 21 — the golden street, the strong walls and bulwarks — to describe the "Righteous Nation" that New England was, is still, and should be in the future.

But that is not all. Mather expands his sermon to address not only New England but America as a whole, and he describes America in mythic and prophetic language not far removed from Columbus's visions and the geography of the T-O maps:

> I have been Surprised at the Reading of a Passage in a Pagan Writer, who flourished more than Fifteen Hundred years ago. Tis *Aelian*, a Grecian Writer, who says, That in Times long preceding his, there was a Tradition, that *Europe* and *Asia* and *Africa* were encompassed by the Ocean; But without and beyond the Ocean, there was a *great Island*, as big as *They*. And in that Other World, there was an huge CITY, called Ευσεβυς. THE GODLY CITY. In that CITY, Sayes he, they enjoy all Possible *Peace* and *Health*, and *Plenty*: And, he Sayes, *They are without Controversy a very Righteous People*; So *Righteous*, that they have God marvellously coming down among them. I know not what well to make of a Tradition so very *Ancient*, and yet having Such an *American* Face upon it. All I will say, is thus much. There are many Arguments to perswade us, That our Glorious LORD, will have an HOLY CITY in AMERICA; a *City*, the STREET whereof will be Pure GOLD.[33]

Mather combines two elements especially potent in the rhetoric of American exceptionalism subsequently: classicism and apocalyptic, using both Aelian's *Varia Historia* and the Revelation of John to mythologize and glorify America, the holy city.

Mather emphasizes the righteousness, wealth, and divine blessing of America the New Jerusalem, and these form the essential characteristics of the nation in apocalyptic discourse ever after, manipulated and recycled in different ways to fit the moment. The conception of America as God's heavenly city may be traced back to Davenport and Cotton, and further back, through different national and religious networks, to Columbus. And after Puritan colonialism, apocalyptic language courses through the patriotism and call to martyrdom of the American Revolution, with ministers using Revelation's militant Christ imagery to inspire American forces.[34]

From the Revolution up through the Civil War, politicians, preachers, and pundits also envisioned America as a New Israel and Zion, another identity of the New Jerusalem. Joseph Smith and his followers sought to build the holy city where the saints would gather. It was during the Civil War that Julia Ward Howe wrote "The Battle Hymn of the Republic" with the apocalyptic opening lines: "Mine eyes have seen the glory of the coming of the Lord: / He is trampling out the vintage where the grapes of wrath are stored."[35] These lines use the blood-soaked winepress imagery of Revelation 14:14–20 and its allusion to Isaiah 63:1–4, describing the slaughter of the war in terms of God's terrible judgment and wrath.

Heavenly imagery and metaphor continue with American expansion westward, justified by the conception of Manifest Destiny and divine fiat. And as U.S. colonization reached the California coast, Washington Gladden (1836–1918), a prominent preacher and minister in Ohio, declared in 1890 the end of exploration and the beginning of the holy city, which would be built in America's heartland:

> The circuit of the earth is completed; migration has come to its term; here, upon these plains, the problems of history are to be solved; here, if anywhere, is to rise that city of God, the New Jerusalem, whose glories are to fill the earth. O, let us not forget what foundations we are laying, what empires are to stand upon them; and in the fear of God and the love of man let us build here a city in whose light the nations of the earth shall walk; whereinto kings may bring their glory and honor; into which there shall enter nothing that worketh abomination or maketh a lie.[36]

In Gladden's words the language of Mather and Cotton's American exceptionalism appears again—the city of God, the light for the nations, the paraphrasing of Revelation 21.

And as American history grows, American territory expands, and its population diversifies, an origin story of the nation begins to ossify around the narrative of the Puritans, their heavenly mission, and the safe haven of America, the New Jerusalem. In this narrative, the "Pilgrims" become conflated with the Puritans, emphasizing the *pilgrimage* made by a saintly people who come to a sacred land while suffering hunger, cold, and sickness but who endure in order to create a model civilization.[37] This is a unifying, homogenizing, and inspirational genesis myth that celebrates a "national character" symbolized by white and Protestant New England, while it obscures the genocide of Native peoples, the violence of slavery, and the bloodbath of the Civil War.

This origin story connects each author, orator, or preacher who evokes it with a mythical past, justifying claims and ambitions with "founding" principles touted as quintessentially American.[38] The Pilgrim/Puritan story thus finds its way into campaign speeches and onto the Senate floor while it also provides the aesthetics for a national holiday and triggers nostalgia for a "simpler time" and things American "as apple pie."

## The Shining City upon a Hill

One particular strand of Puritan apocalyptic exceptionalism is a phrase from a once forgotten sermon that reappears in the 1960s and becomes the most famous expression of American exceptionalism by the end of the twentieth century: the "city on a hill" of John Winthrop's (1587–1649) sermon "A Model of Christian Charity." The sermon, delivered in 1630 by the Puritan leader before he arrived in America, was actually not much noted at the time it was given and had practically disappeared from print, as Abram Van Engen has detailed in his history of the phrase. It was the historian Perry Miller who dusted off the phrase and used it to frame American exceptionalism and mission, and it was John F. Kennedy who then used Winthrop's sermon and the phrase "city on a hill" on the national stage. Kennedy invoked Winthrop in his 1961 "City upon a Hill" speech as president-elect, likening the country's mission and challenge to that of the Puritans arriving in Massachusetts.[39]

But while it may seem that this particular phrase suddenly pops up—like the skeletons turned up by Hurricane Sandy on the New Haven Green—"a city on a hill" and the larger metaphor in which it's embedded have haunted the continent from the moment of European discovery and invasion. Like the thousands of bodies buried in the New Haven Green, the metaphor of America as the New Jerusalem lies in the soil of U.S. national identity, feeding its discourse.

And no other public orator has harvested the ripe fruit of the metaphor as masterfully as Ronald Reagan, who deftly connected the biblical phrase with Revelation 21 in an apocalyptic vision of American immigration that American politicians have imitated ever since. From 1979 to 1989, Reagan used variations of the phrase—"city on a hill," "city upon a hill," and "shining city upon a hill"—over thirty times in political speeches, more than any other president up to that point and since. His most famous use of "shining city upon a hill" appears in his farewell speech to the nation, January 11, 1989, a speech many view as his best, one that pithily and poetically encapsulates the core ideology of his presidency. The phrase appears at the end of the address, and Reagan cites Winthrop as its source, as he often did. Reagan says: "The past few days when I've been at that window upstairs, I've thought a bit of the 'shining city upon a hill.' The phrase comes from John Winthrop, who wrote it to describe the America he imagined. What he imagined was important because he was an early Pilgrim, an early freedom man. He journeyed here on what today we'd call a little wooden boat; and like the other Pilgrims, he was looking for a home that would be free."[40]

Here Reagan invokes the American origin myth, conflating the Puritan John Winthrop of the Massachusetts Bay Colony with the Pilgrims of Plymouth Rock. With just the brief description of Winthrop on "a little wooden boat" and "looking for a home that would be free," Reagan conjures up the mythical Thanksgiving story and the patriotic notion of an American spirit hard-bitten and dauntless in its pursuit of freedom.

To those who "know their Bible"—another very American phrase—it might seem that Reagan cited the wrong source for "city upon a hill." Winthrop may have used those words, but they come from the Bible—from the Sermon on the Mount in the Gospel of Matthew. The phrase "city on a hill" (πόλις . . . ἐπάνω ὄρους κειμένη) of 5:14 is part of a pair of metaphors used to describe Jesus's followers: "You are the salt of the earth. . . . You are the light of the world" (5:13, 14). These are not obscure verses but sentences containing other phrases that are famous in their own right—"salt of the earth," "light of the world"—following right on the heels of the Beatitudes, perhaps the most famous portion of the Sermon on the Mount. For Reagan to cite *Winthrop* as the source of "city on a hill" certainly seems as if he is "ignoring the scriptural basis of this proclamation."[41] On the surface, Reagan seems to bypass mention of the Bible in order to emphasize the American genesis story, focusing on the patriotic Pilgrim narrative rather than something explicitly scriptural.

But Reagan the Great Communicator was also "the Evangelical's President," courting votes from evangelical Christians through alliances with the Moral Majority and the Christian Right, Billy Graham, Jerry Falwell, and Pat Robertson. To omit the Bible at this moment would be to miss an opportunity once more to include a voter base known for their insistence on biblical foundations and the inerrancy of scripture. This was a voter bloc Reagan had all but promised to champion, a group further gratified by his proclamation of 1983 as the "Year of the Bible."[42] Was Reagan simply done courting votes, as he was with his presidency? Was it simply not the time and place to narrow the broad sweep of his speech to the confines of scripture?

Either of these interpretations might seem correct if Reagan had ended his speech simply with the description of John Winthrop seeking "a home that would be free"—but the address continues. If the audience considers the following paragraphs of the speech closely with reference to the Bible, then it becomes clear that Reagan craftily invokes *both* a broad, patriotic founding myth *and* specific allusions to important Bible verses. And any evangelical Christian worth their salt would recognize the verses Reagan alludes to—evangelical Christians of the 1980s were, after all, trained via Bible memorization curricula and camps, practiced "sword drill" races to find scripture references, and listened to *Back to the Bible* and *Thru the Bible* radio programs.[43]

The paragraph following the John Winthrop description of Reagan's "Farewell Address" reads:

> I've spoken of the shining city all my political life, but I don't know if I ever quite communicated what I saw when I said it. But in my mind it was a tall proud city built on rocks stronger than oceans, wind-swept, God-blessed, and teeming with people of all kinds living in harmony and peace, a city with free ports that hummed with commerce and creativity. And if there had to be

city walls, the walls had doors and the doors were open to anyone
with the will and the heart to get here. That's how I saw it and see
it still.[44]

What city does Reagan describe here if not the New Jerusalem of Revelation 21? Reagan positions himself as the apocalyptic seer—he has a vision
and tries to "communicate what he sees" when he sees that "shining city"
that is "God-blessed." It is set on a great foundation ("built on rocks stronger
than oceans"), filled with a diverse multitude ("teeming with people of all
kinds"), enriched by the world ("with free ports that hummed with commerce"), with a wall and gates that stand open ("if there had to be city walls
the walls had doors and the doors were open").[45]

Compare this to the details of Revelation 21:

> Then I saw a new heaven and a new earth. . . . It has the glory of
> God and a radiance like a very rare jewel, like jasper, clear as crys-
> tal. It has a great, high wall with twelve gates. . . . And the wall of
> the city has twelve foundations, and on them are the twelve names
> of the twelve apostles of the Lamb. . . . The nations will walk by its
> light, and the kings of the earth will bring their glory into it. Its
> gates will never be shut by day—and there will be no night there.
> People will bring into it the glory and the honor of the nations.
> (Rev 21:1, 11–12, 14, 24–26)

In Revelation we find the model for Reagan's vision—the seer, John of Patmos, beholds the shining and blessed city ("it has the glory of God and a radiance like a very rare jewel"), built on strong bedrock ("twelve foundations"),
filled with people from everywhere ("the nations"), buzzing with commerce
and full of wealth ("kings of the earth will bring their glory," "people will
bring into it the glory and honor of the nations").[46] There's a wall ("a great,
high wall"), and there are doors ("with twelve gates"), but these doors are
never shut ("Its gates will never be shut by day—and there will be no night").

Thus, in two short paragraphs, Reagan manages to introduce the Pilgrims narrative, the Puritan preaching of John Winthrop, and the identification of America with the New Jerusalem. He thereby picks up not only

the centuries-old thread of Puritan apocalyptic expectations but also that of twentieth-century U.S. evangelicals, who were obsessed with end-times predictions and apocalyptic glory. Reagan continues to weave these threads together in the next paragraph: "And how stands this city on this winter night? More prosperous, more secure, and happier than it was eight years ago. But more than that: after two hundred years, two centuries, she still stands strong and true on the granite ridge, and her glow has held steady no matter what storm. And she's still a beacon, still a magnet for all who must have freedom, for all the pilgrims from all the lost places who are hurtling through the darkness, toward home."[47]

How stands the city at night? Here Reagan returns to the imagery of Matthew 5:14, astutely connecting the verse with the New Jerusalem, a connection contemporary biblical scholars had noted.[48] The city on a hill, because of the light of its habitations, "cannot be hid" (Matt 5:14), and it shines eternally as a "beacon" to others. So America, the New Jerusalem, is the radiant haven "for all the pilgrims," and here Reagan once again ties in the Pilgrims while also reemphasizing the United States as a sacred, safe, light-filled pilgrimage site, in contrast to "the lost places" and "the darkness."

Here also, with the invocation of "pilgrims," Reagan picks up a thread from the beginning of the "Farewell Address," that of immigrants and refugees. The image he begins the speech with is the other vision he sees in that upper window of the White House: that of "a leaky little boat . . . crammed [with] refugees from Indochina hoping to get to America." A sailor on the USS *Midway*—a serviceman, "young, smart, fiercely observant,"—spots this boat, and a rescue of it commences. When one of the boat people sees the sailor aboard ship, he greets him saying, "Hello, American sailor. Hello, freedom man."[49]

This vision prepares the audience for the city on a hill vision at the end. It introduces details of a dichotomy that Reagan later presents in grand, sweeping strokes at the conclusion. On one side—coming from a "lost place" and sailing in "the darkness"—crowd the refugees in desperate need. They come from "Indochina," and they speak an awkward, unidiomatic English: "Hello, freedom man." On the other side, in contrast to the "crammed" leaky boat, is the powerful USS *Midway*, a seafaring extension of the proud city on a hill. On it stands the American serviceman, a man who is "hard at work," who patrols, rescues, and shelters. He can and does offer entry to the boat people.

At the end of the speech, Reagan returns to this duality and the symbols and phrases of the opening narrative—contemplation at the White House window, a wooden boat, a sailing Pilgrim—but there is one slight but revealing change in the contours of the story. John Winthrop is the Pilgrim, he sails on a "little wooden boat," but Reagan calls *him* the "early freedom man." Although Winthrop is himself literally an immigrant to American shores in the seventeenth century, he does not prefigure the Indochinese boat person—the immigrant—but instead *the American serviceman*, already belonging to the New Jerusalem. Reagan's Winthrop does not look for rescue but is identified as the rescuer since he is a "freedom man," the name coined by the boat person. In other words, Winthrop, by some birthright, is at home already on the inside of the walls of the city on the hill even as he is sailing toward it, in contrast to the boat people "from all the lost places . . . hurtling through the darkness."

All these threads Reagan weaves together in the speech to form a large tapestry: an exceptional, yes, but also an apocalyptic America as the New Jerusalem. And this glorious image comes with an ever-present duality of within and without, insider freedom man and outsider refugee. Reagan uses the language of Revelation's New Jerusalem because it was already a ruling metaphor of American immigration that identified the nation as the shining city on a hill with walls and gates. The elements of Reagan's "Farewell Address" cohere as a result of centuries of apocalyptic American identification with the New Jerusalem.

The contours of that metaphor and its role in Revelation's theology and narrative play out into numerous elements and idiosyncrasies of U.S. inclusion and exclusion, at its borders and in its processes of naturalization. Many of these apocalyptically tinged elements are evident in the paragraphs of this presidential speech quoted above, to wit: the innate belonging of some people groups to the city, as represented by John Winthrop, white, male, English, Protestant, and presented as a singular subject, as is also the case of the lone brave sailor; by contrast, the identification of foreignness—through speech and squalor—with peoples of Asia, who are outside and presented en masse ("crammed"); the necessity ("if there had to be") of walls and boundaries, with gates that are welcomingly open but are essentially mechanisms of exclusion; and an emphasis on merit as the pathway to entry ("with the will and the heart to get there"), which is contradicted by those with the birthright of belonging. These are the primary elements of the metaphor of America the New Jerusalem: its exclusion of those deemed unclean, its contradictory processes for entry and naturalization, and the walls and gates at its borders.

# On the "Island of Immortals"
## The Apocalyptic Exclusion of Chinese Immigrants

On a clear, crisp, September morning in 1868, or the seventh year of our Emperor Tongzhi, the mists lifted, and we sighted land for the first time since we left the shores of Kwangtung over sixty days before. To be actually at the "Golden Gate" of the land of our dreams! The feeling that welled up in us was indescribable. I wonder whether the ecstasy before the Pearly Gates of the Celestial City above could surpass what we felt at the moment we realized that we had reached our destination.

*— Huie Kin,* Reminiscences *(1932)*

This place is called an island of immortals,
When in fact, this mountain wilderness is a prison.

*— Anonymous, "Poem 23," carved in a detention center wall of Angel Island*

### Bones and Bodies

Toano, Nevada, lies between foothills, close to the Utah border, in an arid desert landscape dotted with sagebrush. It is now a wilderness with no structures still standing, but in 1870 it was a town connected by the Central Pacific Railroad to the city of Elko, Nevada, about seventy-five miles away. January 5, 1870, was probably a cold day, but railway workers in Toano likely preferred the chill considering the cargo they were loading onto a six-car train headed west to Elko and on to San Francisco. They had to ensure that each car was packed with the remains of dead Chinese railroad workers—packed as full as possible. This was so the Central Pacific Railroad could be well paid for the load, according to the *Elko Independent,* a twice-weekly newspaper that ran from 1869 to 1872: "We understand that the Chinese companies pay the Railroad Company ten dollars for carrying to San Francisco each dead Chinaman. Six cars, well stuffed with this kind of freight, will be a good day's work." The paper goes on to state with the same astonishing callousness, "The remains of the females are left to rot in shallow graves, while every defunct male is carefully preserved for shipment to the Occident."[1]

The western section of the transcontinental railroad had reached completion the prior year—largely through the labor of Chinese workers. The remains of the laborers who had died, whether by sickness, in construction accidents, from harsh conditions, or by outright murder, were collected for shipment back to China.[2] Not all bodies made it across the Pacific, however. Like the bones of those Puritans buried and forgotten in the New Haven Green, the remains of Chinese workers have come back up to the surface, quite by accident. Such was the case when a landowner began to build a new house on a site in Carlin, Nevada, unearthing the remains of thirteen men.[3] Like the bodies of the Green, these remains belonged to a community of immigrants who had already settled in the area for decades by the time of burial—Chinese miners had worked in Nevada's silver mines starting in the 1850s, after the California gold rush of 1848.[4] But unlike the Puritans of New Haven and New England, the Chinese who came to America did not become part of an essential, patriotic national narrative, nor did they or their descendants by default count as citizens of the United States.

In fact, the same year the bodies of Chinese railroad workers were shipped from Nevada to San Francisco, on July 4, 1870, Congress voted not to allow Chinese immigrants to naturalize when passing the Naturalization Act of 1870. During the Senate debate that preceded the vote, Senator George Williams (R-OR) declared that he could not imagine how anyone would want Chinese people to belong to the nation: "Is there anybody who will say that the Chinese is a desirable population? . . . Mongolians, no matter how long they may stay in the United States, will never lose their identity as a peculiar and separate people. They will never amalgamate with persons of European descent." Williams, in that statement, captures succinctly the racialization of Chinese (and later Asian) peoples as perpetual foreigners throughout their history in the United States, up to and beyond this writing.[5]

The Chinese as un-American foreigners also persists in scholarship of American immigration history. Historian Paul Spickard lays out how U.S. immigration scholars have typically sorted into the "Old Immigration" category (ca. 1820–80) those identified as more similar to English Americans (Irish, Germans, Scandinavians), while the "New Immigration" (ca. 1880–1930) category usually comprises immigrants from southern and eastern Europe and Asia. But this categorization is not based on real immigration data. Scandinavians, for example, immigrated to the United States predominately *after* 1880, while Chinese immigrants arrived in significant numbers only *before* 1882. In reality, these categories of "old" and "new" immigration have been formed, most obviously, along the lines of skin color and hinge on the perception that "true" and "original" Americans are those of English descent. Thus, it is assumed that the farther removed they are from the colonial period, the more divergent the racial and cultural "stock" of the immigrants who arrive. But, in point of fact, more immigrants arrived from Britain in *every decade* from 1840 to 1920 than during the entire colonial period. In fact, there were consistently far more British immigrants to America than Chinese in every decade until 1965. Yet U.S. immigration discourse never complains of the loss of jobs to hordes of British immigrants who might be treasonous royalists. As Spickard says, "The English people were never the immigrants under discussion. . . . The issues for English people were never immigrant issues."[6]

At the end of the nineteenth century, the Chinese were not the latest newcomers, only the greatest perceived threat in the minds of white residents in the western states. With the end of the gold rush in California, the closing of certain mines in Nevada, and the completion of the transcontinental railroad, Chinese laborers moved into other areas of work and their communities continued to expand. While Chinese immigrants had faced discrimination and harassment — social, legal, and civic — since their arrival, the shift of Chinese labor away from the railroads plus the ongoing arrival of Chinese immigrants in California prompted still greater violence and hate against them.[7]

Earlier in the nineteenth century, when the railroad companies needed workers for hard and dangerous jobs, they welcomed and recruited Chinese immigrants. After all, "will the white man, in this country, follow such employments?" asked the *Daily California Chronicle* in 1854. The answer: "Never, if it be possible to procure an inferior people to do them. The Chinese are such a people." These were the workers needed to speed along a settler colonialist and imperialist project cutting through Native lands. Railroad investor and politician Leland Stanford assured President Andrew Johnson in 1865 that the Chinese were "quiet, peaceable, patient, industrious and economical . . . ready and apt to learn all the different kinds of work required in railroad building" and "contented with less wages." Then the Burlingame Treaty of 1868 further opened up immigration and commerce between the United States and China. But on the completion of the railroad in 1869, the labor that Chinese immigrants provided came to be viewed as a threat.[8]

In anti-Chinese speeches before the Senate, opponents of Chinese immigration dwelled on the "hordes" of Chinese who were flooding into the United States, what Senator Thomas Bayard (D-DE) called an "inundation of countless numbers and of a race wholly different," which would "destroy the labor of our own people." The Chinese "inundation" Bayard speaks of never amounted to more than one-twentieth of all immigrants arriving in the United States. Nevertheless, Chinese peoples were the first racial-ethnic group targeted by a nationally enforced immigration law.[9]

The Page Act of 1875 effectively barred Chinese women from entering the United States on the prejudicial grounds that they were sex workers and morally corrupting. Then the Chinese Exclusion Act of 1882 further restricted the entry of Chinese immigrants by denying entry to Chinese laborers. While such legislation may have assuaged fears of an incoming flood of Chinese workers, it did not account for Chinese already living in the country or their vulnerability in an environment of violent racist hatred.[10]

Chinese in America had already experienced violence and expulsion from towns through intimidation and harassment in the 1870s. The brutality reached a climax in the 1880s, during which Chinese were shot, lynched, and tortured, not only in California but in Oregon, Washington, Idaho, Wyoming, and other western territories. In 1885, a group of 150 white men in Rock Springs, Wyoming, killed at least twenty-eight Chinese coal miners, whom they shot, dismembered, and burned alive. In 1887, a gang of white men tortured, mutilated, and murdered at least thirty-four Chinese miners in Hells Canyon, Oregon. No one was ever convicted for this butchery, not in the Rock Springs or the Hells Canyon massacres, or after murders, lynchings, and mass expulsion in Los Angeles, Truckee, and Denver.[11]

This hate manifested itself in legislation in 1884 and 1888, which furthered restrictions on Chinese entry, and in the Geary Act of 1892, which renewed and strengthened the Exclusion Act by requiring all Chinese laborers (which later encompassed all Chinese) in the United States to carry proof that they were in the country legally, thereby implementing the first such federal requirement of documentation.[12] Without a certificate, a Chinese laborer could be forced to do hard labor and be deported, and they could not post bail or testify as a witness in a trial.

The Geary Act was extended in 1902 and extended in perpetuity in 1904. It was not repealed until 1943, by the Magnuson Act, which still limited Chinese entry visas to a minuscule *105 per annum* until the National Origins Formula of 1924, on which the low immigration limit was based, was itself abolished in 1965. In the decades between the passage of the Chinese Exclusion Act of 1882 and the Geary Act of 1904, and ever after, there proliferated depictions of Chinese peoples and China as a looming, pernicious, ugly threat in American political speeches, newspapers, literature, and art: the Chinese had become the Yellow Peril.[13]

## Revelation and Yellow Peril

As in other moments of American crisis and feverish hate, pundits and politicians have made use of the book of Revelation to construct and illustrate the situation, inverting the metaphor of America as the New Jerusalem to emphasize the existence of its enemies and the need for violent exclusion. Yellow Peril tropes fit easily into the apocalyptic imaginaries and narratives drawn from the text of Revelation. At the foundation of apocalyptic Yellow Peril imagery and stories used to exclude Chinese from entry and acceptance in the United States lies the belief of a divine, immutable distinction between white Americans and the Chinese "race."

This belief is at the core of the aforementioned speech against Chinese immigration delivered by Senator Bayard in 1882 before the passing of the Chinese Exclusion Act. Bayard argues that opponents of restrictions on Chinese immigration have only profit in mind and do not care about the plight of (white) Americans. He couches this claim in Christian language: "[The authors of the Burlingame Treaty with China] overlooked or disregarded the difference of race, they overlooked the difference between Chinese and Christian civilization. . . . They saw but one thing—a profitable commerce, and they rushed with haste into a treaty that considered Americans and Chinamen as if they were all of the same race, habits, and characteristics—all equally and alike entitled and fitted to become citizens of the Republic of the United States." However, Bayard argues, "A man cannot faithfully serve two contending governments at the same time." Of course Bayard means the United States and China in the immediate context, but he paraphrases a biblical text that serves his purposes precisely, elevating the conflict to one of spiritual dimensions. The text is found in the Gospels of both Matthew and Luke: "No man can serve two masters; for either he will hate the one, and love the other; or else he will hold to the one, and despise the other. Ye cannot serve God and mammon" (Matt 6:24, King James Version).[14]

Bayard alludes to this Christian text to insinuate that his fellow congressmen serve either China and greed or the United States and God. And the distinction between Chinese and Americans—implied by Bayard to be white and Christian—is too great ever to allow Chinese to immigrate and live in America. God himself, Bayard argues, never intended these "races" to mingle: those enabling Chinese immigration "overlooked the great and *manifest* distinctions between these two nations and their population. . . . Why was there not some mingling of *reverence* in this, why was there not some respect paid to the *finger of the Almighty* when he points out the difference between races of mankind?" The Chinese, in Bayard's view, were a race wholly separate and, more important, unchristian, incapable of belonging to the people of God.[15]

That the Chinese were "pagan" and innately disloyal to America had repeatedly been stated by senators in Congress in decades past. For example, in 1870 Senator William Stewart (R-NV) argued that "until they [the Chinese] renounce paganism, until they renounce imperialism, which this generation will never do, we should not propose to engraft them upon the body politic." During that same session, Senator George Williams (R-OR) denounced the idea of Chinese naturalization: "Imagine such an oath administered to Chinamen, ignorant of God, Christ, the Bible, and the Christian religion; ignorant of the Constitution of the country, its laws, its customs, and its habits!" A proposal that Chinese should be allowed to acquire American citizenship, introduced in an amendment by Senator Charles Sumner (R-MA), was equivalent to worship and sacrifice at an idol's altar, according to Senator Williams: "Ignorance, idolatry, immorality, vice, disease, and prostitution are the *deities* of [Senator Sumner's] theory; and *to them* he is now ready to *sacrifice* the pride and glory of American citizenship."[16]

It is no coincidence that Senator Williams names "ignorance, idolatry, immorality, vice, disease, and prostitution" as the deities identified with the Chinese and China. These vices have characterized "the East" in European and American Orientalism for centuries. And these imagined traits of China and the Chinese play into both their allure and their threat in apocalyptic Yellow Peril discourse. Just as the "Chinaman" could be both the exploitable "coolie" and the destroying horde, so also could China be both the source of high-status luxury goods—silk, tea, porcelain—and the decadent and degenerate Babylon of Revelation, the enemy and antithesis of the New Jerusalem, the Bride of Christ.[17]

The Whore of Babylon, who represents the city of Rome in the ancient context of Revelation, is fleshed out and enrobed in lavish, misogynist detail in the biblical text: "And I saw a woman sitting on a scarlet beast that was full of blasphemous names, and it had seven heads and ten horns. The woman was clothed in purple and scarlet, and adorned with gold and jewels and pearls, holding in her hand a golden cup full of abominations and impurities of her prostitution, and on her forehead was written a name, a mystery: 'Babylon the great, mother of whores and of earth's abominations.' And I saw that the woman was drunk with the blood of the saints and the blood of the witnesses to Jesus" (Rev 17:3–6).

Here appear all the characterizations of China in the anti-Chinese discourse of the Senate in the 1870s and 1880s: pagan idolatry, decadence and dissipation, greed, sexual corruption and prostitution, impurity and filth, and—most threatening of all—the conquering and consumption of Christian peoples, the saints and witnesses of Jesus.[18] While the U.S. senators did not explicitly call China the Whore of Babylon, the likening of China to the apocalyptic Whore and to the enemies of God's kingdom is obvious. And for cartoonists and novelists of the time, who had more room for poetic license and range than U.S. senators, the imagery and horror of Revelation provided a vast resource for anti-Chinese illustrations and literature.

Pierton Dooner's *Last Days of the Republic* (1880), possibly the first Yellow Peril novel published in America, tells a cautionary tale of continued importation of "coolies" for economic profit and the spread of Chinese populations beyond the American West into New England and the South. This infiltration allows Imperial China to invade the United States slowly until "the coil of the Asiatic serpent was gradually encircling the entire body of the victim, now virtually within its grasp." Soon, Chinese armies march across the nation; unlike the "Caucasian" soldier who fights "when military glory is the promised reward," the Chinese soldier instead "loves luxury" and "above and beyond all these, he worships gold." This effete militia, driven by greed, overwhelms the American armies with sheer numbers and brutality. As it finally makes its way to Washington, the novel concludes: "The Republic had fought its last battle; and the Imperial Dragon of China already floated from the dome of the Capitol."[19]

In this fearmongering novel, Babylon-China wins, demonstrating the consequences of the idolatrous worship of mammon rather than God. The final image of the dragon flying over the Capitol building is the Qing Dynasty flag of China at the time, which featured a Chinese *long* (龍 Cantonese: *lung*). Whereas in Chinese cultural tradition, the *long* symbolizes power, blessing, the emperor, water, and rain, Europeans had, by the nineteenth century, equated the *long* with the demonic dragon and serpent of the Bible, and of Revelation in particular.[20]

In Revelation, the dragon first appears in chapter 12. It is "a great red dragon, with seven heads and ten horns, and seven diadems on his heads"

(12:3). This is the Beast threatening to snatch away the child born of the Woman Clothed with the Sun, but he is defeated by an army of angels led by the archangel Michael: "And war broke out in heaven; Michael and his angels fought against the dragon. The dragon and his angels fought back, but they were defeated, and there was no longer any place for them in heaven. The great dragon was thrown down, that ancient serpent, who is called the Devil and Satan, the deceiver of the whole world. . . . Then the dragon was angry with the woman, and went off to wage war on the rest of her children, those who keep the commandments of God and hold the testimony of Jesus" (12:7–9, 17). The dragon, along with its various permutations seen in the Beast of the Sea (13:1–10) and the Beast on which rides the Whore of Babylon (17:3), is ultimately cast into the lake of fire, where it is destroyed (19:19–20:3).

This is the draconic Satan that European and American imagination equated with the ancient *long* of China and Chinese peoples. For example, British missionary and diplomat to China George Tradescant Lay documented a Spring Festival procession in 1841 as follows:

> But the pleasure of contemplating such shows and such devices is strongly marred by the thought, that the choicest gifts of Providence, the graces of human life, and the refinements of art, are made to move in procession to honour the Devil; for there he was under the semblance of a huge dragon, "the old serpent" [Rev 12:9], just as he appeared to our first parents when he persuaded them to break their pledge with their Maker. . . . [The Chinese] have been still more faithful in handing down from father to son the abominable worship of Satan, with all its insignia and ostentatious parade.

In this typical European interpretation, China is a Satanic kingdom and enemy of the Christian West, although Tradescant Lay hopes it can be defeated in battle by the forces of heaven: "Moral culture in China seems, with all its intrinsic and extrinsic defects, to have made a *breach* in some of the *outer walls of Satan's kingdom*, which missionaries will take advantage of, when a sufficient number shall have arrived in that country to carry on *the siege* in the regular way." Regardless of these tiny "breaches" in the "walls of Satan's kingdom" open to missionary proselytizing, white American and European discourse would continue to depict China as Revelation's great dragon, menacing the West—up to the present day.[21]

Dooner's *Last Days of the Republic* depicts the "Asiatic serpent" and the "Imperial Dragon of China" overtaking the United States. Robert Woltor's 1882 novel, *A Short and Truthful History of the Taking of California and Oregon by the Chinese in the Year A.D. 1899*, goes even further, making explicit use of Satan and the text of Revelation.[22] The story begins by depicting Chinese immigrants in the same grossly exaggerated way senators were doing in Congress, describing Chinese laborers inundating every business and service industry, in mines, shops, and households, throughout the West.

In the novel, all Chinese workers are organized by the fabled Six Companies of San Francisco and spread everywhere while government officials and businessmen ignore Chinese population growth on the West Coast because of their greed and eagerness for greater commerce and profit. Onto this scene, in 1898, arrives Prince Tsa, admiral of the Chinese navy, "sail[ing] inward through the Golden Gate," which is both the strait in the San Francisco Bay and an allusion to the United States' identity as a divine and heavenly land. West Coast officials and leaders greet him with much pomp and fanfare, and a friendly relationship between the United States and China grows, despite an outcry raised by white American workers.[23]

At the end of 1899, Prince Tsa visits San Francisco again with an ironclad fleet, bearing many lavish gifts and throwing "balls and banquets of extraordinary splendor." Finally, the prince gives one last sumptuous feast on December 31, 1899, on the evening of the turn of the century, inviting the entire government, civic, and social elite aboard his gorgeous ship. There, these leaders find themselves hosted with Oriental luxury, with "gold and silver ornaments, ebony carvings, embroidered screens, and satin draperies, and on every side attendants robed in tunics of spotless silk." Only toward the end of the feast do the guests hear a clamor and roar coming from the shores of the Bay, but by then the attendants have stripped them of all their weapons and they are trapped aboard. The prince then reveals what has been taking place on land, and when he gives his speech, the author states,

"Prince Tsa bore less resemblance to a human being than he did to Milton's Satan."[24]

While these guests were feasting on board, a conspiracy of all Chinese peoples throughout the West went to work, in every shop, eating house, and household, poisoning their white employers and neighbors, so that soon their dead bodies filled houses and streets up and down the West Coast. This mass poisoning echoes the plagues of Revelation, such as the poisoning of rivers and springs (8:10–11) and the turning of the sea, rivers, and springs into blood (16:3–7). Prince Tsa spares the lives of those aboard his ship—those guilty of worshipping the mammon of the East—but only so that they may evacuate all remaining "Americans and Europeans" from California and Oregon. The author ends by warning his readers that China will subjugate the world, as already foretold in Revelation: "In this liberal-minded age . . . we hesitate to draw upon the Apocalypse for quotations in support of these opinions, but those who believe in revelations may find much to support them in prophetic predictions."[25]

The narrator goes on to describe the discovery of a great Chinese sword in San Francisco. It is sheathed in a scabbard carved as a dragon with its jaws open, so that the double-edged blade issues out of it, and on its blade seven copper rivets are fastened, shown to match the seven stars of the Pleiades. The narrator states: "Now, it is somewhat curious that in the sixteenth verse of the first chapter of the Revelation of St. John the angel who held the keys of hell and death is thus partially described: 'And he had in his right hand seven stars: and out of his mouth went a sharp two-edged sword: and his countenance was as the sun shineth in his strength' [Rev 1:16]." In a strange twist, the storyteller thus identifies Revelation's holy Son of Man with the demonic Prince Tsa, who "comes from Oriental regions, where the sun first shines on earth . . . and that with his right hand he draws from its dragon-mouthed scabbard a two-edged sword, whose blade is marked symbolic of the Seven Stars."[26]

Despite the author's conflation of the Son of Man with the demonic, it is clear that Prince Tsa and the draconic kingdom of China are harbingers of the apocalyptic destruction of the United States. Woltor concludes by emphasizing, again, the argument that satanic forces are at work in the

THE DRAGON'S CHOICE

Fig. 4. W. A. Rogers, "The Dragon's Choice," *Harper's Weekly*, August 18, 1900, cover image.

immigration of Chinese to San Francisco, and he again evokes the New Jerusalem, declaring that "the Black Dragon has forced the passage of the Golden Gate."[27]

This is the same Dragon-as-China depicted in political cartoons such as W. A. Rogers's "The Dragon's Choice" (figure 4), which appeared on the cover of *Harper's Weekly* on August 18, 1900, at the climax of the conflict between the Boxers and the Euro-American alliance.[28] The image shows the menacing Beast breathing smoke from its mouth, standing over villages on fire—a dragon taking its menacing stand on the seashore (Rev 12:18). Facing it with calm stoicism is Uncle Sam: white haired, muscular, dressed in sailor whites and adorned with stars, aboard a mighty white ship, a strong bulwark, with cannon aimed and ready. The bestial, raving, dark, satanic China is challenged by the human, rational, white, and angelic United States and presumably the European countries of the Eight Nations Alliance, its allies in the conflict.

A few years prior to Rogers's "The Dragon's Choice," Hermann Knackfuss depicted "The Yellow Peril" (*die Gelbe Gefahr*) (figure 5) in imagery even more explicitly drawn from Revelation. Knackfuss's illustration circulated first in the *Leipziger Illustrierte Zeitung* in Germany in 1895, then, after gaining popularity throughout Europe, was printed stateside in *Harper's Weekly* in 1898. Knackfuss based his drawing on a sketch by Kaiser Wilhelm II, who had commissioned the piece. The kaiser reportedly had a nightmare in which he saw this vision, an apocalyptic warning against the encroachment of Asia—especially Japan (a rising military threat) and China—on the European nations. On the right-hand side of the illustration looms a colossal flaming Buddha—and, like the Whore of Babylon, seated on the seven-headed Beast (Rev 12:3), the Buddha rides black storm clouds that form a menacing dragon with glowing eyes.[29]

The perspective of the audience is directed to several European nations represented as white goddesses and women warriors, dressed in a mix of nationalist and Greco-Roman symbols. They stand in the foreground on a precipice, under a shining white cross; leading them is the archangel Michael, portrayed with typical iconography: with wings, Romanesque armor, and a flaming sword. He extends an arm in a sweeping gesture toward the battlefield, upon which he will soon lead them to war, just as he does in Revelation against the great dragon, Satan (12:7–9).[30]

Captions in French and English below the illustration warn: "Nations Européennes! Défendez vos biens sacrés!" ["European Nations! Defend your sacred goods!"] "Nations of Europe! Join in the defence of your faith and your homes!" The implications of this and other Yellow Peril illustrations in cartoons and literature are clear: the demonic Orient will seize and

Fig. 5. H. Knackfuss, "The Yellow Peril," *Harper's Weekly*, January 22, 1898, 76. (Beinecke Rare Book and Manuscript Library, Yale University.)

destroy lands, white cultures, and white womanhood unless the Christian West wages holy war against it.

But the dragon does not fight alone. As it says in Revelation, "Michael and his angels fought against the dragon. The dragon *and his angels* fought back" (12:7). As expressed in both Dooner's and Woltor's novels, Imperial China may be the dragon driving the attack, but it is the "horde" of sneaky, ruthless Chinese who form the terrible army descending upon the land. This is in fact how Chinese immigrants are described in an Oregon newspaper in 1892, on the eve of the ten-year deadline by which the Chinese Exclusion Act had to be renewed. *The Dalles Daily Chronicle* describes the Chinese threat in apocalyptic terms, playing on the designation of China as "the Celestial Kingdom" (天朝 Cantonese: *Tin Jiu* / Mandarin: *Tian Chao*) and the slur "Celestial" to refer to Chinese people. Under the headline "A

Celestial Horde," it reads: "The woods are full of Chinese over in Canada. It is said the denizens of the Flowery Kingdom, in large numbers, are dodging behind trees and hiding in sequestered nooks, ready to make a break for the United States the minute the clock strikes 12 on the night of the 3d." The Chinese lurk just beyond the borders, an evil, angelic host of another realm, ready to descend—literally, from Canada!—to invade at the stroke of midnight on doomsday.[31]

Fueled by such apocalyptic imagery and rhetoric in newspapers, Yellow Peril literature, and speeches on the Senate floor, Congress passed a spate of laws from 1875 to 1904 to restrict and exclude Chinese immigrants. For fear-mongering white nativists, the notion of America as the New Jerusalem conveniently evoked images of walls and battle and the threat of monstrous invaders. How easy it was then to identify the Chinese—who were already seen as alien and unassimilable in the Euro-American imagination—as a demonic horde about to breach the walls of the New Jerusalem and destroy it.

## Waiting at the Golden Gate

San Francisco fog blankets the Bay almost every morning, sometimes melting away as the sun rises. Huie Kin watched these mists dissolve over the water as he waited aboard ship to enter the Golden Gate Strait on a September morning in 1868. He had set sail from Guangdong over sixty days before, and the sight of land filled him with a marvelous sense of fulfillment and arrival. When he wrote his memoir, *Reminiscences of an Early Chinese Minister,* sixty-four years later, he too described his immigration to America in apocalyptic language. But instead of the onslaught of demonic invader or pestilential outsider, Kin saw his arrival as a fulfillment of an eschatological promise, as the arrival of someone who looks forward to belonging in the blessed realm: "To be actually at the 'Golden Gate' of the land of our dreams! The feeling that welled up in us was indescribable. I wonder whether the ecstasy before the Pearly Gates of the Celestial City above could surpass what we felt at the moment we realized that we had reached our destination."[32] Writing this toward the end of his life, Kin, who had been baptized at the age of twenty and went on to serve the Chinese Christian community in New York City, imbues his first sight of America with Christian language, using the dominant metaphor of America as the New Jerusalem.

But after the initial hope and excitement of seeing the shores of the "Celestial City," Kin encountered the violent and fearful reality faced by Chinese immigrants in the 1870s and '80s. "The useful and steady Chinese worker," Kin recalls, "became overnight the mysterious Chinaman, an object of unknown dread." Not allowed to enter the heavenly city, the Chinese were instead abandoned to the flames, like the fate of anyone "whose name was not found written in the book of life" and so "was thrown into the lake of fire" (Rev 20:15). So Kin's recollections of the terrible persecution of Chinese is laced with flames: "There were long processions at night, with big torchlights and lanterns, carrying the slogan 'The Chinese Must Go,' and mass meetings where fiery-tongues flayed the Chinese bogey."[33]

Kin recollects that anti-Chinese agitator Denis Kearney reportedly called for the Chinese to be hurled into damnation by saying: "There is no means left to clear the Chinamen but to swing them into eternity by their own queues [traditional Chinese braid], for there is no rope long enough in all America wherewith to strangle four hundred millions of Chinamen." Chinese immigrants lived not in the golden light of the Celestial City but in the red glow of flames and the dreaded darkness of night: "We were simply terrified," Kin writes. "We kept indoors after dark for fear of being shot in the back. Children spit upon us as we passed by and called us rats."[34]

The terror and persecution remembered by Kin came right before the passage of Chinese restriction and exclusion laws. After they were passed, it became possible to implement policies to keep out immigrants—namely, Chinese laborers. But implementation and enforcement required practical realities such as detention centers, guards, and immigration officers to make judgments regarding eligibility to enter. After the Exclusion Act of 1882, only Chinese deemed to be teachers, students, tourists, diplomats, and merchants or those whose family members already were residents of the United States were allowed in. Officials were needed to determine whether an immigrant met the criteria.

Bureaucracy creates tedious procedures and difficulties, prolonging the purgatory of waiting either for entry to or exclusion from the country. The hundreds of Chinese still arriving in San Francisco after the passage of restrictive laws were forced to wait, for weeks and sometimes months, before they were free to enter or were deported.[35] Governments at the federal, state, and local level had made almost no preparations for the detention of Chinese immigrants. They were therefore held at various locations under various conditions, all of them awful.

Since the Pacific Mail Steamship Company ran the major shipping lines transporting Chinese immigrants, many of their vessels became floating detention centers, holding Chinese until they could be investigated. The Pacific Mail's grounded ship the *Columbia* was also used as a quarantine detention center for ships like the *Altonower* and "her horde of infected coolies," whom city officials refused to let on land to be treated at hospitals (in contrast to infected white passengers). But when the United States invaded the Philippines in 1898, the Pacific Mail's ships were needed to transport troops; they could no longer detain Asian immigrants because they had to be used to invade Asia.[36]

The Pacific Mail therefore transformed some of its dockside buildings into "the Shed," the infamous detention center on San Francisco's Pier 40. Chinese immigrants were crammed into this space for weeks at a time, in a building described in a telegram by San Francisco Special Inspector Fred Watts as "death trap unsanitary." Indeed, it threatened to erupt into an inferno when one night a mob, part of the anti-Chinese crowd spurred on by Kearney, set portions of it on fire. Those not held either on a ship or in the Shed could be held in the San Francisco County Jail, about which a white reporter in 1903 wrote: "The darkness and filthiness of this Chinese detention area is beyond description. . . . The smell was hard to describe and the place was like hell on earth."[37]

Chinese women arriving unaccompanied at port went neither to the death trap nor to hell but to the "Angry Angel." This was Donaldina Cameron, who ran the Presbyterian Mission House in San Francisco and who raided Chinatown's brothels and housed Chinese women. Some of the women staying at the Mission House called her "Old Mother" (老母 Cantonese: *Lou Mou*), while other Chinese dubbed her "Jesus Woman" and "Foreign Devil" (番鬼 Cantonese: *Faan Gwai*). She eventually came to be called "Chinatown's Angry Angel," and a colleague claims that to the Chinese women she sheltered she "seemed an angel of deliverance."[38]

While Cameron certainly saved many Chinese women from enslavement, she also helped perpetuate stereotypes of Chinese sexual depravity through the "rescue" stories she told. What is more, she partnered with law enforcement and immigration officials so that the Mission House also became a detention center, where Chinese women could be inspected, interrogated, and either deported or placed under her supervision. Cameron herself understood the home as a kind of detaining purgatory for Chinese "girls," from where she hoped "the wise Providence that has guided their destinies thus far [may] bring them safely through all their perils into His Kingdom at last." This sentiment conflates the outer world of America and the heavenly world of the divine, both of which Cameron hoped would be the eventual destination of her wards.[39]

But what the women's Mission House, the county jail, and the Shed could not provide was a way to keep the threat of the Chinese horde *outside* the walls of the Heavenly Kingdom until their fates could be determined. Since Chinese immigrants were detained on the mainland, they could also try to escape—to break quarantine and infiltrate the country. Notes could also be smuggled out of detention centers—which is what one prisoner with a Hawaiian birth certificate and claims to citizenship did when he was detained and slated to be deported in 1904. This was Sun Yat-sen, who managed to send a secret message to leaders in the Chinese community so that he could eventually be released.[40]

Officials subsequently chose a new location to hold immigrants arriving at San Francisco Bay, a place deemed desirable in the same way as Alcatraz: as an inescapable, insular prison. This locale was also imbued with apocalyptic overtones, matching the heavenly inclusion or exclusion anticipated and encountered by immigrants—and in keeping with the U.S. gatekeeping of the New Jerusalem. This was Angel Island, lying north of Alcatraz in the San Francisco Bay. Ironic happenstance and heavenly ideation would have it that the threatening "celestial horde" must be held back at the mystical Isla de Los Angeles.

There they would be imprisoned before they set foot on the mainland beyond the Golden Gate Strait, which itself was first named Chrysopylae, Greek for "Golden Gate," recalling the ancient Chrysoceras, the Golden Horn harbor of Byzantium, and, more ancient than that, the Golden Gate of Jerusalem, derived from the early Christian work *The Infancy Gospel of James.*[41]

John Frémont, the man who christened the Strait, also envisioned "the day when riches of the Orient would flow through the gate," riches of foreign nations, like the tribute of "every nation" that enters the New Jerusalem in Revelation.[42] "The nations will walk by its light, and the kings of the earth will bring their glory into it. Its gate will never be shut by day—and there will be no night there. People will bring into it the glory and honor of the nations" (Rev 21:24–26). Of course, the wealth of the Orient, as we have seen, also calls to mind Revelation 18 and the merchants and ships bearing gold, jewels, and riches for decadent, exotic, and degenerate Babylon (11–13).

The Angel Island detention center embodied exactly this apocalyptic ambiguity of American immigration. Unlike Ellis Island, memorialized in arrival stories of the "nation of immigrants," the purpose of Angel Island was not to "process" immigrants but to exclude them. The announcement of its opening regurgitated the national discourse of hospitality and American moral uprightness while it simultaneously enacted the national policy of racist exclusion. So the *San Francisco Chronicle* predicted in 1909 that when immigrants arrive at Angel Island, the "newcomers from foreign shores will probably think they have struck *paradise.*"[43] This language echoes the expectations of Columbus and his paradisial visions, but those outside the golden city experienced quite a different reality. From the perspective of Chinese travelers, Angel Island could be anticipated as the mythical "Island of Immortals" of Chinese fables but experienced as a hellish jail guarded by foreign devils (鬼佬 Cantonese: *gwai lou*).[44]

This is the sentiment expressed in one of the many poems carved by detained Chinese men on the walls of the barracks of Angel Island Immigration Station between 1910 and 1940:

> This place is called an island of immortals,
> When in fact, this mountain wilderness is a prison.[45]

So although San Francisco and California were nicknamed "Gold Mountain" (金山 Cantonese: *Gam Saan* / Mandarin: *Jin Shan*) in Chinese—and even now San Francisco is called "Old Gold Mountain" (舊金山 *Gau Gam Saan* / *Jiu Jin Shan*)—this shining city could also be a symbol of exclusion. Another barracks carving reads:

> I bought an oar and arrived in the land of the Golden Mountain.
> Who was to know they would banish me to Island?[46]

What Chinese immigrants found on Angel Island were not open doors, free ports, and inclusion in the New Jerusalem, as Ronald Reagan would tout in his vision of the shining city on a hill. Instead, they found themselves herded into segregated quarters—men separated from women and Europeans separated from "Orientals." They were subjected to humiliating physical examinations, because they and other Asians were believed to carry more infectious diseases than other races. They endured hours of interrogation in order to prove their identity and their right to enter the country. Every Chinese detainee had to stand trial, guilty until proven innocent, and each case was investigated and analyzed, files and paper trails carefully sifted. The average case took two to three weeks to process before a judgment was pronounced, but some cases dragged on for months upon months. One woman was detained for twenty months before all her legal options were exhausted and she was deported back to China. Those who successfully gained entry had usually been subjected to interrogations lasting day after day. One twelve-year-old boy, whose case was taken up to the federal courts, endured hearings that generated eighty-seven pages of testimony.[47]

The Angel Island Immigration Station detained Chinese and other arrivals from 1910 to 1940. Even at the end of its time as an immigration detention center, Chinese testimonies of the place do not tell of improvements or of a "paradise." One Chinese man, part of a student delegation, wrote in 1939 that the island "should be called the Devil Island" because of the humiliating and needless physical examinations and the misery of those detained. Another student, a Chinese woman, wrote that same year: "We were to go to the immigration station, Angel Island; unfortunately, we were not able to find any angels there, but we did see many heartless human beings."[48]

There was one "Angel of Angel Island," Katharine Maurer, who served as a deaconess there from 1912 until its closure as an immigration detention center. But despite her angelic presence on Angel Island, the "Angry Angel" in Chinatown Donaldina Cameron, and even the "Fighting Angel," missionary to China and Bible translator Absalom Sydenstricker (the father of novelist Pearl S. Buck), no angelic power could transform America's rejection and exclusion of Chinese immigrants as a heathen horde at its gates.[49] Even after the repeal of Chinese exclusion in 1943 and the Immigration and Nationality Act of 1965, which abolished the National Origins Formula, the identification of Chinese with unassimilability, national threat, and disease continues to this day.

## Apocalyptic Exclusion Expanded

Restriction and exclusions laws, mob violence, Yellow Peril literature, and dramatic congressional speeches all targeted the perceived threat of China and Chinese immigrants. But the apocalyptic discourses present in all of these affected many more groups of people than the Chinese hoping to enter the United States. The creation of Chinese exclusion laws effected a shift in immigration processing and created systems, officials, bureaucracy, and policing that have become essential to American immigration ever since.

The laws restricting and preventing Chinese immigration were the first federal immigration laws systematically enforced, which required a specialized government agency and officials dedicated to the task. Anti-Chinese immigration laws necessitated more than just the inspection of U.S. customs collectors at ports; they led to the establishment of the Office of the Superintendent of Immigration (1891), which became the Bureau of Immigration (1895), split into the Bureaus of Immigration and Naturalization (1913), which in turn recombined to become the Immigration and Naturalization Service (1933), which was eventually replaced by Customs and Border Protection, Immigration and Customs Enforcement (ICE), and U.S. Citizenship and Immigration Services (2003).[50]

The necessity for reentry permits, identification cards, and papers to prove admissibility also established systems of documentation and interrogation at entry points. The processes for determining entry or exclusion created systems for determining criminal offenses and punishments, and laws for deportation. On a deeper, more insidious and pervasive level, these exclusion laws and their enforcement also began the rapid crystallization of the idea of *being illegal* in America. The national exclusion of a specific ethnic group proclaimed explicitly and indisputably that entry through the gates of America was based on race—understood to be essential, God-ordained, and immutable.[51]

Of course, the link between American identity and race—that is, whiteness—is already clear in the history of U.S. citizenship and naturalization, which had excluded indigenous and Black peoples more than a century before the Chinese exclusion acts. The victims of the two foundations of the United States, genocide and slavery, Native and Black peoples were already forcibly within the gates of the New Jerusalem—imprisoned and murdered for its construction but deemed essentially unqualified to be citizens. The anti-Chinese legislation from 1875 onward established who must stay *outside* the gates and against whom the walls must be defended: the heathen, invasive, and threatening hordes. As Edward K. Valentine (R-NE) argued in Congress on March 18, 1882: "In order to protect our laboring classes, the gate . . . must be closed."[52]

Once the U.S. government shut the gate, the powerful within could insist that it remain shut: "Hereafter," ran one 1882 *Chicago Times* piece, "we are to keep our hand on the door-knob, and admit only those whose presence we desire." Through the first half of the twentieth century, the United States held the door ever more tightly closed, as restrictions on immigration from East, Southeast, and South Asia climaxed with the Immigration Act of 1917, which established the Asiatic Barred Zone, ruling ineligible for entry most immigrants from Asia, the Pacific Islands, and parts of the Middle East. The 1917 act also established literacy requirements for entry, effectively keeping out classes of unwanted people from all over the world.[53]

The success of apocalyptic anti-Chinese rhetoric in creating legislation, bureaucracy, and detention policies made its arguments and tactics a blueprint for anti-immigrant and anti-non-white discourse in America ever after. These essential rhetorical moves include invoking the invasion of the Dragon and the Yellow Peril and the racialization of Chinese as a heathen horde, ungodly and virtually inhuman. Expanding beyond Yellow Peril in literature, novelists also wrote Black Peril stories, such as King Wallace's *The Next War: A Prediction*, published in 1892, in which a "vast horde" of "Africans . . . Mulattoes, Quadroons and Octoroons" take over America. In another work, published in 1893, armies of "Indo-Chinese, Hindoos, Afghans, Beloochees, Persians, Turks, Arabs," and also Chinese and Africans take over Europe and America. The popularity of such Yellow, Black, and Brown Peril stories is evinced by famed novelist Jack London, who wrote one himself, titled "The Unparalleled Invasion" (published 1910), in which the monstrous threat of China is finally eradicated by the absolute genocide of the Chinese population, followed by "the sanitation of China."[54]

Beyond writing apocalyptic stories of foreign invaders, white American nativists also linked unwanted people groups to Chinese peoples racially, tingeing them "yellow" in suggestive descriptions. Building on the white-black binary used to reinforce the systemic oppression of Black peoples already within the United States, a white-yellow binary was invoked in anti-immigration arguments. This, of course, worked most easily against other East Asian peoples, such as the Japanese and Koreans. Anti-Yellow hatred and rhetoric also came to include South Asians. Indians were described in newspapers in 1910 as "Hindu Hordes" that were "dirty, diseased . . . the worst type of immigrant . . . not fit to become a citizen . . . and entirely foreign to the people of the United States," exactly as the Chinese had been viewed since the mid-nineteenth century. Even certain European groups became "Chinese" if they were undesirable — Italians were the "Chinese of Europe" or "European coolies," while eastern Europeans were said to have been intermingling their bloodlines with "Asiatic hordes." The hateful descriptions of these immigrant groups draw directly on anti-Chinese discourse, which consistently and continually emphasized certain characteristics: filthiness, depravity, diseased bodies, sexual immorality, and their existence as a collective "horde" of virtually nonhuman, bestial beings.[55]

While anti-Chinese descriptions and arguments served as the playbook for subsequent and broader opposition to immigration, that rhetoric borrowed from an even earlier playbook, the ancient text of Revelation, already prominently used in framing American identity, colonization, and expansion. In the early Christian apocalyptic text, those who must be excluded

from the New Jerusalem of Revelation are explicitly described: "But nothing unclean will enter [the city], nor anyone who practices abomination or
falsehood" (21:27a). "Outside are the dogs and sorcerers and sexually immoral and murderers and idolaters and everyone who loves and practices
falsehood" (22:15).[56] Such verses and descriptions provide the key compo-
nents of racist anti-immigrant characterizations: filthiness and being diseased, idolatry and heathen religion, sexual immorality, dishonesty and
violence, and nonhumanness and animality, especially animality associated
with filth, disease, and plague (such as dogs, pigs, rats, and locusts).

The rejection, interrogation, inspection, and humiliation of those seeking entry to America stands in sharp contrast to the promise of paradise, and
Reagan's open doors for those "with the will and the heart" to enter. This
does not signal, however, that America failed as the New Jerusalem but
rather that the metaphor continued (and continues today) to serve the political interests of those using it in immigration discourse: at first the colonizing immigrants and later white American nativists. America as the New
Jerusalem, with its gleaming walls and foundation, set as a "shining city on
a hill," presents a fresh beginning, moral aspirations, promises of wealth,
and assurances of safety and stability. But the appearance of the New Jerusalem of Revelation 21–22 comes after a long narrative of violent warfare,
plagues, and judgment. Implicit in the purity of those within the city walls
is the exclusion of the "impure" without, the "dogs and sorcerers and sexually immoral and murderers and idolaters" (Rev 22:15).

The imagining of America as the New Jerusalem did more than elevate
America as the city on a hill and cast a golden glow on its founding and its aspirations. This vision also effectively *shrunk* the country. Discourse identifying
America as the heavenly city contracts a vast nation into a unified, compact
space, traditionally and historically bounded by walls. This does several things
at once: it creates the impression of crowdedness and scarcity, and it fore-
grounds boundary as defining identity, which makes belonging an either/or enterprise and creates the danger of infiltration and invasion. It is no mistake that
while spacious skies and amber waves of grain are invoked to celebrate America's beauty, the discourse of immigration—and of minoritized peoples—deals
mostly in cities and urban settings, ghettos and hordes, filth and disease.

# PART TWO

# Disease and Plague

# THREE

# "Nothing Unclean Will Enter It"
## Apocalyptic Epidemiology and Exclusion

Its gates will never be shut by day—and there will be no night there. . . .
But nothing unclean will enter it, nor anyone who practices
abomination or falsehood.

—*Revelation 21:25–27*

And it seems God hath provided this Country for our Nation, destroying the
natives by the plague, it not touching one Englishman.

—*John Smith, on the 1616–19 epidemic (1635)*

When we see this fatal scourge of pagan, mahommedan, and anti-christian
lands lighting upon our shores, and feel the first blow here at the heart of this
aspiring nation, we may not forget that the moral influence of this city is felt to
the extremity of the land.

—*Rev. Gardiner Spring (1832)*

## Invading Disease, Invading Enemies

The language of disease is one of invasion. Viruses and bacteria as described in textbooks and news stories alike do not neutrally enter a body
but *infiltrate* it, first through vulnerable points of entry on the boundaries of
a body (for example, mouth, nose, eyes, open wounds). Then, a pathogen—
literally, "producer of suffering"—might breach the walls of individual cells,

the myriad units constituting the attacked body. It takes no great leap of imagination to view this as indeed an "attack," with enemies "marching" down windpipes and "hijacking" cell mechanisms, while white blood cells form a "front line" on the battlefield. But, as Susan Sontag writes, "The effect of the military thinking about sickness and health is far from inconsequential." The metaphor of war, in dramatizing and narrativizing disease, "overmobilizes" and "overdescribes" such that "it powerfully contributes to the excommunicating and stigmatizing of the ill."[1]

War-themed dramatizations of disease cast survivors as heroes—but those who die or continue as disabled consequently play the role of those not strong enough or not brave enough, so that they lose not only life or ability but also a moral contest. "Fighting" cancer or COVID-19 becomes a test of personal merit, a struggle to "dominate," rather than simply the experience of disease within a nexus of physical, economic, social, and cultural realities.[2] And if a person must "fight" a disease, someone who "loses the battle" easily becomes a "loser" and personally to blame because of their habits or lifestyle or, further down that road, their moral depravity. This is why Sontag and many others reject the use of military language in epidemiology.

Alongside the stigmatization of those who suffer and die comes the categorization of these individuals into groups understood as especially susceptible to disease, socially and sexually deviant, disgusting in hygiene, or all of the above. AIDS, known as the "homosexual disease" in its first decades, was seen in the United States as belonging to a depraved community that deservedly suffered a divinely inflicted, apocalyptic plague.[3]

But in the full story of AIDS in America, the disease did not *originate* with "homosexuals," but came from *outside*. While at first the American public feared a group within their national borders, scientific discoveries of the virus's origins among West African primates drew attention to dangers lurking outside those borders. The conjunction of *Africa, monkeys, plague,* and *sexually transmitted* coalesced in American public imagination into a new nightmare full of racist fear, playing on a "subliminal connection made to notions about a primitive past" that "cannot help but activate a familiar set of stereotypes about animality, sexual license, and blacks."[4] AIDS became evidence of the bestial depravity of Africans outside the United States, who also appeared to have co-conspirators among depraved Black Americans inside the country.

The equation of sickness with the Other is, of course, nothing new. During the Black Death, Rhineland city leaders targeted Jews for slaughter, accusing them of poisoning wells and spreading the plague. In the third century CE, the philosopher Porphyry blamed Christians—and their neglect of Asclepius and the gods—for causing a plague.[5] But while these peoples constituted an Other, they were not groups delineated as alien foreigners from abroad. Indeed, it was their integration in society that was part of the problem, so that the only way to appease the gods and/or safeguard society was the expulsion or destruction of the enemy already within.

The discussion here focuses on the fear of enemies *outside* the city walls as the carriers of plague, on the perception of peoples wholly "new" and Other in the American context as the main cause of disease. The earliest immigrants to America, white Europeans, understood indigenous peoples as the "new" and Other, and thereby especially prone to the diseases that ravaged their populations—even though they themselves were the invading foreigners. Once established in the land, later generations of white Anglo nativists maligned subsequent immigrant groups they rejected as especially prone to sickness. These beliefs were informed and supplied by the metaphors and theology of the book of Revelation, which depicts those outside the walls of the New Jerusalem as "filthy" and immoral, to be barred from entry. White colonials and nativists, having imagined America as the shining new city of God, naturally produced—and continue to produce—a theologized anti-immigrant discourse that associates "foreigners" with plague.

It was after the European explorers happened upon the American continents that ideation of disease focused blame not only on the Other but on the Other as an outsider. The figure of the diseased foreigner came into sharp focus due to several new realities of the American context: the relative boundedness of the "New World," lying between the Atlantic and Pacific Oceans; advances in travel by ship and, thus, the coming together of people groups heretofore separated by vast distances; and the speed by which they could be mutually introduced.[6] Under these conditions of the New World, the

European blame of disease on the Other morphed to become the American blame of disease on new arrivals. But the first arrivals, who indeed brought disease with them, did not see themselves as wreaking ruin on Native populations but as given a divine weapon.

## The Sword of the Lord

When the explorers and later colonists arrived in the Americas, they not only murdered indigenous populations by their own hand but introduced tiny "colonizers" as well. The actions of these European first immigrants mirrored simultaneous, microscopic events carried out by the pathogens they brought, as these sought to "(1) colonize the host; (2) find a nutritionally compatible niche in the host body; (3) avoid, subvert, or circumvent the host's innate and adaptive immune response; (4) replicate, using host resources; and (5) exit and spread to a new host."[7]

This is a description taken from a standard microbiology textbook, describing the "successful" pathogen, one able to "maximally exploit" the host and multiply rapidly. Perhaps the metaphor of colonization more accurately describes the course of disease than the metaphor of warfare. In any case, the new European immigrants, like the viruses they carried, exploited the Native host and its resources and multiplied so that they decimated, by sword and disease, on average 90–95 percent of each Native group they encountered. In Jamestown, Virginia, the Native population decreased from twenty-five thousand to two thousand between 1607 and 1700, while its colonist population grew from zero to around one hundred thousand. To be sure, some colonists also suffered from disease strains new to them, such as malaria, but the pathogens they brought with them wrought far greater destruction on Native populations.[8]

Far from seeing themselves as the diseased Other and foreigner, however, the first European immigrants interpreted the death of the Native population as part of a glorious destiny. In New England, epidemiology was based in large part on theology, framed by an apocalyptic mission to establish God's kingdom on earth. Puritan minister Increase Mather credited prayer and God's hand with the felling of the Native "heathens" by disease:

How often have we prayed that the Lord would take those his Enemies into his own avenging hand . . . and send the destroying Angel amongst them. This Prayer hath been heard; For it is known
that the Indians were distressed with famine, multitudes of them
perishing for want of bread; and the Lord sent sicknesses amongst
them, that Travellers have seen many dead Indians up and down
in the woods that were by famine or sickness brought unto that
untimely end. Yea the Indians themselves have testified, that
more amongst them have been cut off by the sword of the Lord in
those respects, then by the sword of the English.

Colonist Daniel Denton (1626–1703) similarly saw divine will at work in the
death of Native populations in New York: "Where the English come to settle, a Divine Hand makes way for them, by removing or cutting off the Indians, either by Wars one with the other, or by some raging mortal Disease."[9]

Increase Mather's son Cotton Mather further explained how this mortal-
ity made way for the establishment of God's people, ridding the land "of
those pernicious creatures to make room for *better growth.*" Puritan discourse portrayed the colonists as the Israelites reaching the Promised Land
on which to construct God's kingdom in the New World. Cotton Mather
writes, "This at last is the spot of *earth* which the God of heaven *spied out*
for the seat of such *evangelical,* and *ecclesiastical,* and very remarkable
transactions," where the Puritan fathers attempted "in the American hemisphere to anticipate the state of the New-Jerusalem."[10] Of course God would
clear the way for its foundations to be built.

These colonial quotations combine allusions to Israelite history and
apocalypticism that create a divine narrative and justification for the invasion and settlement of New England and beyond. In this discourse, the colonists, and the Puritans in particular, rhetorically equate themselves to the
Israelites coming to the Promised Land—"spying it out"—as the Israelite
heroes Joshua and Caleb do the land of Canaan in Numbers 13–14, reporting: "The land that we went through as spies is an exceedingly good land. If
the Lord is pleased with us, he will bring us into this land and give it to us"
(14:7–8). This "errand into the wilderness," to borrow the title of a sermon

delivered by Samuel Danforth (1626–74) of Massachusetts in 1670, was not only to establish the colonists in the land but also to eradicate the Native peoples there before them.[11] The colonists were aided by disease, the "sword of the Lord," which cleared the land of its Native population—a weapon with which God also threatened the Israelites themselves if they were disobedient: "I will bring the sword against you, executing vengeance for the covenant; and if you withdraw into your cities, I will send pestilence among you, and you shall be delivered into enemy hands" (Lev 26:25).

The agricultural metaphor used by Cotton Mather of clearing the land for "better growth" suits the Israelite analogy of invading the land of Canaan, since God commanded the Israelites to empty the land lest any remaining indigenous people become a pestilent growth: "But if you do not drive out the inhabitants of the land from before you, then those whom you let remain shall be as barbs in your eyes and thorns in your sides" (Num 33:55). But the culling of Native peoples for "better growth" even better parallels metaphors in the New Testament that have, in the history of their interpretation, become supersessionist over and against Jewish peoples.

Metaphors from the Hebrew Bible prophets comparing disobedient Israel (and others) to a vineyard of rotted grapes and vegetation to be cut down are repeatedly evoked in the texts of the New Testament to warn of a cutting off, culling, and winnowing of growth destined for apocalyptic fire and destruction. By contrast, the "better growth"—the vines that bear fruit, the nourishing wheat, or the well-planted seed—endures and flourishes. Everything else must be cut down, as in the gruesome scene of Revelation 14, when "the angel swung his sickle over the earth and gathered the vintage of the earth, and he threw it into the great wine press of the wrath of God. And the wine press was trodden outside the city, and blood flowed from the wine press, as high as a horse's bridle, for a distance of about two hundred miles" (19–20).[12]

The decimation of indigenous peoples by plague could certainly be understood in these divine and apocalyptic terms: depictions of terrible devastation ("Travellers have seen many dead Indians up and down in the woods") are also claimed to be God's will. The clearing of the land by sickness made way for the "plantations" of the Puritans. These are not the agricultural estates with the same name most associated with the American South but the communities called "plantations," that is, plantings of God's people as "better growth" by Pilgrim and Puritan colonizers, such as Plymouth Plantation or the "plantation" of New Haven. These communities were "plantings" of God's people, namely, Pilgrim and Puritan colonizers, who embodied the "better growth" that Cotton Mather envisioned.[13]

Once established as God's plantations, however, New England colonists no longer played the role of new arrivals and the beginners of God's work: they became rooted natives in their own eyes, no longer spying out and invading but responsible for the *defense* of God's city. In terms of disease, what had once been the weapon of God to clear the way before them turned into a threat at the gates of the holy city.

## Apocalyptic Epidemiology

By the third generation of English colonists, perceptions of sickness had shifted due to changes in scientific thinking along with phenomena relating to continuing immigration to America's shores. Most colonists in the eighteenth century believed that toxic vapors arising from decay caused disease, and it made sense to them that the poor, who lived in dirtier, more dilapidated dwellings, should fall sick, since they had greater exposure to the "miasma." This belief that a filthy and harmful environment caused disease was known as the "localist" position (since it points to local environs as the root cause of sickness) or the "anticontagionist" position (when it cites the environment as the *only* cause of sickness, exclusive of contagion).[14]

But it became apparent to colonists, as their populations gained immunities to diseases present in America and lived to witness wave after wave of new, vulnerable immigrants arriving, that *newcomers* most often became ill. The idea of contagion grew so that, as Alan Kraut notes, a "melding of miasmatic theory with a growing fear of contagia served to bind the cause of disease *directly to the sufferer.*"[15] In other words, both localists and contagionist theories of disease blamed the immigrants: they were either the spreaders of disease, lived in such squalor that it gave rise to miasma, or both. In either case, the sick and sick-making foreigner was to blame.

Disease stalked the land no longer as God's Angel of Death, clearing the way, but as the filthy outsider, threatening the now established city of God. Conceptions of immigrants as the unclean outside the walls of New Jerusalem grew easily from existing theology and ideas of church membership. John Davenport, states Cotton Mather, "did now at New-Haven make *church purity* to be one of his greatest concernments and endeavours . . . he used a more than ordinary exactness in trying those that were admitted unto the communion of the church: indeed so very thoroughly, and, I had almost said, severely strict, were the terms of his communion . . . that he did all that was possible to render the renowned church of New-Haven like the New-Jerusalem."[16]

Davenport guarded entry to the New Haven church as if it were—indeed, *as*—the New Jerusalem, although, Mather notes, Davenport found it "impossible to see a *church* state, whereinto there 'enters nothing which defiles' [Rev 21:27]."[17] Mather here describes Davenport's process for admitting persons to membership in the New Haven church, judging them by their professions of faith and points of theology. But the underlying language of purity and defilement presents a prime example of the widespread and age-old conflation of Christian morality and righteousness with physical purity, cleanliness, and health. This is unsurprising given that the foundational text of the Christian New Jerusalem, Revelation itself, also conflates cleanliness with righteousness, and filthiness and disease with sin and immorality.

Throughout Revelation, those on the side of God, who ultimately dwell within the walls of the New Jerusalem, are depicted as wearing white robes, symbolizing—in times modern and ancient—cleanliness, purity, and wealth. White robes are given to the faithful who conquered, who have not "soiled their clothes" (3:4), who are "sealed" as God's chosen, and who are virginally and thus also morally pure (14:4). These and all who live in the New Jerusalem have washed their robes in the "high powered detergent" that is the blood of the Lamb (7:14, 22:14). Having clean, washed robes is in fact a requirement for entering the New Jerusalem: "Blessed are those who wash their robes, so that they . . . may enter the city by the gates" (22:14). The white cleanliness of the robes is a visual mark of the citizenship and legitimacy enjoyed by those who entered through the heavenly gates. The robes also signal, then as now, the elite status of those who do not engage in labor that would stain their clothes, who can afford such raiment, and who are habituated to healthful environs with cleansing water. The text conflates these aspects of class and outward appearance with righteousness and divine salvation.[18]

Conversely, those outside the walls of the New Jerusalem are hopelessly evil and dirty, in sharp contrast to the righteous within. This antithesis is proclaimed by an angel in a pair of couplets:

> Let the evildoer still do evil,
> and the filthy still be filthy,
> and the righteous still do right,
> and the holy still be holy. (Rev 22:11)

These lines, imitating the structure of classical Hebrew poetry, underline the conflation of "evildoer" (ὁ ἀδικῶν) with "the filthy" (ὁ ῥυπαρός) and "righteous" (ὁ δίκαιος) with "the holy" (ὁ ἅγιος). At the same time, they define filthiness as the opposite of holiness, also to be understood as purity.[19]

The filthy evildoers outside the city walls may be grouped with the worshippers of the Beast who are afflicted with disease after the first bowl of God's wrath is poured out: "So the first angel went and poured his bowl on the earth, and a foul and painful sore came on those who had the brand of the beast and who worshiped its image" (Rev 16:2). Those outside the New Jerusalem are also the sexually immoral, murderers, and idolators (Rev 22:15). And in contrast to those inside, who are clothed in luxuriant, clean white robes, their opposites outside are described as "wretched, pitiable, poor, blind, and naked" (Rev 3:17).[20]

This is a description of suffering—they are "wretched" and "pitiable"—but furthermore a description that denotes poverty, for those who are "poor" cannot, as the Son of Man instructs, "buy from me gold refined by fire so that you may be rich, and white robes to clothe yourself" (Rev 3:18) and so they remain "naked." Since they are blind, they are also disabled, and since they are poor, they cannot access medicine by buying, as instructed, "salve to anoint your eyes so that you may see" (Rev 3:18).

While this description serves primarily as a warning to a lukewarm church at the beginning of Revelation, it becomes clear in the ensuing narrative that those who do not (or cannot afford to) clothe themselves in robes washed by the blood of the Lamb not only suffer poverty and shame but go on to commit violent and revolting acts. They do not wash white robes in the blood of the Lamb but rather imbibe what is abominable, for when the second and third bowl of God's wrath poured on the earth turns all its waters to blood (Rev 16:3–4), an angel declares of those who worship the Beast:

> Because they shed the blood of saints and prophets,
> you have given them blood to drink.
> It is what they deserve! (Rev 16:6)

And so, together with the drunken Whore of Babylon, those outside the walls of the New Jerusalem drink the blood of corpses (Rev 16:3–6), the blood of martyrs (17:6), and the wine of prostitution (17:2). They are thus utterly revolting, both ritually and morally impure, poor, dirty, evil, and diseased.[21] Therefore these accursed, both polluted and polluting, stay eternally quarantined outside the city gates.

Those committing abominations, kept outside the New Jerusalem, cannot access the glories within, which are ironically the very things they would need as the wretched, impure, diseased, and unclean. Within the walls lies healing, cleansing, and purification: there is a river of the Water of Life running through the center of the city (Rev 22:1–2), and the Tree of Life grows on either side, bearing nourishing fruit and leaves for healing (22:2). Thus the "filthy [will] still be filthy," seeing through the open city gates the water for cleansing and the trees for healing but forever out of their reach, for "nothing accursed will be found there any more" (22:3).

The purity of the New Jerusalem in Revelation served as inspiration for the moral and theological purity to which Davenport and others aspired in New England church communities. But Revelation's consistent conflation of evil and idolatry with filth and plague impacted ideals not only of church membership but also of civic membership. That is, white nativists also began to exclude new immigrants and forbid their entry on the same grounds as those barring the way to the New Jerusalem: based on identifying certain immigrants as diseased, immoral, and disabled. The combination of epidemiology associating new immigrants as disease-prone and the discourse of America as God's city to be guarded converged in the formation of America's first exclusionary immigration laws.

The Massachusetts Colony began to shut its gates to those who might defile it in the year 1700. The colony passed a law explicitly barring entry to the sick and disabled, declaring shipmasters liable for any passengers who were "impotent, lame, or otherwise infirm, or likely to be a charge [burden] to the place" and who could not provide security or procure a surety for their support." This law was strengthened in 1724, so that any town in Massachusetts, not only port towns, could refuse entry to "poor, vicious, and infirm persons," an echo of Revelation's "wretched, pitiable, poor, blind, and naked" (3:17).[22]

The categories of the "poor, vicious, and infirm" exhibit the same ancient combination and conflation of these characterizations, signaling the belief that if one is poor, one must be vicious (that is, immoral) or infirm; or if one is infirm, one must be vicious and poor and therefore deserve it, and so on. This circular association of poverty, immorality, and sickness is evident in the continuing attitudes of nativists in colonial America and after independence.

## Disciplined by God's Plagues

In 1793, yellow fever struck Philadelphia and continued to do so regularly until 1805. The inhabitants of the city blamed various "foreign" groups: Germans, French refugees escaping the slave revolution in Haiti, and immigrants from the British West Indies. No matter whom they blamed, however, Philadelphians in the main believed God had inflicted the disease, its arrival perhaps also indicating the arrival of the eschaton. "At length," reads one Philadelphia pamphlet, "the sword of [God's] indignation, the two-edged sword of wrath [Rev 1:16] is unsheathed." Presbyterian minister Ashbel Green told his congregation during the 1798 breakout of the fever, "It is predicted that 'in the last days perilous times shall come' [2 Tim 3:1]. Those days it is our lot to behold."[23]

While most clergymen and much of the general public viewed yellow fever as divinely inflicted, a minority of scholars turned to the history of plagues to determine the cause of the disease. Viewing America as the heir to Greece and Rome, these academics naturally looked to Homer, Thucydides, Livy, Procopius, and even Edward Gibbon's *Decline and Fall of the Roman Empire* for clues. Arguably the most prominent source, on account of his literary stature, detailed description, and important historical context, was Thucydides and his recording of the Plague of Athens in the fifth century BCE. Thucydides notes that the sickness that swept Athens during the Peloponnesian War reportedly had first broken out in Ethiopia:

> It first originated, it is said, in Ethiopia above [upstream of] Egypt. Then, it descended on Egypt and Libya and most of the King's land. It struck the city of the Athenians suddenly, and at first it infected men in Piraeus, so that they said the Peloponnesians had put poison in the cisterns, since there were no wells there yet. Afterward it also reached the upper city, and now far more people died. Let every man, both doctor and layman, say what he thinks about it, about from where it is likely to have come, and for what reasons he thinks it had such power to produce so great a disaster: I will only say how it happened.

As Thucydides seems to foresee, doctors and laypersons have indeed debated and hypothesized the cause of the Plague of Athens, up to the present. American scholars at the end of the eighteenth century were no exception.[24]

Even before the horrible outbreak of yellow fever in 1793, Philadelphian doctor Thomas Bond had postulated that the sickness was the very same as that of Athens: "The yellow fever which I take to be exactly the same distemper as the plague of Athens, described by Thucidides, has been five different times in this city since my residence in it." In detailing the 1793 outbreak, noted scholar and doctor William Currie cited Bond's argument to insist that the disease spread by contagion, especially contagion as imported from foreign places. He begins his treatise, *A Sketch of the Rise and Progress of the Yellow Fever*, by locating the initial outbreak at wharves receiving ships from the West Indies, including from Havana, Curaçao, and the Turks—places with predominantly Black enslaved populations. Currie excerpts Bond's remarks on Thucydides above, and the ancient account of the Athenian plague fits nicely into his argument of contagion by importation. Thucydides does note, after all, that the disease had allegedly traveled to Athens from far-off Ethiopia, a land in classical literature symbolic of remoteness, Black peoples, and the demonic.[25]

Localists (or anticontagionists), however, used Thucydides to argue the exact opposite, that both yellow fever and the Athenian plague arose from the *environment*, not contagion. Elihu H. Smith, a young Yale College graduate, argued that the way Thucydides refers to the report that the disease came from abroad shows that "he thought it entitled to very little credit." Via analysis of Thucydides' account, Smith concluded that it was the characteristics of ancient Athens's locale and urban atmosphere that gave rise to the disease, not contagion from elsewhere. He claimed that Philadelphia was similar to ancient Athens in its climate, position near the sea, crowdedness, and so on, so that "a due consideration of every circumstance cannot but impress the mind with a deep conviction of the unity of cause" for both cities. Additionally, Smith stated, "If local causes originated a pestilence in Athens, local causes may generate a Yellow Fever in Philadelphia and New-York."[26]

In the sphere of medical debate, the localists won during the Philadelphia yellow fever pandemic: they published and publicized their arguments more aggressively, and they appealed more to the scientific rationale of the time. Prominent localists like Smith and Noah Webster (of dictionary fame) roundly criticized the contagionists, including James Tytler, who postulated that both plagues, Athenian and Philadelphian, were divinely inflicted. Tytler was subsequently censured by medical professionals as a result.[27]

But if the localists prevailed, did this mean an end to blaming epidemics on immigrants and foreigners? Did it curb the belief that God punished via plague? Did it stamp out the idea that disease was a sign of God's wrath and the end times? It absolutely did not. It did not matter whether immigrants were the persons causing contagion or living in locales that did: as the filthy undesirable, they were a focus of blame either way. That they were blamed in apocalyptic terms, as we have seen and shall see, is tied to America's enduring identity as the New Jerusalem, the founding metaphor for American exceptionalism.

Therein lies the reason why localist scientific argument most certainly did not end belief in God's punishment of the United States by disease. The localists likened American cities to others in world history at a time when patriotic narratives stressed American *exceptionalism*. To argue that "New-York, and some other cities and towns of North America, are beginning to suffer what other cities and towns in ancient and modern times have undergone before them" was to undermine the hillside below the Shining City upon a Hill. "A New World, same as the Old World" was and is not the inspiring motto politicians wish to champion.[28]

Instead, popular discourse largely ignored localist arguments that America was just like other places that had experienced epidemics. Politicians, preachers, and newspapers continued to uphold the narrative of American exceptionalism even, or rather especially, during epidemics. They claimed that America's suffering was *also* exceptional: like the chosen Israelites whom God punished for disobedience, so America, being held to a higher, divine calling, must endure greater punishment through pestilence when found disobedient and in need of chastening. After all, God states in Revelation, "I reprove and discipline those whom I love" (3:19a). The spread of disease was thus transformed from a medical phenomenon into proof of God's special attention and a warning against disobedience, including *allowing the infiltration of the disobedient*. Proponents of American exceptionalism thus insisted that God's wrath was not focused on Athens or Rome or London but on *America*—on Philadelphia, on New York, on San Francisco. This is not the divine wrath that obliterates evil cities, such as Sodom and Gomorrah, but the wrath that disciplines the holy beacon and example to the rest of the world in order that it expel the sickness and evil that has infiltrated and defend against further disease threatening to invade.

After the yellow fever epidemic, cholera arrived in 1832 as the next great disease to plague the United States. Despite the conclusions of scientists from the yellow fever outbreaks, many Americans still believed cholera to be God's punishment. "Atheists may deny," stated a New York newspaper editorial, "but the intelligence and piety, the real wisdom among us, will ac-

knowledge the providence of God. . . . They *feel* that God is chastising us."
And because America was God's chosen nation, so much more would God's
discipline be visited upon it until its people repented. Thus proclaimed a
pamphlet, "The highest privileges ever granted to a people have been by
multitudes neglected and scorned. . . . Iniquity runs down our streets like a
river." This could not stand, that the New Jerusalem should no longer flow
with the River of Life but with a River of Sin.[29]

Apocalyptic epidemiology, in spite of contemporary scientific views, thus
heightens America's status as God's city while intensifying fear of the sick
and filthy invader—the unwashed immigrant, the immoral, the idolator at
the gates. The logic of a bounded city—that it must be defended, that it excludes by borders, that it creates insider and outsider identities—comes
with the metaphor of the New Jerusalem. And the book of Revelation itself
emphasizes this logic throughout via the themes of plague and filth, playing
on the circular association of disease with dirt, poverty, and sin.

## "Blessed Are Those Who Wash"

In the American context, the apocalyptic conflation of dirt, poverty, sin, and
disease was easily aimed against immigrants. During the 1832 cholera outbreak
in New York City, the Reverend Gardiner Spring gave a sermon echoing Revelation in identifying disease with idolatry. He located the "fatal scourge" as
coming from "pagan, mahommedan, and anti-christian lands" and arriving on
American shores and New York in particular, the heart of the country and the
center of its godly example to the rest of the world. Spring exhorted his audience to repentance and renewed righteousness, believing the last days had perhaps already begun, when the righteous "shall be purified, and made white"
and "the wicked are to be *shaken out of the earth.*" He implied that the epidemic and the turmoil in the city were one of the end-time plagues, stating that
the *"seven vials and the seven last plagues* are not yet all poured upon the
earth." Thus, one had better repent and win inclusion in the heavenly city
rather than be grouped with the foreign diseased destined for destruction on
the outside: "The righteous shall be received into the kingdom of their Father,
and the wicked of every name shall be cast into the lake of fire," he concluded.[30]

Irish Catholic immigrants were among the "idolaters" blamed for bringing disease to America, especially during the cholera epidemics of the 1830s–60s, which seemed to afflict the Irish population disproportionately. As Catholics, they were suspected of "obey[ing] their priests as demigods," in the words of one xenophobic author. The Irish, moreover, were supposedly lax in hygiene and thus also in morality. And because it had been their "lifelong habit" to bow to the gods of Catholicism, particularly the anti-Christ figure of the pope, pundits doubted their ability to assimilate to Protestant American ways.[31] The Irish thus fit the closely associated categories describing those to be kept out of God's city: the idolatrous, the filthy, and the diseased. As such, they were proclaimed unassimilable to American ways of life as characterized by correct Protestant worship, morality, health, and cleanliness.

In the effort to process a surge of Irish and other immigrants and to prevent sickness from entering the United States, New York's Emigration Landing Depot opened at Castle Garden in 1855, located six miles away from the city. Officials implemented quarantining procedures including inspection, isolation, and detention, which were soon copied and implemented across other U.S. ports.[32]

Besides the Irish, cholera was also linked with other unwanted immigrants arriving in New York City, and Castle Garden was seen as a first line of defense in a war defending America. In an 1883 cartoon that ran in the magazine *Puck*, the figure of Death arrives at Castle Garden by ship (figure 6). He is wearing caricatured Turkish dress with the word "CHOLERA" spelled out on his belt. On the shore, the New York Board of Health aims a bottle of carbolic acid at the ship, fighting disease and its carriers as they would invaders in battle, with a front line of soldiers and a row of cannons. Though the cartoon points to changes in the medical understanding of disease — it is carbolic acid and not prayer, after all, that is aimed at the ship — this does not mean that apocalyptic imagination and association ceased.[33] Pragmatism and scientific knowledge may have gained ground since the 1830s, but the theological and apocalyptic rejection of the foreigner as unholy and diseased remained powerful. It is, after all, Death who rides the bowsprit, ready to cut down the brave city behind its great white wall, and this infiltrating specter comes in the guise of an unwanted immigrant.

PUCK.

THE KIND OF "ASSISTED EMIGRANT" WE CAN NOT AFFORD TO ADMIT.

**Fig. 6.** F. Graetz, "The Kind of 'Assisted Emigrant' We Can Not Afford to Admit," *Puck*, July 18, 1883, 326. (Philadelphia Museum of Art, Library and Archives.)

Of course, the desire to keep infectious diseases outside a nation's borders is an understandable desideratum, not necessarily tied to racist hate. But in the case of the United States, the introduction of health inspections at ports of entry and the use of medical expertise to screen immigrants created a new way to exclude groups of people that shunted responsibility onto "science." Even seemingly objective medical diagnoses could serve nativist interests. On account of such screenings and the socio-scientific values they touted, American citizenship was conflated with healthfulness, just as in the New Jerusalem. And so also dirtiness and disease—real or not—became essential characteristics of peoples considered inadmissible and unassimilable to American life. Thus crossing through the golden door to America at Ellis Island, which opened as a processing center for immigrants in 1892, required a health inspection to weed out the infectious, the mentally ill, and the deformed.[34]

But when immigrants were allowed to enter the country, their domestic cleanliness and personal hygiene habits also had to meet the standards of the New Jerusalem. Indeed, just as "washed robes" marked those who could enter the heavenly city of Revelation (Rev 22:14), fresh laundering, personal hygiene, and good housecleaning became "American" traits touted by public health officials and inspectors. People who were deemed to exhibit these traits or deemed capable of adopting them could, in the eyes of health officials and social workers, assimilate and become "American." But in reality, it was prejudice, racism, and white supremacist ideas, not the actual hygiene of certain people groups, that predetermined ideas of assimilability.

Because of their prejudice, nativists blamed Italian immigrants in New York City, particularly from southern Italy, for the spread of tuberculosis in the first decade of the twentieth century and for the polio epidemic of 1916. A study published in 1890 by Richard Mayo-Smith, an economist at Columbia University, is representative of the rhetoric used to blame Italian immigrants for disease: "Huddled together in miserable apartments in filth and rags, without the slightest regard for decency or health, they present a picture of squalid existence degrading to any civilization and a menace to the health of the whole community." Mayo-Smith highlights the same associations identified above in the context of colonial America, linking filth with lack of "decency," disease, menace, and poverty, all graphically represented by the scandalous "rags"— impure, unwashed, beggarly—of the outsiders.[35]

And yet the Italians were not viewed as utterly hopeless. It became the mission of service organizations and health officials to help them "become Americans," as one publication of the Daughters of the American Revolution put it. This phrase comes from the *Guida degli Stati Uniti per l'immigrante italiano / Guide to the United States for the Immigrant Italian,* published in Italian in 1910 and in English translation in 1911. Part of the advice for Italians becoming American, beyond learning English, the rules of citizenship, and basic laws, related to *hygiene and health.* Under "Rules of Health," the first precept is: "Clean water, clean food, clean bodies, clean clothes, clean houses, clean streets keep us healthy." The *Guide* gives this list not just as advice for good health but as essentially American characteristics: "It is the **duty of the citizen** to do everything possible for the good health of himself and his fellows. . . . Where conditions are not hygienic either in the care of water-closets, the disposal of garbage, or the plumbing of houses, complaint should promptly and freely be made to the Board of Health. That is the American way, and in America you should do as Americans do." The text does not specify whether the "American way" refers to hygienic practices or surveillance, but nativists may have thought both were necessary patriotic duties. Certainly clean, washed clothes and bodies, and the expulsion of those defiling such cleanliness, symbolized to those guarding the gates who belongs in America-the-New-Jerusalem.[36]

Interestingly, the *Guide* gives explicit testimony of the established acceptability of other immigrant groups at that moment in time (1910). In the chapter "Land of the Immigrant," the author pronounces:

> The Irish and Germans of those days [the 1850s] came to us as poor as the Italians, the Russians, or the Greeks of to-day. Like these, too, they began to make their living humbly by hard and honest work. They have forgotten the poverty, unhappiness, and oppression that drove them away from the old world. They have prospered, and *they are now all Americans.* They have all had their defects because they are human beings, but they have still had qualities that have helped make this country great and respected throughout the world.
>
> And so to-day America greets the Italians.[37]

This quotation assumes a more positive understanding of Italian (and Russian and Greek) immigrants as able to make the same transformation as Irish and German immigrants sixty years earlier. It characterizes Italians as *human*, with human rights and needs. The perception of an immigrant group as *human* is not a given, as shown in the last chapter and also as demonstrated by the cartoon "The Fool Pied Piper," from a 1909 issue of *Puck*, a political humor magazine (figure 7).

In the "Fool Pied Piper," Uncle Sam leads rats out of Europe toward the United States. These human-headed rats display the headwear and objects of caricatured peoples of southern and eastern Europe as well as of Turkish

THE FOOL. PIED PIPER.

**Fig. 7**. Samuel D. Ehrhart, "The Fool Pied Piper," *Puck*, June 2, 1909, centerfold. (Library of Congress Prints & Photographs Division, Washington, LC-DIG-ppmsca-26380.)

peoples, Roma, and Jews. They wear fezzes and bandanas; they carry torches, knives, pistols, and threatening Black Hand messages of the Mafia. Upon their rodent backs is written their criminal identities: "thief," "white slaver," "bandit," "murderer," "fire brand," "kidnapper," "convict," "degenerate," "crook," "criminal." The leaders of Europe cheer their departure in the background. So while the *Guide* hinted that some opinions were changing in favor of greater acceptance of people from southern and eastern Europe, the *Puck* cartoon demonstrates the concurrent view that certain groups coming to America were not just violent criminals but a diseased plague of rats, ready to infect, multiply, and spread.

The Immigration Act of 1917 implemented a literacy test for the purpose of keeping out just such unwashed and pestilent immigrants. The Emergency Quota Act of 1920 sought further to prevent unwanted European immigrants from coming in large numbers by limiting immigrants from any country to 3 percent annually of the peoples of that national origin already in the United States according to the 1910 census. This rate was subsequently reduced by the Immigration Act of 1924 to 2 percent, based on the 1890 census. The 1924 act also barred from entry any immigrants who were legally ineligible to naturalize. That meant the barring of Japanese entry, which was previously allowed as an exception to the Asiatic barred zone established in 1917. Both the 1920 and 1924 laws were championed by Albert Johnson, Republican congressman of Washington and a leading eugenicist.[38]

The purpose of these quotas, based on the National Origins Formula, was to maintain a dominant population of northern and western European ancestry, predominantly those coming from the United Kingdom. While arguing for these immigration laws, Congressman Johnson minced no words regarding the types of people he believed would ruin America, pronouncing the Jews as the most dangerous. He claimed they were "unassimilable" and "filthy, un-American, and often dangerous in their habits." Jewish immigrants had previously been blamed for tuberculosis in New York City in the 1890s, the "White Plague"; decades later it remained an open question as to whether Jews could or should really belong in America.[39]

That ambivalence had deadly consequences. After the immigration quotas were established, the allowed number of immigrants from Germany up until 1937 was less than one-third filled annually. In the winter following Kristallnacht in 1938, however, more than 240,000 Germans, most of them Jewish, applied for visas, yet the annual quota of immigrants from Germany (including Austria at the time) was 27,370. Throughout the Holocaust, the United States did not budge on increasing the quota. Two-thirds of Americans in fact wanted to "keep [Jewish refugees] out."[40]

U.S. consulate officials tasked with processing visa applications used health and disease as grounds for denying Jews escape from Germany. Even before the rush to escape in the winter of 1938, the American consulate in Stuttgart rejected over 60 percent of visa applicants. When an investigation showed that officials there were citing tuberculosis at an unusually high rate, the consul excused the health inspectors for being "overzealous" and confusing flu and bronchitis with tuberculosis. The day after Kristallnacht, one young man, Erich Sonnemann, managed to avoid the Gestapo and make it to the Stuttgart consulate. Everything in his visa application was in order, including a sponsor stateside, but an X-ray revealed a hernia on his left side. Labeled "physically defective," Sonnemann was turned away.[41]

These denials of entry to the United States are connected through a long and complicated genealogy to the racist hatred that in the fourteenth century blamed Jews for poisoning wells in the Rhineland and demonized them as children of the Devil, irredeemable, and barely human. Jewishness was (and is) an unstable identity in the United States, a nation founded on supersessionist theologies for establishing God's kingdom, and antisemites continue to this day to question Jewish belonging in America. This instability of belonging and admissibility is directly connected to notions of disease and invasion—both viral and militant—since "Jewishness" has long been associated with a curse in the blood, passed down through generations (Matt 27:25). Although U.S. immigration health screening did not actually accuse Jews of a satanic heritage, its "overzealous" scrutiny of Jewish health operated on assumptions of Otherness carried in the body.[42]

The instability of Jewish identity and belonging in America had for centuries stemmed in part from this belief that Jewish difference is manifested bodily. So while Jews had therefore been categorized as white in terms of eligibility for citizenship, marriage to other white people, and naturalization, the well-established belief of innate Jewish physical difference rendered their acceptability and assimilability questionable.[43] Thus American immigration discourse associated disease and plague not only with the immoral, dirty, poor, and idolatrous, but also with the unassimilable, whether hidden in the veins or, as we shall see, borne directly on the skin.

# FOUR

# "They Must Go"
## Non-White Peoples as Plague and Pest

And a foul and painful sore came on those who had the mark
of the beast and who worshiped its image.

—*Revelation 16:2*

### Peoples as Plagues

During the outbreaks of yellow fever in Philadelphia from 1793 to 1805, medical experts struggled to ascertain the cause of the sickness, which had also struck American cities at the end of the seventeenth century. Physician William Currie was convinced that the disease had come from abroad, and from the West Indies in particular. He cited literature on the outbreak in 1699 that called the disease "Barbados distemper . . . which had been very mortal in the West India islands."[1] This identification associated yellow fever not only with the tropical and the foreign but also with Black bodies of the enslaved populations in the Caribbean.

But this did not mean that white Americans believed that Black people were especially prone to the disease—quite the opposite. White physicians and scientists believed that Black people were immune to it. South Carolinian physician John Lining stated, "There is something very singular in the constitution of the Negroes, which renders them not liable to this fever." This assumption of the immunity and "hardiness" of Black bodies served to justify slavery by categorizing the enslaved as particularly and naturally suited for hard labor: "The colour of the skin in the negro gives him a decided advantage over the white, by enabling him to endure the scorching heat of the sun with less suffering; whilst he is protected by the very nature of his constitution from the unhealthiness of hot climates. . . . Under such circumstances, negroes are seen working with cheerfulness and alacrity, when the white labourer would become languid and sink from the effects of a torrid sun."[2]

The belief of an essentially different Black body was widespread even in American states that had abolished slavery. For Philadelphian white leaders and physicians during the 1793–1805 yellow fever outbreak, their belief in Black immunity justified their request that Black leaders and community members stay within the city to help with the public health crisis. Black leaders and their community members did so, sometimes at the cost of their own lives. Undying racism led white Philadelphians then to turn around and accuse Black people of stealing from white homes and extorting money from sick white people.[3]

To this, the first Black Episcopal priest, Absalom Jones, and the founder of the African Methodist Episcopal Church, Richard Allen, who were together founders of the Free African Society, responded with a publication detailing the sacrifices of their community during the epidemic and the injustice of such accusations. "When the people of colour had the sickness and died, we were imposed upon and told it was not with the prevailing sickness, until it became too notorious to be denied, then we were told some few died but not many. Thus were our services extorted *at the peril of our lives*, yet you accuse us of extorting *a little money from you*."[4]

The contradictory medical beliefs about Black people and this utter betrayal by the white people they aided would continue through U.S. history. During subsequent American epidemics and public health crises, Black bodies were constructed as both immune but disease-causing, fearsome but invisible, useful but also disposable.[5] Those anxious to preserve the privilege of their whiteness in America have made numerous contradictory medical claims about Black people in order to preserve white supremacy.

With regard to apocalyptic language, however, very little of the discourse associating enslaved and free Black people with disease makes use of the myth or vocabulary of the New Jerusalem. The reason for this may simply be the general discursive erasure of slavery and segregation from America's history. Additionally, the enslavement of Black people by whites, the realities of the Civil War, and then Jim Crow and segregation do not fit the pilgrim versus heathen or insider versus outsider dynamics of the heavenly metaphor and the shining imagery of American exceptionalism. Certainly some antebellum southern ministers tried to preach a segregated New Jerusalem, depicting Black people in heaven as working "in God's kitchen" or separated from whites. Thus a southern preacher told his enslaved audience: "You slaves will go to heaven if you are good, but don't ever think that you will be close to your mistress and master. No! No! there will be a wall between you; but there will be holes in it that will permit you to look out and see your mistress when she passes by. If you want to sit behind this wall, you must do the language of the text 'Obey your masters.' " This theology was absolutely rejected by those to whom it was preached, and enslaved Black people had their own visions of what a just heaven would be.[6]

But the metaphor of the New Jerusalem could easily be used against non-white immigrants newly arriving in America—and it was, endlessly. The previous chapter covered the complex of immigration and apocalyptic plague used at the beginning of American colonization against Native people and then pivoted to target incoming Irish, southern and eastern Europeans, and especially Jewish people. The efforts to exclude these immigrant groups were clearly prejudiced against non-northern Europeans, but it was not tied to skin color.

As American immigration policy incorporated new health standards as requirements for admission, American identity became even more tightly bound with whiteness and "purity," not just racially but *hygienically*. Whiteness meant Americanness, and Americanness meant cleanliness, and cleanliness had, for millennia, been associated with the color white, whether of skin or clothing or materials, literal or figurative. As historian Suellen Hoy writes: "Cleanliness became something more than a way to prevent epidemics and make cities livable—it became a route to citizenship, to becoming American. It was, in fact, confrontation with racial and cultural outsiders that transformed cleanliness from a public health concern into a moral and patriotic one."[7]

This concept of cleanliness extended beyond the contiguous United States and beyond the walls of the heavenly city. The agents of American imperialism in the Pacific also used health and hygiene as weapons of colonization, with the invocation of leprosy as a primary tool of their arsenal. In both Hawai'i and the Philippines in the late nineteenth and early twentieth centuries, U.S. officials identified indigenous and non-white residents with leprosy, isolated the diseased in leprosaria (leper colonies), and separated offspring from infected parents. American and European scientists themselves had created the link between leprosy and non-whites by categorizing the disease (among others) as "tropical," never mind that leprosy had been known in Europe through the Middle Ages. This classification bound the disease to the Global South and handily labeled Native populations as essentially diseased and in need of white intervention, colonization, and civilization. The intentional, consistent use of the term *leprosy* rather than other current, scientific names for the disease, such as Hansen's disease or *Mycobacterium leprae*, evoked biblical narratives of lepers and leprosy that cast those afflicted with the disease in Hawai'i and the Philippines as "unclean" and sinful while simultaneously framing colonization as Christlike and missional.[8]

In this way, even as the United States claimed Hawai'i and the Philippines as its territories, American public discourse created an abhorrence of Hawaiian and Filipino peoples, their immigration to the mainland, and the importation of their goods, when these were seen as a commercial threat. Thus one editorial printed in U.S. labor publications in 1909 warns against the importation of cigars from the Philippines by conjuring the specter of the plagued leper and marshaling racist tropes of tropical indigence:

> Now every soldier knows the uncleanliness of the average Philippino, and if you ask him he will tell you that many a poor fellow came home in a box by too close association with them, as they are poison to the white man. They are all affected with a skin disease and a large majority are covered with open sores and scars. Leprosy, beri-beri, cholera, bubonic plague and other infectious diseases, are, as everyone knows, prevalent there. They sit half naked

and work and scratch, while the air is rank with the smell of decayed fish and coconut oil, which the women use on their hair.[9]

The author draws on a common web of associations to arouse disgust, in particular the association of skin disease, leprosy, poverty, filth, and nakedness.

The anecdotal description of the "average Philippino" above has little scientific value but relies instead on *biblical* language to effect repulsion. Beri-beri, cholera, and bubonic plague are not skin diseases, whereas *Mycobacterium leprae* attacks and damages peripheral nerves, leading to skin conditions such as discoloration, inflammation, rashes, and growths. Leprosy does not primarily cause "open sores," but the author evokes pustulous sores to disgust the reader. More importantly for our present purpose, the author borrows a cluster of biblical phrases and images to characterize the diseased Filipino. This description includes the term *leprosy* itself, used (inaccurately) in English translations of the Hebrew Bible (for ṣāraʿat, צרעת, for example, Lev 13:1), which is linked to sores and boils, often inflicted by God as punishment, especially as a plague (for example, Ex 9:8–11). "Leprosy" (*lepra*, λέπρα) also appears in the New Testament as an ailment to be cleaned (not healed) by Jesus (for example, Matt 8:2–4). But the phrases "open sores and scars" and "sit . . . and scratch" most particularly recall not leprosy but rather the abject poverty of Lazarus in Luke 16:20–21, whose sores or festering wounds (*helkos*, ἕλκος) are licked by stray dogs, and the miserable Job, who sits and scrapes his Satan-inflicted/God-permitted sores (šəḥîn, שׁחין) with a potsherd (Job 2:7–8).[10]

The group of key words ("unclean," "leprosy," "sores," "naked," "scratch") overlaps with biblical language of the unclean, outcast, plagued, and divinely punished. And although Lazarus and Job are sympathetic, pitiable characters, their appearance also inspires disgust, reinforcing the thrust of the newspaper description that the Filipinos (and their goods) are pestilential and "poison to the white man." Furthermore, the description of an entire people who "are *all* affected" by skin disease invites comparison with whole people groups struck down by God, like the Egyptians (Ex 9:8–11), who suffer from boils. It also evokes the apocalyptically diseased, namely the worshippers of the satanic Beast who bear his mark, upon whom God's wrath is poured, causing "a foul and painful sore" to break out on their skin (Rev 16:2, 10–11).

The rhetoric of disgust employed against Filipinos and Hawaiians, who are described not only as diseased but also as consumers of what is foul— "decayed fish" and "coconut oil" in the above example—and who live, half-dressed, in squalor, reinforces the prevailing discourse and builds on the metaphor of America as the New Jerusalem.[11] This discourse of disease echoes the exclusionary rhetoric of disgust in Revelation: those excluded from the heavenly city are divinely struck down by painful sores (16:2, 11), drink the blood of corpses, and must eat the dead animals of the sea (16:3–6). These wretched rejects wander outside in shame and nakedness (16:15), like dogs (22:15) in their filthiness and filthy ways.

The rhetoric of disgust surrounding leprosy and other "tropical" diseases in American anti-immigrant discourse inspired a revulsion to peoples of the Global South, predominantly Black and Brown peoples. Tuberculosis, in marked contrast, was deemed a more "civilized" disease, that is, a disease that afflicted white people in the United States and Europe. Hence, it was nicknamed "the White Plague," an apt label on several levels. People dying of tuberculosis, especially white women, were often romantically portrayed as virginal and refined by sickness into something pure, white, and spiritual. Thus, if those within the New Jerusalem must fall ill, then their disease must be framed in a way that further qualifies them as citizens of the city, making them pure, virginal, and white like a bride (Rev 14:4, 7–8), clean and clothed in washed, white robes (Rev 7:9, 14; 22:14), mimicking the Celestial City, itself "the bride, the wife of the Lamb" (Rev 21:9). Into this pure and crystal-clear bride (Rev 21:11) must not enter plagued peoples—and peoples seen as plague.[12]

Not only does the conceptualization of America as the New Jerusalem emphasize the need for city defenses against plague from without, this ideation also stresses purification and cleansing *from within*. Emphasis is placed not just on the gates that guard against plague-carrying outsiders, but also on constant washing and flushing out by an internal flow of water. In Revelation 21:1–2, the River of the Water of Life springs from its source at the throne of God and flows through the city, symbolizing (among other things) the cleanliness of the waterways of the city and the continual flushing out of its pristine and pure golden streets (Rev 21:21). This pure and life-giving river is presented in implicit contrast to that other city of Revelation: Babylon, that is, Rome with its famous sewer, the Cloaca Maxima, which dumped sewage into the Tiber River and spewed filth onto the streets in times of flood.[13]

The metaphor of the New Jerusalem, with its imagery of walls and water, enemies without and purity within, imports into America-the-New-Jerusalem the logic of urban planning, both ancient and modern, along with urban anxieties and urban fears. In cities both of the first century and of the nineteenth, twentieth, and twenty-first, barriers were erected to separate the diseased and dying from the healthy, whether by means of defensive borders or internal mechanisms of expulsion. Immigration discourse, shaped by this urban logic, trades in the fear of pestilence, over-crowding, miasma, and the figure of Death riding the prow of incoming ships (figure 6 in the previous chapter).

Thus the unwanted peoples of Europe coming to America in "The Fool Pied Piper" cartoon in the previous chapter (figure 7) are depicted as rats: they are a pestilence of city life and a premier symbol of urban disease. The cartoon conflates pests, vice, and unwanted immigrants. Their bestial de-piction, recalling associations from throughout American history and the strategic rhetoric of disgust and exclusion in Revelation neatly groups to-gether the filthy, the sinful, and the dogs.

Against these plagued peoples, America as the Celestial City is idealized as a unified and bounded space, with boundaries that mark absolute inclu-sion and exclusion. Inside the city there is one throne, one river, at the banks of which gather the saints, all with the Lamb's name written on their foreheads, and all wearing white robes. Identity within the New Jerusalem is uniform, even if the inhabitants had once come "from every nation" (Rev 7:9). Like this heavenly city, the United States, when understood as a se-cure, bounded city with a unified, uniform "native" population, must abso-lutely defend against the infiltration of disease, filth, and plague. And if these are primarily the unassimilable, one of the most unassimilable peo-ples in American imagination are the Chinese.

## "Stagnant Water, and Dirty Clothing and Filthy Bodies"

In 1862, at the young age of twenty-one, Ephraim S. Wells purchased a pharmacy in Jersey City, New Jersey. He had apprenticed as a druggist since the age of twelve, and he came into his fortune during the 1870s and 1880s, when Americans eagerly and indiscriminately purchased patent medicines with their empty promises of health, beauty, and vigor. Wells, however, was in the business of death—that is, his premiere moneymaking product caused it: Wells made rat poison, and an effective one at that, since it comprised only white arsenic and some negligible fillers. Wells's genius lay not in his pharmaceutical concoctions but in the advertising for his products, which he proudly claimed were all written and designed by himself. These ads appeared throughout the United States in magazines and on trade cards in the late 1870s and throughout the 1880s. While some depicted humorous scenes of unemployed cats and bereaved rats, one ad ingeniously combined product marketing with racist politics (figure 8).[14]

Centered in this advertisement for pest poison stands a caricatured Chinaman about to eat a rat, while holding another ready in his left hand. Above them reads the slogan, "They Must Go," referring, of course, both to the rats and to the Chinaman. The text is an obvious allusion to the political slogan "The Chinese Must Go" coined by Denis Kearney of the Workingmen's Party of California in 1877. Wells's advertisement uses a common nativist trope for foreignness, the consumption of what is considered vile, to identify both the Chinese and rats as pests, implying that the poison—ingested by rats that are then ingested by Chinese—can work effectively to rid the buyer of both. The Chinaman's queue, a traditional Chinese symbol with political significance, sticks out behind the man's head, its angle and curves mirroring the tail of the rat he is about to eat.[15]

Wells was not the first American to portray the Chinese as a literal pest on the level of "rats, mice, bed bugs, flies, roaches" (the pests the poison was advertised to kill in figure 8). In 1878 the San Francisco satirical magazine the *Wasp* ran a cartoon titled "Uncle Sam's Farm in Danger" (figure 9) by the illustrator George Keller. This cartoon participated in the fearmongering against Chinese refugees fleeing the Northern Chinese Famine of 1876–79.

**Fig. 8.** Ephraim S. Wells, "Rough on Rats," Forbes Co. advertisement, Boston, ca. 1880s. (CPA Media Pte Ltd / Alamy Stock Photo.)

UNCLE SAM'S FARM IN DANGER.

SEVENTY MILLIONS OF PEOPLE ARE STARVING IN THE NORTHERN PROVINCES OF CHINA. ALL WHO CAN DO SO ARE MAKING PREPARATIONS TO COME TO THE UNITED STATES. LOOK OUT FOR THE GRASSHOPPERS, UNCLE SAM !

**Fig. 9.** George Frederick Keller, "Uncle Sam's Farm in Danger," *Wasp*, March 9, 1878. (The Bancroft Library, University of California, Berkeley.)

In it, Chinese immigrants do not just consume pests as an implied pestilence themselves, they *are* a literal pest, embodying a horrifying plague. Depicted as a swarm of consuming grasshoppers, the Chinese are like a biblical plague of locusts, particularly the plague described in Revelation 9:7, which covers the earth after the fifth trumpet of God is blown. Like the apocalyptic locusts, the Chinese insects have "faces . . . like human faces," their queues are "like women's hair" as long braids, and the queues simultaneously resemble "tails like scorpions, with stingers" (Rev 9:7) and stick straight out of the backs of their heads like an insect's appendage.

Further linking the cartoon to the apocalyptic imagery of Revelation is the demonic figure of Famine, driving the grasshoppers on with a cord of whips. Famine and the grasshoppers appear in shades of pale green, the color of the fourth horse of the Apocalypse, which Death rides over the earth to kill with "sword, famine, and pestilence and by the wild animals of the earth" (Rev 6:7–8). Only a simple farm fence stands in the way of the horde of Chinese locusts, a sign of weakness at the U.S. border and of U.S. immigration policy. In the apocalyptic-diseased American imagination, the Chinese embody the horrors of Revelation visited upon the earth.

Advertisements and cartoons such as Wells's "Rough on Rats" and Keller's "Uncle Sam's Farm" rely on decades of anti-Chinese hate, particularly a racist hatred that links Chinese peoples with disease and filth as pests. Official anti-Chinese action based on identification of Chinese with pestilence is documented as early as 1854, when a sizeable community of Chinese had formed in San Francisco, causing alarm among white city dwellers. One Dr. William Rabe, during a San Francisco Common Council meeting, drew attention to "the Chinese and their filthy quarters," and the Committee on Health and Police were instructed to investigate the complaint. That same week, a news article had discussed a wave of cholera then sweeping the United States; the author theorized that cholera spreads through "a poisonous gas" that develops in "some filthy locality, or where air is stagnant, and that there it diffuses, being breathed into the lungs." Consequently, the author states, there is "little doubt that it will make its appearance, and may in some of our filthy localities like the Chinese quarters of the city, sweep off considerable numbers."[16]

Doctors, politicians, and news media viewed Chinese people with disgust and published their views broadly. The *New York Daily Tribune* described Chinese peoples in 1854 as "unclean, filthy beyond all conception," claiming that "the Chinese quarter of the city [of San Francisco] is a byword for filth and sin." The California State Board of Health pronounced in 1862 that Chinese entry into the United States would cause national decay and declared in 1870–71 that intermingling with "a sensual and depraved people" would guarantee the passing on of "hereditary vices."[17] Public discourse blamed Chinese for disease and sickness, relying on these perceptions of foreignness linked with degradation and plague.

In the late 1860s and during the '70s and '80s, San Francisco suffered several smallpox epidemics, and some Chinese immigrants were found carrying the disease when they arrived at the city ports. Hysteria also grew over the spread of leprosy beginning in the 1870s. Medical officials claimed it was an "essentially Chinese disease," and the Board of Health deported dozens of Chinese diagnosed with leprosy from 1871 to 1883.[18] In 1883, the *Wasp* ran "San Francisco's Three Graces," a cartoon depicting the specters of Malaria, Smallpox, and Leprosy looming over the city of San Francisco, with the *Altonower*, a ship that had carried immigrants with smallpox, arriving in the harbor (figure 10). These giant phantasms of disease, demonic and bestial, tower above the city, threatening its lone, brave church with its crucifix, representative of the pious citizens who must guard against such corrupting invaders. Leprosy, the "Chinese disease," is a caricatured Chinaman, sporting a queue. From his left hand flows something white labeled "Chinatown." This may be the disease itself poured out on the "filthy quarters," echoing the image of the angel who pours plague from the bowl of God's wrath on those who worship the demonic Beast (Rev 16:2).

The white object streaming from the Chinese specter's hand may also be a flowing cloth, a piece of laundry, symbolic of a key employment of Chinese immigrants as launderers. By the date of the "Three Graces" cartoon, 1883, anti-Chinese polemicists, politicians, and cartoonists had spread numerous rumors that Chinese workers cleaned and pressed laundry in filthy ways, claiming they spit saliva from their mouths onto cloth for ironing. The San Francisco Board of Health conducted investigations into the city's laundries in 1896–97 at the behest of committee member Dr. H. Hart. Hart postulates in a contemporary medical journal that Chinese launderers could be spreading "consumption, syphilis or skin diseases" through "mouth spray" and the filthiness of their work areas. Hart further identifies Chinese laundries as "opium dens," and implies they corrupt "whites of both sexes" who "are frequenters of the places by day and by night." The article concludes by announcing a "repugnance to wearing a Chinese-washed garment," and asks the Board of Health to investigate the danger to white families.[19]

For Chinese living in the United States, their identification by white society as diseased, pestilent, and corrupting meant the constant surveilling and policing of their homes and businesses, accompanied by the threat of invasive fumigation, unsafe quarantine and isolation, removal from one's home to segregated hospital quarters, and deportation. Health inspections continued after the establishment of the Angel Island detention center, which boasted larger facilities that could house new, more invasive procedures (pro-

**Fig. 10.** George Frederick Keller, "San Francisco's Three Graces," *Wasp*, May 26, 1883, cover image. (The Bancroft Library, University of California, Berkeley.)

cedures that were never routine at Ellis Island). The island's health inspectors separated Asian men and women, made them strip naked, and demanded fecal samples for bacteriological scrutiny. The U.S. Public Health Service began bacteriological examination of Asian immigrant feces at Angel Island in 1910, focusing on evidence of hookworm, threadworm, and, beginning in

1917, liver fluke. The focus on parasites that are undetectable except through microscopic examination stoked fears that Chinese and other Asians might appear healthy but pass on invisible parasites once they entered America. This further intensified, in historian Nayan Shah's words, the "conflation of the internal parasite and the social parasite."[20]

The Chinese body, the Asian body, and all unwanted bodies that had to be kept from entering the United States were identified not only as carriers of parasites but also as indistinguishable from pests, disease, and plague themselves. Health officials focused investigations on immigrant neighborhoods, including Irish, Italian, Jewish, Chinese, Japanese, and Mexican over the decades, and pronounced these environs to be especially conducive to fostering disease, as if these peoples *were themselves* diseases that thrived in such places and posed a danger to America.

In describing the "filthy quarters" of San Francisco's Chinatown as likely to harbor cholera, news writers identified the neighborhood as a place of "stagnant water, and dirty clothing and filthy bodies."[21] These three elements—impure water, dirty clothes, and filthy bodies—are continually emphasized in American public discourse that associates unwanted immigrants with plague and disease. They are also the key characteristics of the damned and their destruction in the book of Revelation, in which waters turn to poison (8:10–11) and blood (11:6, 16:3); idolators either do not wash their robes (3:4), live in shameful nakedness (3:18, 16:15), or dress in degenerate scarlet and purple (17:4, 18:12, 16); and the sinful suffer from painful sores (16:2, 11) or degrade their bodies with sexual immorality (21:15).

The New Jerusalem of Revelation and its citizens present the opposite characteristics. Through the city flows the pristine River of the Water of Life (22:1–2), from which the blessed may drink, the blessed to whom "springs of water" have also been given (21:6, 22:17). The holy, that is, citizens of the New Jerusalem (3:4–5, 4:4, 7:9), angels of God (15:6, 19:14), and the Son of Man (1:14), are dazzlingly clean and wear white robes, and their bodies are virginal (14:4) and holy, healed by the fruit of the trees of life growing along the river (22:2).

That American anti-immigrant discourse should use the same elements as Revelation to describe white citizens as pristine and the unwanted as filthy is not merely happenstance or due to a universal human association of the foreign and unwanted as dirty. The long and persistent use of the New Jerusalem, God's city, to imagine America had incorporated into immigration discourse the vocabulary of purity, filth, health, and disease in distinctly Christian modes. This is especially apparent when analyzing stories of redemption, in which individuals become qualified for inclusion in America. Such feats occur through *personal* and *individual* conversion to Protestant Christianity, not through the acceptance of a whole population by American society. The construction of race in America, particularly as it pertained to non-white races, is inseparable from the designation of "heathen" peoples, as Kathryn Gin Lum has shown.[22] Thus, the category of "the heathen Chinee" marked an entire people group as quintessentially idolatrous, even if an individual could still be saved through cleanliness and godliness.

## "God's Love, Pure Air and Sunshine"

Such is the case of individual Chinese women described by white missionary women working to save souls from prostitution and filth. Chinese women had effectively been barred from entry to the United States by the 1875 Page Act, which operated on the assumption that they were by default prostitutes, by choice or by force. In his arguments in favor of the bill, Senator Horace Page (R-CA) urged Congress "to place a dividing line between vice and virtue" and pass a law that would "send the brazen harlot who openly flaunts her wickedness in the faces of our wives and daughters back to her country."[23]

Chinese women who already lived in the country or managed to gain entry after 1875 continued to be described as sexually depraved, corrupting, and furthermore as diseased. They came to be designated in such monstrous terms that the Chinese Harlot resembled the Whore of Babylon of Revelation herself. One medical writer, Mary Sawtelle, describes syphilitic Chinese prostitutes in 1878 as receiving "thousands nightly" to commit "beastly acts," just as the Whore of Babylon received "the kings of the earth [who] have committed sexual immorality with her" (Rev 18:3).[24] White men were warned to keep away from the diseased Chinese women, just as an angel of heaven warns those looking on the destruction of Babylon: "Come out of her, my people, so that you do not take part in her sins, so that you do not share in her plagues" (Rev 18:4). And officials and pundits portrayed Chinese prostitutes not only as dangerously contagious but also as spiritually demonic. San Francisco supervisors in 1885 deemed Chinese prostitution "the most abject and satanic conception of human slavery."[25] Sawtelle, in writing to white women, warned them of diseases their husbands could contract from Chinese prostitutes, a "demon to destroy her husband by her side, to inoculate her pure blood with poisonous virus."[26]

But into these satanic dens of Chinese prostitution ventured white women missionaries like the "Angry Angel" Donaldina Cameron, discussed in chapter 2, and, before her, Emma Cable of the Chinese Mission Home. Cable's narration of a Chinese woman's apartment in a Presbyterian report begins with a description of the dark and dank surroundings as the opposite of the ideal Christian environment of "God's love, pure air and sunshine." After a period of evangelization, the Chinese woman converts, and Cable describes the transformation of Christian conversion primarily through the complete change in the woman's habitation: "To-day we find her in a cheerful room . . . which she has thoroughly cleaned, whitewashed and papered." Cable describes other such conversions similarly: "Instead of darkness we have air, light, sunshine, birds and flowers. Rooms enlarged and beautifully furnished, walls papered [and] floors carpeted." As historian Shah notes, "Ideas of cleanliness, sanitation and middle-class white material culture were conflated as indicators of Christian belief and 'civilized' behavior."[27]

But the language of these conversion stories not only draws on white American material culture and ideals of hygiene, it also uses the symbols of salvation and citizenship in the New Jerusalem of Revelation: the washing of water, clean white robes, and pure, healthy bodies. One 1900 missionary account describes the San Francisco home of Mrs. Wong Lee, a Christian convert, and her family in precisely these terms. When the visit occurs, Mrs. Wong Lee is doing exactly what heavenly citizens should do: the laundry for her family, and " 'seven children do make a lot of washing.' " Mrs. Wong Lee's hair is "glossy and smooth," she and her children are dressed neatly and cleanly in clothes that are "a triumph of laundry work," and everything speaks of white Christian cleanliness, washed by pure water: "The floor was white as scouring could make it [Mark 9:3]; the windows shone, the curtains were snowy [Isa 1:18; Rev 1:14], and on the neatly papered walls were Scripture texts, and a picture of Christ blessing the children." The children cradle the new baby in the sunshine, another feature of Christian cleanliness and an echo of the shining New Jerusalem. The visit ends with purified saints singing "the immortal hymn," in imitation of saintly song at the throne and dwelling of God (Rev 5:11–14, 15:2–8).[28]

In America as in the New Jerusalem, "Blessed are those who wash their robes, that they will have the right to the tree of life and may enter the city by the gates" (Rev 22:14). The great irony, of course, is that the primary washers of robes in the American West, the Chinese, could not find acceptance or admittance. The more they washed, the more white Americans accused them of contaminating not only their own robes but also white Christian robes and spreading the plague. As a heathen people, they could not gain admittance or acceptance; they could do so only as individual converts. In particular, if a Chinese woman allowed white women mission workers to highlight their own virtue through proselytizing, she could hope to attain inclusion if she washed everything as white as snow and transformed her home with "God's love, pure air and sunshine."

## "A Class Who Habitually Shunned Water"

In touting the attractions of the city of Los Angeles and Southern California, government officials and a U.S. president also described the area as possessing clean water, pure air, sunshine, and God's blessing. In 1879, Los Angeles health officer Walter Lindley boasted that residents of the city "have the health-giving sun almost every day in the year, we have the ocean breeze just properly tempered by hills and orange groves, we have the best altitude for health, we have pure water pouring down from the mountain stream . . . we have in fact everything that God could give us to make this a healthful city." Here sound echoes of the glorious light, running river, and fruit trees of the New Jerusalem, along with the gifts of God, which evince a "healthful city." In a 1903 visit to the region, President Theodore Roosevelt praised

Southern California in similar terms: "I have enjoyed to the full getting into your beautiful State. . . . Here I am in the pioneer community of irrigated fruit growing in California. . . . You have made this city [Riverside] and its surroundings a veritable little paradise."[29]

But what pleases President Roosevelt the most are not the streams of water irrigating fruit trees. Roosevelt emphasizes the *people* who lived in this paradise, and not just any people. The president says: "I like *your stock*, and I am glad it is not *dying out*. . . . I admire most of all the men and women of the country. It is a good thing to grow citrus fruits, but it is even a better thing to have *the right kind of citizenship*. I think you have been able to combine the very extraordinary material prosperity with that form of the *higher life* which must be built upon material prosperity if it is to amount to what it should in the long run."[30]

Roosevelt addresses the mayor of Riverside and his "fellow-citizens," hence, a white audience of U.S. citizens and exactly the type of "stock" he believes is "the right kind" of "higher life" that should benefit from the prosperity of this "veritable paradise." The president implies between the lines of his speech that this paradise must *not* foster the wrong kind of stock, people who are not a higher life, and who would prevent Southern California and the United States from becoming "what it should be in the long run." The year of Roosevelt's speech, 1903, is the same year in which the U.S. Public Health Service began categorizing Class A diseases in immigration inspections as "loathsome and dangerous," contagious, and necessary to exclude, and Class B conditions or diseases as marking an immigrant "likely to become a public charge." These classifications of immigrants at U.S. entry points served to deny entry to exactly the "stock" that Roosevelt implied should not flourish in America, lest there be a "dying out" of white American citizens.[31]

The magnitude of the threat that such unfit peoples posed for paradise, that is, California, was also the message and warning of Health Officer Lindley in 1879. He praises Los Angeles as having all the God-given elements of the Celestial City except for one crucial problem. "We have in fact everything that God could give us to make this a healthful city and yet we allow that rotten spot—Chinatown—to grow and pollute the air we breathe and poison the water we drink." Chinatown, Lindley claims, "is the crying sanitary *evil* of Los Angeles."[32]

Soon after Lindley's report was written, Congress began to pass restrictive laws against Chinese immigration, and in their wake other people groups also faced exclusionary immigration laws, particularly those identified with the Chinese as part of the "Yellow Peril." As the Chinese population in Los Angeles and Southern California shrank, accusations of pestilence and contagion shifted their focus to Japanese communities. These communities had grown in number because of the compromise of the U.S.-Japan Gentlemen's Agreement of 1907, which restricted Japanese immigration overall but allowed Japanese wives to enter the country to join their husbands. As Japanese farms grew more productive and successful, fearmongering pundits blamed the Japanese for sickness. Just as Chinese launderers were accused of spreading plague through the unhygienic treatment of laundry, Japanese farmers were rumored to spread sickness through their produce. Echoing Lindley's declaration of Chinatown as a "crying sanitary evil," Los Angeles County health officer John Pomeroy published an article in 1920 titled "Japanese Evil in California," in which he decried the population growth of an inferior race that would lead to "a large American citizenship, yellow in color." Such sentiments enabled laws aimed at preventing Japanese and other Asians from owning land ("alien land laws") to pass in 1913 and 1920, hindering the growth of Japanese communities; and the Immigration Act of 1924 prevented Japanese immigration altogether.[33]

Besides the Chinese and Japanese in Southern California, the other main people group that was demeaned, ostracized, and accused of spreading disease were Mexicans. Since the U.S. War with Mexico / Intervención estadounidense en México (1846–48) and the Treaty of Guadalupe Hidalgo (1848), which added most of the present-day American West and Southwest to U.S. territory, Mexican identity in U.S. territory was an unstable entity. The Treaty of Guadalupe Hidalgo granted Mexicans already residing on territories ceded to the United States the right to citizenship and to be "protected in the free enjoyment of their liberty and property." But while legally "American," Mexican identity was constructed as "non-white" and remained unstable and vulnerable in Southern California.[34]

As Chinese and Japanese populations dwindled in Southern California due to immigration restrictions, employers needed a different population to work as cheap, exploitable labor. Mexicans' utility as a new workforce prevented the worst exclusionary immigration laws aimed previously at Asians from being directed at them.[35] Nonetheless, they were still labeled by public health officials as especially prone to disease and subjected to intense inspection and physical disinfection measures in their communities and at the U.S.-Mexico border.

In 1916, Mexican workers had become a primary source of labor for the construction of railroad lines in Southern California and the Southwest for Southern Pacific Rail; the Chinese "coolie" had been replaced by the Mexican "peon," now the primary exploitable labor for such work. An outbreak of typhus (a disease spread by lice and ticks) at a railroad construction camp north of Los Angeles catalyzed inspections and disinfecting treatments not only at Mexican workers' camps but also at the U.S. border. Two years before, a health official had already warned that "every individual hailing from Mexico should be regarded as potentially pathogenic," and the outbreak of typhus set in motion bodily inspection and disinfection at camps and for those crossing the border.[36]

The California State Board of Health outlines its inspection procedure in its October 1916 bulletin thus: "Occupants of the camps are deloused by baths and by rubbing with kerosene. Their clothing is immediately boiled, the most important part of the process. All cases of the disease are promptly quarantined and contacts are held in detention for a period of twelve days, after being freed from lice." This health bulletin also warned, like Lindley and Pomeroy, that California, despite its "favorable economic and hygienic conditions," might be under threat from disease because of "filthy conditions, especially personal uncleanliness." Hence, "places where Mexicans congregate should be watched very carefully and kept free from lice. . . . Should any suspicious cases be found . . . control of the disease should be immediately put into force." The identification of Mexicans as personally unclean and requiring surveillance repeats the racist associations used against the Chinese and Japanese, demonstrating how such discourses, using apocalyptic paranoia, are "repackaged, re-energized, and relegitimized."[37]

Entrance into the United States was still possible for Mexican immigrants—like those entering the New Jerusalem, they could still cross the border if they "washed their robes," literally. But white racial constructs of Mexican identity held that the Mexicans were a people who did not wash; they were, as a L.A. County health report stated, a "class who habitually shunned water." Thus the Public Health Service forced immigrants to wash at the border by establishing the El Paso Disinfection Plant in January 1917, and planned for other stations in Laredo, Eagle Pass, and Brownsville. Medical inspectors at these plants made travelers strip naked to be examined for "vermin infestation, for eruptions of any sort, enlarged glands or any abnormality." If lice were found, men had to shave their heads and burn the hair, while women had to apply kerosene and acetic acid to their hair and scalps. Thereafter, according to a doctor on site, "the person is passed on to the shower baths, where the bathing process is supervised by an attendant and then passed into a rear room in which the clothing is received back through an opening in the wall after having been disinfected by steam and dried in a vacuum."[38]

This account barely speaks to the actual horror experienced by those who underwent the process. It was not a spa treatment where one was "bathed with soft soap and warm water," as the El Paso Herald boasted. As the examples cited above amply attest, delousing immigrants at the time usually involved kerosene. It was about as dangerous as one would expect: one El Paso prison delousing in 1916 resulted in a building explosion in which nearly all the prisoners burned to death. Later travelers who passed through the El Paso Disinfection Plant describe a horrific experience. José Burciaga, for example, states in an interview, "You see, when someone entered they doused him with something. What a nightmare! And then there was more: men, women, they shaved everyone. . . . They bathed everyone, and after the bath they doused you with cryolite [sodium aluminum fluoride], composed of some sort of substance, it was strong." At one point in the 1920s, travelers were further fumigated with Zyklon B pesticide, the same substance later used in Nazi gas chambers. Nevertheless, migrant workers crossing the border underwent this procedure to obtain the "bath certificate" that allowed them to work—certificates that expired after one week.

This was the washing regimen required to enter the New Jerusalem by the gates.[39]

In October 1924, bubonic and pneumonic plague affected two Mexican neighborhoods in Los Angeles, both of which were placed under quarantine, as was the harbor, as a precaution. A November 8, 1924, article in the *Los Angeles Times* reported the deaths of two Mexicans linked to pneumonic plague. The same article describes the rationale of health officials' decision to launch a campaign to examine and exterminate rodents in the area in an effort to curb disease. One official tells the newspaper, "As long as this rodent population remains in California we are in danger of outbreaks of plague ... this plague is not unexpected, Los Angeles is exposed to three lines of attack—from the ground squirrels in the north, from the rats which may be imported from the Orient and from the rats which may be imported by train from Mexico. This epidemic is the first gun fired by the enemy. To spike the enemy's gun, it is necessary to reduce our rodent population below the threshold of infection and to keep it reduced."[40]

This statement, following the details of the plague in "Mexican areas" and reporting the Spanish names of the two deceased, seems to blur the lines between literal rats to be exterminated and Asian and Mexican peoples, whose numbers many felt ought also to be suppressed. The mention of an "enemy" and the "enemy's gun" makes it particularly clear that the speaker has wandered away from discussing literal rats, conceiving of the problem rather as a foreign and invasive threat.

Once again, the unwanted immigrant becomes indistinguishable from the disease-bearing pest, threatening a pure, hygienic America. And this association of Mexican peoples as a disease-carrying plague only grew stronger during the Great Depression, when whites resented and feared the presence of Mexicans as a threat in a time of economic hardship. It is during this time that Mexican identity, once wavering between American and foreign, depending on context and political exigencies, became squarely foreign. During the 1920s and 1930s "Mexican" became synonymous with "alien" and was presumed most likely "illegal." Through this transformation, the undeserving "alien" now threatened to take "American" jobs.[41]

Sanitary officers of the late nineteenth century and the U.S. Public Health Service of the 1910s and 1920s led the way to this shift in racial construction by continually associating Mexicans with disease and plague. In addition to bubonic and pneumonic plague and typhus, officials also identified Mexicans as particularly susceptible to tuberculosis, and exaggerated accounts of Mexicans pouring over the border in the "thousands" stoked fears of massive disease outbreaks. The fear of disease and the fear of scarcity during the Depression coalesced with white racial constructions of the Other to cast Mexicans as the latest plague invading the land. Moreover, federal laws and immigration systems that determined entry and status had crystallized around certain concepts of immigrant identity since the first federal restriction and exclusion law of 1875. At this junction of disease, economic hardship, immigration law, and racial construction, Mexican identity became associated with illegality. "Disease, then," historian Natalia Molina states, "was used not just to marginalize Mexicans but also to criminalize them. . . . Illness and illegality could be merged into a single condition: disease marked Mexicans as illegal."[42]

At the federal, state, and local level, the U.S. government used the conception of the illegal Mexican to justify the deportation of hundreds of thousands of Mexicans and Mexican American *citizens* to Mexico. Deportation programs began in Los Angeles, where the county hospital became a primary location for identifying individuals to deport. There, Mexicans seeking medical care could be diagnosed both as diseased and as seeking charity and, hence, also as a public charge, something long excluded in American immigration policy. As these deportation programs developed, the list of diseases and conditions for which someone could be deported also grew, so that Mexicans could also be deported for having a venereal disease, arthritis, broken bones, and more.[43]

These justifications for deportation make it obvious that *actual* public health and science were not the drivers behind immigration and deportation policy but rather the white supremacist belief that only whites belong in America. This belief consistently equates American identity with white identity, which is assumed to be clean, pure, and Protestant Christian. By contrast, non-whites must be filthy, diseased, pestilential, and sinful, just as those outside the New Jerusalem are idolaters, sexually immoral, and dogs.

The deportation of Mexicans continued beyond the Great Depression, even though the Bracero Program began in 1942 to bring Mexican workers back into the country as agricultural workers.[44] The fruitful trees of paradise had to be harvested. California, the Sunshine State, and other fields and farms of America continued the God-blessed production of food, just as in the New Jerusalem the trees of life bear twelve kinds of fruit, a new crop each month, with healing leaves to be picked as well (Rev 22:2). Mexicans were welcome into America-the-New Jerusalem as exploitable laborers, but their inclusion could be revoked and their names stricken from the Book of Life, and health was an effective justification for such banishment.

In the biblical city, the qualifications of those entitled to eat from the trees of life as citizens of the holy city are clearly laid out. The text states: "Blessed are those who wash their robes, so that they will have the right to the tree of life and may enter the city by the gates" (Rev 22:14). Entering by the gates implies legal entry, conducted in broad daylight (there is no night in the city: Rev 21:25) and with no need for hiding or climbing walls. This type of entry is the "right" (ἡ ἐξουσία) afforded to those who have washed, to whom the harvest of the trees is also granted. Yet the launderers and fruit-pickers of America, the Chinese, Japanese, Mexican, Asian, and Latin American immigrants, did exactly this labor but never attained the stable, inviolable citizenship of white Americans, the creators of the New Jerusalem narrative for the United States. Non-white immigrant identity, through the discourse of racist public health narratives and their transformation into law, has been essentialized as those "outside," the "dogs" and the "filthy" (Rev 22:15), those with "foul and painful sores" (Rev 16:2).

## "And Then Came a Plague, a Great and Powerful Plague"

After the National Origins Act of 1924, medical inspections at U.S. ports of entry gave way to health exams of immigrants in their countries of origin—except at Angel Island and at the U.S.-Mexico border, where officials had always conducted far more aggressive and invasive inspections than at Ellis Island. Even after the wave of deportations during the Great Depression and the closure of Angel Island in 1940, medical inspections and the harmful fumigation of Mexican migrants continued under the guest-worker Bracero Program into the 1960s. To this day hospitals still serve as hubs of health-based deportations to Mexico and Latin America, which are sometimes carried out by private companies operating without transparency.[45]

And while the list of inadmissible diseases and health conditions at U.S. ports of entry has narrowed substantially, the apocalyptic language and racist reasoning that depicted the Chinese as a horde of locusts and framed Mexicans as the filthy unwashed remain ever ready and reusable to stoke fears during times of turmoil and disease. This is made clear in recent memory during the Ebola epidemic in West Africa in 2013–16. The American hysteria over the disease and racist fears about African immigrants, accompanied by cries for a travel ban, far exceeded the reality in the United States, in which there were only eleven cases, two fatal. The stigmatization of African immigrants came easily from long associations of foreigners with disease. The fact that the targeted immigrants were also Black further exacerbated long-held American conceptions of Black identity as bestial and criminal.[46]

Even more recently, the COVID pandemic again revealed the U.S. association of the outsider with disease, all within an apocalyptic frame. As with any widespread disaster, but especially epidemics, end-times decoding of the coronavirus through the lens of Revelation sprang up quickly across multiple media. One article published as early as January 30, 2020, was titled "The Wuhan Coronavirus and the Bible's Prophesied Disease Pandemics." By late spring of 2020, Google search results for "COVID-19 Book of Revelation" returned almost 40 million results, since, as biblical scholar Stephen Moore aptly puts it, "This is what Revelation is for, this is what Revelation does."[47]

Language issued by the White House did nothing to assuage fears of an apocalyptic disease: President Trump, after downplaying the threat of the virus against all scientific evidence, made an about-face on Twitter on May 3, 2020, to announce a "plague" and to predict America's triumph over it. He tweeted: "And then came a Plague, a great and powerful Plague, and the World was never to be the same again! But America rose from this death and destruction, always remembering its many lost souls, and the lost souls all over the World, and became greater than ever before!"[48] Channeling the prophetic voice of a seer, Trump begins the tweet with dramatic, apocalyptic phrasing ("And then came a Plague") that echoes Revelation when the seer beholds the awful. For example, "Then I saw another beast" (13:11) or "Then I looked and there was the Lamb" (14:1). But above all Trump mimics the words of the seer at the beginning of the passage of the Seven Last Plagues: "Then I saw another portent in heaven, great and amazing: seven angels with seven plagues, which are the last, for with them the wrath of God is ended" (15:1).

The end of the plague, Trump predicts, will mark the end of an old world and the rise of an exalted America, "greater than ever before." And while souls must be lost in such a powerful plague, they will be remembered, even as they are sacrificed to reveal a greater America. In referring to those who will die, Trump uses not only biblical and apocalyptic language but also the apocalyptic language of Ronald Reagan. "Lost souls all over the World" is an echo of the end of Reagan's farewell speech, when he speaks of "all the pilgrims from all the lost places." In contrast to Reagan's evocation of America as a shining immigrant refuge, however, Trump presents America the New Jerusalem as rising above the destruction *without* the "lost souls." The greatness for which America is destined does *not* include those who are suffering and near death. This is simply a matter of course, since the outsiders come from "lost places"—or, in Trump's language, from "shithole countries."[49]

The implicit disregard for human life and the vulnerable evident in this tweet was borne out in Trump's ensuing identification of the virus with Chinese peoples; Trump repeatedly referred to the virus as the "China virus," the "China plague," and "Kung Flu." From March 2020, when shutdowns due to COVID-19 began in earnest in the United States, to March 2022, harassment and hate crimes against Asian Americans and Pacific Islanders surged. The organization Stop AAPI Hate received over 11,500 reports of hate incidents targeting Asian American Pacific Islander peoples. The Yellow Peril, the pestilent horde, the Asian in America was again to blame for a plague.[50]

And then, as if history were indeed repeating itself, the blame shifted to migrants at the U.S.-Mexico border. Although travel restrictions to the United States had been in place since February 2020, and the Centers for Disease Control invoked Title 42 to deny asylum to refugees on the grounds of combatting contagion, a resurgence of COVID-19 infections from the new Delta variant of the virus in the summer of 2021 was quickly blamed on immigrants at the southern border. On July 14, 2021, Senator Ted Cruz (R-TX), blamed the spike in infections on immigrants at the border and the Biden administration's supposedly lax border policies. Cruz stated: "We're seeing COVID positivity rates rising in South Texas. We're seeing COVID positivity rising in Laredo. We're seeing COVID positivity in San Antonio. Just yesterday, I spoke to the mayor of Uvalde, Texas, who said as a result of the illegal immigrants being released—in Uvalde they're seeing COVID positivity spiking up. And Biden wants to release even more COVID positive illegal immigrants. This is lunacy."[51]

There is no evidence that the spike in the virus was related to immigration at the border, although there is certainly evidence that a lack of vaccination and masking in the United States led to mutations and increased the transmissibility of COVID. Nevertheless, a September 2021 report showed that Americans believed immigrants and tourists were a top reason for the spike in infections. As for blaming President Biden's immigration policies, the Centers for Disease Control and Prevention under the Biden administration in fact extended the implementation of Title 42, and the administration launched a deportation program of Colombian immigrants under the border rule in March 2022.[52]

The most significant result of medicalizing immigration policies and the border has not been to protect Americans from disease but to racially construct non-white groups—Asians, Latin Americans, Africans, and others—as foreign and, furthermore, illegal. The implementation of medical inspections at the border went hand in hand with the proliferation of bureaucracy, procedures, and documentation needed for entry and naturalization. These institutions in turn broadened and reinforced the conception of the illegal and undocumented person. The medicalization of the border also more clearly defined and conceptually hardened the lines drawn between the United States and Mexico and at ports of entry, such as at the detention centers of Angel Island and Ellis Island.[53]

The New Jerusalem metaphor enabled the identification of unwanted peoples with apocalyptic plague. And the threat of these pestilent invaders then justified the use of documentation and hardened borders to exclude them. As we shall see, bureaucratic paperwork and barriers also figure in the book of Revelation, and their heavenly terminology, logic, and dynamics likewise come into play in American immigration and naturalization.

# PART THREE

# Requirements and Categorizations

# FIVE

# The Book of Life and the Book of Deeds in American Immigration and Naturalization

Then I saw a great white throne and the one who sat on it; the earth and
the heaven fled from his presence, and no place was found for them. And I
saw the dead, great and small, standing before the throne, and books were
opened. Also another book was opened, the book of life. And the dead
were judged according to their works, as recorded in the books. And the
sea gave up the dead that were in it, Death and Hades gave up the dead
that were in them, and all were judged according to what they had done . . .
and anyone whose name was not found written in the book of life was
thrown into the lake of fire.

*—Revelation 20:11–15*

And the mention of a book, in this case, may be supposed an allusion to the
Public Registers, used in Cities, Countries, Kingdoms, and with almost all the
Civilized Nations of this World; where the Names of such as might have any
claim to future Privileges, are usually Enrolled. . . . This is the Book of Life.

*—Cotton Mather,* Unum Necessarium *(1693)*

## "And Books Were Opened"

Crammed with the awesome, fantastical, bizarrely beautiful, and gro-
tesque, the Apocalypse of John presents spectacle upon spectacle to
the reader. In Revelation 19, the Rider on the White Horse, with flaming
eyes and robes dipped in blood, captures the Beast with seven heads and
ten horns and casts it and its false prophet into the lake of fire (19:11–20).

Then an angel descends to bind Satan with chains, sealing him in a pit for a thousand years—the millennium during which Christ reigns (20:1–6). This episode, as well as a short summary of Satan's return and final destruction (20:7–10), concludes the warfare, violence, plague, and calamity of the book. After the passing of heaven and earth, into the void descend a new heaven and a new earth, and the city of God, the New Jerusalem (21:1–2). But between the final destruction of Satan and the arrival of the New Jerusalem there is a narrative caesura, a loaded pause in the drama and pageantry. It is like the breathless break in the music at the end of Handel's "Hallelujah" chorus, separating the busy interwoven chanting and hymnody—with apocalyptic lyrics taken from Revelation 19:6, 16, 11:15—and the final triumphant *Hallelujah*, sung in unison with a thundering roll of timpani.[1]

In the narrative pause of the text, there is no fighting, no singing, no proclamation, no angelic explanation. There is almost no sound and no color, except for the awaiting lake of fire that burns with sulfur. But this liminal scene, between the struggle and the triumph, is itself an awesome spectacle: a spectacle of ultimate, all-encompassing bureaucracy. This is the Judgment of the Dead, an apocalyptic administrative scene with the supreme bureaucrat seated and ready to process the dead—*all* the dead, all who have ever died, whether by land or sea, both "great and small" in fame, stature, or age. All these dead stand before the judge, presumably waiting to be processed individually since judgment rests on one's deeds ("judged according to what they had done" [20:13]) and the listing of one's name in the Book of Life (20:15). Unless this office also operates at supernatural speed, the wait itself, standing before the throne, would be a punishment.[2]

This is the most bureaucratic scene in the New Testament canon. As a liminal scene between the destruction of Satan and the entrance of the New Jerusalem, it acts as a gateway, both structurally within the narrative and literally as the process through which the dead must go in order to enter the heavenly city or be cast into the lake of fire. But what exactly determines the fate of each of the dead? As is typical with any bureau, the procedure begins with records—a database, so to speak—and Revelation's database consists of books: "Books were opened" (20:12). The text further reveals, as mentioned above, that there are two types of books: those that record the deeds of the dead, which I will call the Book of Deeds, and the Book of Life. But how do these two types of books jointly determine entry or exclusion? Is an entry in the Book of Life predicated on deeds? If so, why are both types of books examined at this judgment? How can the two work simultaneously? Does the Book of Life overrule the Book of Deeds?

The previous chapters have explored the apocalyptic exclusion and rejection of immigrant groups as related to the description of those forbidden entry into the New Jerusalem, "the dogs and sorcerers, and sexually immoral and murderers and idolaters, and everyone who loves and practices falsehood" (Rev 22:15). Those chapters explore how American nativists adopted the strategies of Revelation, that is, the identification of unwanted people groups as plagues, diseased, pagan, and sexually dangerous, in order to build social and political movements for their exclusion.

This chapter analyzes the bureaucratic mechanisms for entry and exclusion in American immigration and naturalization—laws, policies, and documentation—in conversation with the gatekeeping logics deployed before the gates of the New Jerusalem, that is, the records of the Book of Deeds and the Book of Life. As with the preceding analyses in this book, the influence of the book of Revelation on American concepts and requirements for immigration and naturalization is sometimes obvious in direct quotations or the use of imagery and sometimes palpable through a shared discourse or underlying conceptualizations. But in any case, inasmuch as American policies of immigration and naturalization have treated Protestant Christianity as the assumed religious identity of "Americans" to the exclusion of other groups, it has in rudimentary principle excluded on the same grounds as the judge of Revelation, that is, based on Christian religious worship or identity. And the category of religious worship and identity in American history deeply imbricates constructions of race and ethnicity.[3]

## Soil, Blood, and Sacrament

The laws and policies of the American colonial period have their roots in English law. With regard to citizenship and naturalization, English law, until 1350, held that the place of a person's birth determined their allegiance and citizenship, which was inalienable.[4] Thus citizenship rested upon the soil of birthplace and was a matter beyond one's action or choosing; it was determined, it could be said, by destiny.

In 1350–51, under the reign of Edward III, it was declared that those born to English parents "in Parts beyond the Sea" (*De natis ultra mare*), that is, outside of England, would inherit English citizenship, enjoy all the rights afforded to those born on English soil, and were "in Ligeance," that is, owed loyalty to the king.[5] Citizenship was thus expanded to include, for example, the children of ambassadors born outside England and those born within the king's dominions, which would come to include the American colonies. But these rights remained strictly a matter of birth, by soil (one's birthplace) and by blood (one's parentage). Whether by chance or destiny, people found themselves citizens without choosing or meriting such rights.

In 1610, a foreigner could naturalize by the "mere Grace and Favour" of the king, but in that same year, under James I, this was restricted by law to be granted only to "such as are of the Religion now established in this Realm," that is, Protestant Anglicanism. Thus, citizenship became possible beyond the vicissitudes of destiny and was within reach through one's actions, that is, by gaining the special favor of the monarch (as far as that lies in one's power) and by proving one's religion and worship through the sacrament of the Lord's Supper. As the law states: "No person or persons of what Quality, Condition, or Place soever, being of the Age of Eighteen years or above, shall be naturalized or restored in Blood, unless the same person or persons have received the Sacrament of the Lord's Supper within one Month next before any Bill exhibited for that Purpose; and also take the Oath of Supremacy and the Oath of Allegiance in the Parliament House before his or her Bill be twice read."[6] This explicitly tied citizenship and naturalization, beyond soil and blood, to the sacrament of Communion and Protestantism.

Since English colonization of America began under the rule of James I, these were the laws in place, so that those born to English parents in the colonies were also English citizens. An act passed under William III in 1698–99 expanded this circle to include persons born in English colonies to parents who were *not* English citizens.[7] This effected two significant transformations of symbolic, political, and economic import: first, this act claimed American colonial soil as English soil, and it therefore would produce English peoples of inalienable allegiance. Like the soil on which Cadmus sowed the dragon's teeth, American colonial soil became the ground of a new autochthony. It was a land where an alien immigrant population could be transformed into an English and then a distinctly American and "native" population, as if having lived there always and belonging to the soil. Second, this meant that all heritable wealth and, most significant, American land itself, passed from populations in the colonies of diverse citizenship to English citizen children. Both these effects served to erase, on mythic and practical levels simultaneously, the histories, lives, and land of indigenous peoples. The expansion of destiny-oriented citizenship by birthplace to include the colonies was an expansion of imperial territory.

In 1709, Queen Anne further increased the possibilities of naturalization for foreigners by allowing German Protestant refugees to naturalize; many then sailed for America to settle ultimately in Pennsylvania. The Foreign Protestants Naturalization Act required only that the foreigner take an oath and the Lord's Supper. Although the law was repealed in 1712, its effects were not.[8]

These two rites of naturalization, the oath and the sacrament, were retained as key elements in a law, which came to be known as the Plantation Act, passed under George II in 1740. The act made it possible for aliens to naturalize in the American colonies if they had resided there for seven years, swore the oath, and took the Lord's Supper. The law also allowed concessions for Quakers and Jews, who were not required to say the phrase "upon the true Faith of a Christian" in the oath or to take the sacrament. Long-held English legal practice also makes it likely that Jews in the colonies were permitted to swear naturalization oaths on the "Books of Moses" or the Old Testament instead of the Christian Bible. Concessions were not made, however, for "Papists," that is, Catholics. Thus, at this point in English and American history, under a supersessionist paternalistic attitude, Jewish peoples were considered less politically dangerous than Roman Catholics.[9]

Whereas the laws discussed above governed English citizenship and naturalization in the colonies, each of the colonies had its own set of laws regarding immigration, civic inclusion, and rights. These ranged from highly exclusive regulations, as in New England, where immigrants could be turned away if deemed "poor, vicious, and infirm," to more relaxed systems, as in South Carolina, where aliens already residing or coming to the province could "enjoy all rights, privileges . . . as if they had been born of English parents within this Province" if they swore an oath of allegiance to the English sovereign and an oath against "popery." In New York, a ban on Catholic naturalization to the province was strictly enforced in at least one circumstance, in 1683, when the governor barred the entry of two French Catholics, who were deported back to Canada.[10]

The requirement that one confess Protestant Christianity was thus a consistent theme in colonial laws for entry and naturalization. Another consistent theme was the requirement for official record-keeping in a list or book. Massachusetts laws from 1700 to 1731 required "a perfect list or certificate" showing every passenger arriving on a vessel and a "record in the council books" for all foreign Protestants sworn in by oath. The Plantation Act of 1740 similarly required that all who were naturalized in America have their names registered "in a Book or Books to be had and kept for that Purpose in the said Office, for publick View and Inspection as Occasion shall require."[11]

The writing of names in these books for entry and inclusion consistently rested on the same facts of destiny (one's birthplace or bloodline) or deeds (one's spoken oath and sacramental worship). That naturalization could occur at all and through one's own actions presented a fundamental shift from common law before the fourteenth century, allowing factors beyond birthplace to determine citizenship. The Plantation Act of 1740 thus allowed entry into the "Book of American Citizenry" not only for those fated from birth to be citizens but also for those who had merited inclusion by their deeds: by oath, sacrament, and duration in the land.

### "He Showed Me My Name Written in Letters of Blood"

At the same time as the Plantation Act of 1740, American colonials were also obsessing about whether their name might be recorded in another book of citizenry: the Book of Life. In the electrically charged atmosphere of the Great

Awakening and in the decades of its aftermath, numerous men and women had terrifying visions where they encountered both Satan and Jesus and where they beheld their own names written in Revelation's Book of Life. One anonymous account from Hebron, Connecticut, in 1742 tells how the writer was transported by a dove to the top of a mountain to behold "God the son seated on a throne of Glory." The writer states that "Christ then looked on me and asked me why I looked so sorrowful. I could not answer one word. Then he, taking up the book, he showed me my name written in Letters of blood."[12]

That same year, in nearby Lebanon, Connecticut, two children, a girl and a boy, beheld a shared vision wherein they both arrived at the heavenly city. The boy stated that Jesus met him inside the city and showed him the Book of Life, while the girl recounted that she saw the boy reading a book "bigger than any Book they had ever seen in the World," on which in "Golden Capitals" were listed the names of saints.[13]

Tales of such visions circulated not only among parishioners and in letters between ministers in New England but also in newspaper accounts and pamphlets, as public religious leaders and pundits weighed in for or against the credibility and orthodoxy of these mystical experiences. The *Boston Evening-Post* ran an account in March 1743 of a disturbance during a church service in Mendon, Massachusetts, when several attendees had visions and were shouting and howling and jumping on the pews. One servant or enslaved girl told of a vision in which she descended into hell and was rescued by Christ, who "took her by the Hand, led her out, and carried her up to Heaven, and shewed her the Book of Life, where she saw a great many Names, among which were her Mistress's, and that the Book wanted but two Inches to be fill'd up, and that CHRIST told her, that if the *good Work* which was carrying on upon Earth Succeeded, he should come to Judgment in a short Time." The writer of this newspaper article adds to the end of this account: "Oh! Wretched Delusions!"[14]

While the bulk of historic accounts of Book of Life visions come from up and down New England—from Massachusetts, Connecticut, New Hampshire, and Maine—similar visions occurred in Nova Scotia, upstate New York, Kentucky, and Ohio. The Book of Life visions that began during the Great Awakening endured for decades, in places far from New England, as shown by this description of "New Lights" Baptists of the Carolinas Back-country, written by Anglican minister Charles Woodmason in 1768–69:

> The Giddy, and the Ignorant the Enthusiastic and Superstitious, whom [itinerant preachers] judge they may draw round them, such are *decreed* to be sav'd—And their Names are wrote in the Lamb's Book of Life—because they read it there. I ask'd some of these deluded Persons, thus infatuated, thus impos'd on, How these Persons, and when, and where they read and saw this Book of Gods decrees when at the same Time, they could not read the *Psalter* when laid before them? . . . The Answer given, was,— That the finger of God pointed it out to them.

Like the writer of the account of the young woman's Book of Life vision in the *Boston Evening-Post*, Charles Woodmason describes these visions of Backcountry settlers with incredulity and scorn. How, he asks, can these un-educated people claim to read their names in the heavenly book if they can-not even read? But beyond the disbelief and disquiet caused by the supernatural and claims of divine knowledge received directly from Christ, perhaps more disturbing to Woodmason and other religious leaders was the implied *theology* of the visions of the Book of Life.[15]

Protestant denominations in eighteenth-century America, whether Con-gregational or Anglican or Baptist, held to a doctrine of election, that is, the belief that God chooses only some people and not others for salvation and eternal life, without regard to their actions. Given the doctrine of election, an aspect of the doctrine of predestination, the idea that an individual could receive a divine, privileged surety of one's election was considered any-where from unseemly to verging on the blasphemous. For some church and civic leaders of New England, with their heritage of distinguishing between the earthly "visible church," containing both predestined damned and saved, versus the "invisible church" of those elected by God, these individ-ual announcements of registration in the Book of Life seemed highly unor-thodox and threatening to church order.[16]

Furthermore, there appeared in some of these visions the existence of blank pages in Revelation's Book of Life, pages *yet to be filled*. The girl of the *Boston Evening-Post* account claimed to have seen "that the Book wanted but two Inches to be fill'd up, and that CHRIST told her, that if the *good Work* which was carrying on upon Earth succeeded, he should come to Judgment in a short Time." And according to the boy and girl who had a shared vision, the Day of Judgment was coming soon because "the Book of Life was filled up, wanting about One Page . . . and when that was fill'd up, the Day of Judgment was to come."[17]

These unwritten pages of the Book of Life portended not only an imminent Day of Judgment but also indicated that names were continually being added to the Book, which contradicted the doctrine of predestination. The ongoing addition of names hinted that human action was at least partly responsible for inclusion in the list. This notion is further emphasized by the admonitory tone of the visions, implicitly exhorting people to carry on "*good Work.*" This idea went against the orthodox Protestant teaching of salvation as destiny, via the election of God, and instead indicated that salvation was possible through human action or merit. These visions, observes historian Douglas Winiarski, "rendered obsolete the classic morphology of conversion" in that they gave, in the words of contemporary pundits, "infallible Assurance" of salvation, which liberated visionaries and congregants from "old Stingy puritan Doctrines."[18]

Thus, while the pathway to citizenship expanded in the American colonies beyond the destinies of birthplace and blood, so also the citizenship registry of the New Jerusalem expanded in charismatic, revivalist understanding to include souls beyond those elected and predestined for eternal life.[19] This is not to say that these expansions directly influenced each other, but they reflect a similar and simultaneous shift in fundamental processes and possibilities for belonging, while using closely related vocabularies of destiny and merit containing similar contradictions. That is, both colonial civic and religious belonging continued to uphold the principles and doctrines of fate—birthplace, parentage, election, and predestination—yet also allowed inclusion by deed—oaths, sacrament, worship, and catechism.

Of course, it would be anachronistic to categorize colonial naturalization and Protestant Christian salvation separately as "civil" and "religious" transformations. To be a naturalized citizen in the colonies was to be a Protestant

Christian: one had to perform the rite of the Lord's Supper and swear on one's Christian faith, just as one had to perform almost identical rites, usually with the addition of baptism, for Christian conversion. These actions did not eradicate the notion that citizenship, whether earthly or heavenly, was also conferred by circumstances of fate, nor did the idea of innate, essential belonging tied to birth, blood, and election obsolesce: these ideas endured, in spite of the contradictions. In fact, they proved to be as enduring as bedrock, as will be discussed below.

On a practical level for colonies and their churches, however, the principle of inalienable allegiance to one's birthplace would not encourage immigration and grow the labor force, or expand colonial territory, just as divine and unascertainable election would not foster church participation or expand congregations. In practical terms, belonging to church and state had to be expanded beyond inclusion by fate and add inclusion through deeds in order to grow the population, contradictions be damned. Thus American ideas and policies of citizenship and belonging grew along contradictory trajectories of predestination and action, fate and deeds.

The entry procedures and databases of the book of Revelation itself also operate in the same contradictory fashion as in colonial civic and religious practice. The ancient text and its representation of heavenly citizenship and belonging present the same fundamental contradictions and hidden logics crisscrossing centuries of American naturalization and immigration.

## Heavenly Bureaucracy: Ministry and Mystery

Revelation is crowded with mention of other texts, including letters to the seven churches (2–3), a sealed scroll (5:1–8), an edible scroll (10:2–10), the books of judgment (20:12–15), and even a reference to itself as a text, along with an anathema against those who might dare to change it (22:18–19). These texts, like the throne room and the armies of God, present an apocalyptic version of imperial power, reflecting and amplifying the reach, might, and mechanisms of empire for rule and administration on a divine and eschatological level. The scroll sealed with seven seals functions like an imperial decree, but on an omnipotent scale, so that when Christ the Lamb

unseals it, its mere opening calls forth emissaries to enact God's will immediately (5:6–6:17).[20]

Likewise, the books consulted at the Judgment of the Dead in Revelation
21 function in ways similar to imperial registries and lists, as do the heavenly
books of other Jewish apocalypses, some from which Revelation takes its inspiration. The heavenly books of judgment, like the lists of empires and governments, demonstrate and execute the power of bureaucracy: namely, the
power to surveil, gather data, maintain records, enforce procedures, and ob-
fuscate with impunity the Kafkaesque logics in operation. The question of
which came first, earthly or heavenly bureaucracy, is not the issue here.
Giorgio Agamben notes: "Sometimes, as in Tertullian's writings, the administration of worldly monarchy is the model of the angelic ministries, whereas
at others the celestial bureaucracy furnishes the archetype of the worldly.
What is decisive, however, is that long before the terminology of civil administration and government was developed and fixed, it was already firmly
constituted in angelology. Not only the concept of hierarchy but also that of
ministry and of mission are . . . first systematized in a highly articulated way
precisely in relation to angelic activities."[21]

Suffice it to say for this discussion that the celestial bureaucracy of Revelation (and its Jewish literary forebears) had, by the time of the establishment of the United States, been a part of the ideation and implementation
of earthly governments for centuries. Characteristic of the administration of
the Kingdom of Heaven—whether in the ancient text of Revelation, in the
history of its interpretation, or even today in jokes, television, novels, and
comics featuring "celestial bureaucracy," is the combination and conflation
of *ministry* and *mystery*.[22] That is, heavenly administration consists of a hier-
archical, data-laden bureaucracy that exerts and exhibits its power by its
very inscrutability.

In Revelation, the nature and function of the Book of Life exhibits precisely this combination of ministry and mystery. The narrating seer highlights the Book of Life throughout the text as both a threat and a promise. It
is a comprehensive database and its effects are absolute in the most apocalyptic sense, but the details of its operation remain unclear. The first mention of the Book of Life occurs in the letter to the Church of Sardis, dictated

by the Son of Man: "If you conquer, you will be clothed like them [the worthy] in white robes, and I will not blot your name out [ἐξαλείψω] of the book of life; I will confess your name before my father and before his angels" (3:5). Thus it appears that entries in this registry are not necessarily permanent, that their continued listing is contingent on behavior, on "conquering," which, in the context of the letter, seems to mean obedience and repentance (3:3).

If erasure is a threat, how did the names appear in the Book of Life in the first place? Allusion to the time of their registration is made in Revelation 13:8, when the diabolical Beast has risen from the sea and been given authority to rule: "And all the inhabitants of the earth will worship [the Beast], everyone whose name has not been written *from the foundation of the world* in the book of life of the Lamb that was slaughtered." And again, in Revelation 17:8, an angel tells the seer that "the inhabitants of the earth, whose names have not been written in the book of life *from the foundation of the world*, will be amazed when they see the beast, because it was and is not and is to come."

These verses also show that worship and obedience determine whether one's name is written in the Book of Life or not—those who worship the Beast are those whose names have *not* been written in the Book of Life. But the record of one's name also appears to be a matter of destiny: names that are *not* in the book have *not* been there from the foundation of the world; this is stated twice. But the registry of names as predestined is potentially contradicted by the warning that one's name can also be *blotted out* of the Book of Life, if one does not obey, repent, and "conquer." The narrative does not further clarify how stable the records are: if one's name is *not* in the Book of Life from the foundation of the world, will that name *never* appear there? This information is not given. But since names may still be blotted out, it seems that inclusion in the registry is predetermined, whereas exclusion from it is not.

The Book of Life in Revelation resembles the Book of Life in other ancient Jewish literature, functioning like the citizenship lists of the ancient Mediterranean world.[23] In Revelation 21:27, the inhabitants of the New Jerusalem are "only those whose names are written in the Lamb's book of life." And like other ancient literary descriptions of the Book of Life, the way one's name is registered in it remains unclear, although one biblical psalm indicates that birthplace determines citizenship in Zion (Ps 87:5–6):

> And of Zion it shall be said,
> "This one and that one were born in it,"
> For the Most High himself will establish it.
> The Lord records, as he registers the peoples,
> "This one was born there."

Thus, within the Book of Life literary tradition the concept of birthright citizenship does exist, which is consistent with the notion of destiny as determining belonging. As biblical scholar Leslie Baynes states, "A person may be enrolled as a citizen of Zion strictly because of the luck of birth."[24]

In summary, the main elements of the Book of Life in Revelation are as follows: it is a list of names; it has existed since the beginning ("foundation") of the world and so implies predestination; but the threat of erasure from this book is used to compel allegiance and obedience. The logic of the list remains obscure, a mystery.

The function of the Book of Life is further complicated by the appearance of other books at the Judgment of the Dead, where these books are consulted together: "And I saw the dead, great and small, standing before the throne, and books were opened. Also another book was opened, the book of life. And the dead were judged according to their works, as recorded in the books. . . . And anyone whose name was not found in the book of life was thrown into the lake of fire" (Rev 20:12, 15).

The Book (or books) of Deeds, is therefore a list not of names but of actions attributed to individuals. The ancient historical *comparanda* for the Book of Deeds are not citizenship lists but rather texts like military diplomas that prove an *earned* citizenship or records of a ruler's deeds — *res gestae* in inscriptions and literary works. The literary trope of a divine record of deeds spans different cultural traditions. In Aeschylus's *Eumenides*, for example, Hades is described as a "judge of mortals beneath the earth, and he observes everything with his recording mind."[25]

And like the Book of Life, the Book of Deeds also appears in Jewish apocalyptic literature, usually paired with the phrase "and books were opened," as it is in Revelation. For example, in Daniel 7:10, "The Court sat in judgment, and the books were opened"; or in 2 Baruch 24:1, "And the books will be opened in which are written all the sins of all those who have sinned." In the throne room of judgment in Recension A of the *Testament of Abraham*, one angel writes down all a person's sins, while another writes down all a person's righteous deeds.[26]

If, then, the Book of Deeds is a record of each individual's "works," how does it operate in conjunction with the Book of Life, a destiny-determining list of names? On the one hand, the Judgment of Revelation relies on a cumulative record that requires evaluation, the Book of Deeds. On the other hand, that same book seems irrelevant in the presence of the Book of Life, an absolute list in which names either appear or not, effecting immediate and absolute judgment. It is possible, as in 2 Baruch 24:1 and other literature, that the Book of Deeds of Revelation records only a person's sins, resulting in their erasure from the Book of Life, although the text does not state this. Regardless, nowhere does the text of Revelation indicate that one can be *added* to the Book of Life, only that one can be blotted out from it—and therefore also obliterated as a living being. Therefore, every citizen of the New Jerusalem has been predestined for the city "from the foundation of the world." This bureaucracy operates both through the mystery of fate and the ministry of records, wielding the threat of administrative omniscience and surveillance.

The contradictory cooperation of fate and deeds—or, in Christian theological parlance, election and works—as embodied in these heavenly books has been a source of confusion and debate for centuries.[27] The mystery and ministry of ancient heavenly citizenship records, which themselves are a reflection of procedures and practices of their own historical context, are echoed in American colonial laws as they expanded to include additional pathways to naturalization—via oath and sacrament—thus supplementing the traditions of *jus soli* and *jus sanguinis*. The Plantation Act of 1740 allowed for citizenship to be acquired by *both* destiny and deeds, by birth and by worship, just as the revival visions of the 1740s allowed for both a predetermined heavenly Book of Life and the ongoing addition of names to that registry.

While these American phenomena seem to expand the possibilities of belonging beyond predestination and the luck of birth, certain aspects of destiny remain assumed and unstated in the law of the colonies. What is not spelled out but assumed in the 1740 Plantation Act was being practiced in violent acts on plantations, on the bodies of Black enslaved peoples who could take no oath or sacrament to naturalize and gain citizenship. In that same year of 1740, the South Carolina colony passed the Negro Act, declaring "all Negroes and Indians . . . mulattoes or mustizoes" (unless the latter three were free) "and all their issue and offspring" to be "absolute slaves," that is, property, without the right to raise food, travel alone, learn to write, or earn money.[28]

This legislation was the culmination of centuries of slave laws and practices in England and the colonies. There was no question of citizenship or naturalization for Black or indigenous peoples, regardless of how laws were changing in order to increase the population of the colonies. Black and indigenous peoples did not belong in the earthly Book of Life, which functioned alongside the expanding Book of Deeds offering news paths to citizenship. That is to say, the American Book of Life was not a book of fated enrollment based solely on birth and parentage, but rather on *white* birth and parentage. The American Book of Life, in reality, was a Book of *White* Life. And, as in the book of Revelation, if one's name was not in the Book of White Life, this omission would *always* trump the Book of Deeds: no Black or indigenous person in America, up through the Revolution and for decades thereafter, could swear an oath or take a sacrament to naturalize.[29] They were not in the Book of White Life, which had been written at the foundation of the American world.

## Two Books of Life

The South Carolina Negro Act in 1740 rested in part on the ideas circulated in the Fundamental Constitutions of Carolina, a document sealed in 1669 by the eight proprietors of the Carolina colony and co-authored by none other than John Locke. One prominent feature of the document is its liberality in religious toleration for the sake of attracting settlers to the colony. A key section of the document states, "*Religion* ought to alter nothing in any Man's Civil Estate or Right," which seems to promise religious freedom. But the full text reveals that this precursor to the U.S. separation of church and state also provides justification for the continued Christian enslavement of people. The full argument of this section reads: "Since *Charity* obliges us to wish well to the Souls of all Men, and *Religion* ought to alter nothing in any Man's Civil Estate or Right, it shall be lawful for *Slaves* as well as others, to Enter themselves, and be of what *Church* or *Profession* any of them shall think best, and thereof be as fully *Members* as any *Freeman*. But yet no Slave shall hereby be exempted from that *Civil Dominion* his Master hath over him, but be in all other things in the same State and Condition he was in before."[30]

This precept severed the connection between civic and religious inclusion, in the guise of liberality, so that an enslaved person could not, upon baptism or taking the sacrament, become a free person or a naturalized citizen. This constitution, in the words of historian Tisa Wenger, "suggests how the emerging ideal of religious freedom forged conceptual distinctions between race and religion as newly separable forms of identity."[31] That is, the racialized enslavement of Black bodies could be justified within the realm of civic identity, separate from a religious realm and regardless of the "spiritual status" of Black people's souls. Thus, an enslaved person could take the sacrament as a Christian yet be unable to fulfill the requirements for naturalization because the law declared citizenship possible only for white people.

By the seventeenth and eighteenth centuries, Europeans had classified enslaved African peoples as "non-white," while Europeans themselves had become racialized as "white." How these racial categories should relate to religious belief and identity became a fraught question given the desire of American colonists to maintain Black enslavement and disenfranchisement. In answer, the Fundamental Constitutions of Carolina and subsequent legal and religious opinions explicitly cordoned off religious from racial-civic identity, latching onto a similarly conceived separation of the spiritual from the physical. Thus Black people's Christian conversion and taking of the sacrament would only bring the salvation of their souls, whereas their bodies remained ineligible for citizenship and rights.[32]

Cotton Mather's 1706 pamphlet *The Negro Christianized* spelled this out with overweening paternalism as he admonishes masters to proselytize those they have enslaved: "The greatest *Kindness* that can be done to any Man is to make a *Christian* of him. Your *Negroes* are immediately Raised unto an astonishing Felicity, when you have *Christianized* them. . . . Tho' they remain your *Servants*, yet they are to become the *Children* of God. Tho' they are to enjoy no *Earthly Goods*, but the small Allowance that your Justice and Bounty shall see proper for them, yet they are become *Heirs* of God, and *Joint-Heirs* with the Lord Jesus Christ."[33] Mather delineates exactly how disconnected an enslaved person's civic rights were from their spiritual rights: on the one hand, they are chattel, mere property; on the other, they are children of God. Under colonial law, they cannot own goods, but under heavenly inheritance law, they are royal heirs.

In this passage, Mather uses the inheritance language from Paul's letter to the Romans: "For you did not receive a spirit of slavery to fall back into fear, but you have received a spirit of adoption. When we cry, 'Abba! Father!' it is that very Spirit bearing witness with our spirit that we are children of God, and if children, then heirs, heirs of God and joint heirs with Christ—if, in fact, we suffer with him so that we may also be glorified with him" (Rom 8:15–17). Mather uses Paul's distinction between the enslaved, who are unable to inherit, and adoptees, who can, to draw a firm line between enslaved people's earthly status and their spiritual status. In Mather's teaching, as in Paul's, an enslaved person's earthly status is the reality of the *present time*, but this will be changed in the *future* ("they are to *become* the *Children* of God"), at the apocalypse of God when creation shall be renewed and the children of God glorified (Rom 8:18–25).

This argument is in keeping with the doctrine of Cotton Mather's father, Increase Mather. Increase Mather, in his *New Jerusalem* (transcribed by Cotton), states that the Book of Life has "names written in it, as in a great city there is a book wherein the names of those that are *free men*, that are Denizens of the city are Registered." But this heavenly register does not grant freedom to the enslaved living on earth, which remains "a Valley . . . a Vale of tears" even though the people suffering in that vale "belong to this city of god." So also, Cotton Mather understood the present reality as separate from whatever glories and freedoms might come with future citizenship in the heavenly city. Mather in fact states that there are two Books of Life, the "Book of Life Temporal" and the "Book of Life Eternal."[34]

And Mather sees the status of one's earthly life, governed by the Book of Life Temporal, as borne on the skin of the enslaved, further separating the identity of an enslaved body from the mind or spirit that can be saved. In *The Negro Christianized*, Mather writes, "They that have been Scorched and Blacken'd by the Sun of *Africa*" are able "to have their Minds Healed by the more Benign *Beams* of the *Sun of Righteousness*."[35] This platonic duality writes racialization on the skin, so that the body and its markings belong in the realm of the state, and the salvation and freedom of the soul can only be realized in heaven.

This duality, when enshrined in legal opinion, such as the Yorke-Talbot slavery opinion of 1729, made it possible to baptize enslaved persons without effecting manumission.[36] Thus, missionary activities in Africa, the Caribbean, and other places in the Global South could continue without threatening the slave trade; and this proselytization of "heathens" could serve as a justification for colonization—colonization that could then continue to send enslaved peoples to America and Europe.

Thus, while the naturalization processes of colonial America retained, up until the Revolution, the swearing of a Christian oath and the taking of the sacrament, there emerged during this period two Books of Life: the Book of Life, bearing the names of those who worshipped Christ and were admitted eschatologically to the heavenly New Jerusalem, and the Book of White Life, written from the foundation of America and bearing only those names destined by body and blood to be white enough to have citizenship in the earthly New Jerusalem of the United States. The definition of whiteness would expand and contract with some flexibility, but the one unquestionable identity in American citizenship and naturalization (and enfranchisement) was that of the white, male, English Protestant.

# SIX

# The Book of White Life

If you conquer, you will be clothed like them in white robes,
and I will not blot your name out of the book of life.

—*Revelation* 3:5

The two angels on the left and right hand, these are the ones that write down
sins and righteous deeds. The one on the right records righteous deeds, the
one on the left records sins. . . . The fiery and merciless angel . . . he judges
the works of humankind by fire. And if the fire consumes the works of any
person, the angel of judgment immediately seizes them and casts them into
the place of sinners, the harshest place of punishment.

—*Testament of Abraham* 13.9–13

## To Govern Is to Populate

The baseline American identity as a white, male, English Protestant is
apparent in the debates leading up to the Naturalization Act of 1790,
the first federal naturalization law in the United States. The opening debate
in Congress before the passage of the bill revolved around many issues,
none of which questioned the racialized identity of those who could be
naturalized: "all free white persons." The U.S. government, at the founding of the nation, based citizenship on the luck or fate of being born white.
In Revelation's terms, the American Book of Life—the citizenship registry
based on destiny—was the Book of White Life, written at the foundation of
the American world.

Thus in 1790, there was of yet little debate as to what identity qualified for citizenship. That was obviously the white man. The real debate in Congress leading up to the passage of the first naturalization act focused on what requirements could be set to guarantee that such white persons be upstanding and meriting naturalization. In the terms of Revelation, the Book of White Life had already been written; the task before Congress was to compose the Book of Deeds: what actions would demonstrate that a free white person was "good," "reputable," "worthy," "useful," "honorable," and possessed of "that zest for pure republicanism."[1] In Congress's view, a probationary period of mandatory residency would prove one's worthiness.

The main question remaining for Congress was how long a period of residency would be required. Too short a period would cheapen the privilege of citizenship and invite abuse of the naturalization process; too long would discourage immigration. The statesmen clearly saw the need for greater immigration since they had "a large tract of country to people" and wished to "increase the wealth and strength of the community." This meant setting a reasonable requirement for length of residency, and it also meant expanding slightly the category of whiteness, which would both encourage immigration and promote the liberality of the new United States. Congressman John Page (VA) argued:

> The policy of European nations and States respecting naturalization did not apply to the situation of the United States. Bigotry and superstition, or a deep-rooted prejudice against the Government, laws, religion, or manners of neighboring nations had a weight in that policy, which cannot exist here, where a more liberal system ought to prevail. I think we shall be inconsistent with ourselves if, after boasting of having opened an asylum for the oppressed of all nations, and established a Government which is the admiration of the world, we make the terms of admission to the full enjoyment of that asylum as is now proposed. It is nothing to us, whether Jews or Roman Catholics settle amongst us; whether subjects of Kings, or citizens of free States wish to reside in the United States, they will find it in their interest to be good citizens,

and neither their religious nor political opinions can injure us, if
we have good laws, well executed.[2]

These admirable sentiments against bigotry cast the United States as a nation that had advanced beyond the archaic "superstition" of European nations. They also open the category of "free white persons" to Jews, who
could already naturalize under English colonial law, and Catholics, who
generally could not. The congressman's argument reveals a growing decou-
pling of race—here whiteness—and religion. The inclusion of Catholics,
who under prior English law in the colonies could not have taken the Protestant sacrament, expanded the parameters of naturalization.

But the description of the United States as "an asylum for the oppressed
of all nations" because of its immigration policy was and is a moral grandstanding fiction. Immigration and naturalization laws serve ultimately to create the ideal population as conceived by those who set policy and legislate.
"In the Americas," observed Argentine intellectual Juan Bautista Alberdi, "to
govern is to populate," and in the twentieth century—after waves of immigration restrictions—this saying was modified to state "to govern is to populate *well*."[3] For the first Congress of the United States, to "populate *well*"
meant peopling the land quickly with persons racialized as white. The construct of "white" could include Jews and Catholics for the sake of expediency in peopling the land rapidly with a minimally acceptable population.

This rapid populating of the land with white bodies would also achieve
the aim of pushing indigenous peoples out of U.S.-claimed territories,
which were certainly not lying vacant but rather were the home and ances-
tral lands of Native peoples. For this reason also, the U.S. government conceptualized *jus soli*, the right to citizenship by birthplace, as applicable only
to free white persons, thus denying citizenship to Native peoples (who had
always been born in the land) and to enslaved peoples. This limitation of *jus
soli* for white persons only also transformed the soil of the land so that it created only American citizens, claiming it as essentially American while erasing the history, belonging, and governance of indigenous peoples.

So while the first U.S. federal naturalization acts (the Naturalization Acts
of 1790 and 1795, which required two and then five years of residency) were

far more liberal than any naturalization laws of Europe, their aim was to people the nation quickly in such a way that the newcomers replicated the racial identity of the ruling class. The proliferation of this racial population and their settlement on the land would help guarantee continued white governance and further establish their innate belonging to the land.[4]

How could a nation founded on democratic principles of self-rule and equality of the people so thoroughly exclude and exploit those who were not white? Conventional wisdom, invested in the essential goodness of America and its founding ideals, would answer that the shining foundation of the United States was only marred by the racism characteristic of the time of its establishment, and that eventually justice and democracy would (or will) win the day as the nation left behind archaic racist notions. Critical scholars, however, counter this and argue that racism is built into the very conceptualizations and structures of the nation-state and American democracy. Anthony Marx argues: "Citizenship is a key institutional mechanism for establishing boundaries of inclusion or exclusion in the nation-state. . . . But by specifying to whom citizenship applies, states also define those outside the community of citizens, who then live within the state as objects of domination. . . . Nationhood was institutionalized on the basis of race; the political production of race and the political production of nationhood were linked."[5]

The formation of a citizenry can exclude along lines other than race, but that was not the case in the United States. The country began as a colonial proprietary enterprise over and against indigenous peoples, requiring the labor of Black peoples as property. Thus Matthew Frye Jacobson writes: "Whiteness was tacitly but irretrievably written into republican ideology as well. . . . The new democratic order would require of its participants a remarkable degree of *self-possession*—a condition already denied literally to Africans in slavery and figuratively to all 'non-white' or 'heathen' peoples in prevailing conceptions of human capacity. . . . 'Fitness of self-government' [was] a racial attribute whose outer property was whiteness."[6]

The idea that a nation could be founded at all assumed the right of white colonizers to seize the land from Native people and work it with enslaved Black people. The country was not founded on a social contract of *all* the people, but rather on a contract agreed to by a ruling group that was defined by its exclusion of others (not free, not white). Charles Mills observes that American "citizenship and personhood have overtly or tacitly been defined as white," so that "the role of the state becomes the maintenance of the official sub-personhood of non-whites." This dynamic is reflected, argues Benjamin Ringer, in the upholding of *two* creeds at the founding of the United States and throughout its history: one is the creed of "universalistic, egalitarian, achievement-oriented, and democratic norms and values"; the other is "a racial creed which stressed the separateness of the races and the inferiority of the nonwhite."[7]

These two creeds neatly reflect the dynamics outlined in the discussion of the Book of Deeds and the Book of Life in the preceding chapter. The American meritocratic creed declares that the actions of all peoples are included in the Book of Deeds, so they might merit inclusion and participation in the New Jerusalem. But the American *racial* creed declares that this applies only to those already registered in the Book of White Life, as a result of chance or fate or mysterious divine predestination.

The coexistence of these two books meant, in terms of practical policy, the targeted exclusion of persons who could trouble the principles on which they were predicated. Following the first federal naturalization laws, Congress passed a bill in 1803 banning the immigration (or importation) of foreign Black peoples. Passed near the end of the successful Black revolution in Haiti (1798–1804), the bill was intended to prevent the increase of free Black persons in the United States and thereby any danger of a similar rebellion, particularly in slaveholding southern states. This anti-immigration legislation addressed an identity that was already a contentious issue in the States, that is, the free Black person who occupied the liminal space between the Book of Life and the Book of Deeds. As free people born in or residents of the land, free Black people could satisfy the *deeds required* of citizenship (residency, good behavior, and oath) and merit entry in the Book of Deeds. But as Black people, they were racialized as fundamentally incapable of *embodying* a citizen of the Book of Life, with its privileges of belonging and rights. The free-but-not-white person laid bare the contradictions of the two books, and this troublesome identity triggered the creation of further laws to cover the discrepancy. This reaction to contradiction and ambiguity was to make more explicit that the Book of American Life, that is, the list of who can attain American citizenship, was really the Book of White Life.[8]

In certain states, for example, New Jersey, free Black people could vote as citizens in the early nineteenth century, as could white women. But in the wake of the rebellion and victory in Haiti, and of their *own* successful revolution against England, white male American leaders clamped down on further expansion of freedom and self-rule and increasingly narrowed and made explicit the race- and gender-based parameters of voting and citizenship on the state level, such as in New Jersey, Connecticut, and Pennsylvania.[9] If rebellions for freedom were on the rise, the governing elite wanted to prevent any such uprisings among those they believed incapable of self-rule and a threat to their own power.

Thus, in 1776, John Adams wrote to his wife Abigail when she proposed that women should be allowed to vote: "As to your extraordinary Code of Laws, I cannot but laugh. We have been told that our Struggle [the American Revolution] loosened the bands of Government every where. That Children and Apprentices were disobedient—that schools and Colledges were grown turbulent—that Indians slighted their Guardians and Negroes grew insolent to their Masters."[10] John Adams's laugh intimates that revolutionary action should be permissible only to persons whom he and his colleagues believed were predestined for citizenship rights. The revolutionary spirit he saw on the rise outside of that charmed circle was a danger that had to be stopped. And after decades of state legislation from 1807 to 1850 explicitly denying Black people and other non-whites the right to vote, the Supreme Court Dred Scott decision of 1857 declared definitively that Black people, enslaved or free, did not have the humanity to be citizens, that they were not and could not be registered in the Book of White Life.

But like the Book of Life in Revelation, the Book of White Life can be altered or modified within certain parameters. The names may have been written in it at the foundation of the world, but this does not guarantee their permanence in the registry, since they may be "blotted out" (Rev 3:5). In U.S. immigration history, the category of citizen—beyond the unquestioned inclusion of those who are white, northern European, and Protestant, includes two further categories that might be labeled "legally white" and "sometimes permissible."[11] In apocalyptic terms, the first category, that of the "legally white," is included in the Book of White Life, but its members' belonging is beset by difficulties in the Book of Deeds. The second category, "sometimes permissible," is included in the Book of White Life when it is expedient to U.S. foreign policy or mitigates labor shortages; "sometimes permissible" identities, unlike those of the first category, have not generally become racialized as white and can easily be blotted out.

The category "legally white" includes some identities the U.S. government categorized as white in a legal sense from the founding of the nation. For example, the status of European Jews and Catholics was included in the first congressional debates about immigration, which concluded with legislation that declared them eligible for citizenship because they were necessary for populating the land. Their inclusion in the Book of White Life did not, however, mean their admittance to the United States was always unrestricted or that their sociocultural acceptance in America was guaranteed. Nativist prejudice and suspicion often targeted Jews, Irish, and southern and eastern Europeans as especially diseased and resistant to assimilation. In many cases, white Anglo-Saxon nativism led to violence against these populations, including attacks on Irish, Italian, Greek, and Jewish peoples.[12] It must be noted that the racialization of Jewish people remains highly unstable in the United States, where they continue to be persecuted in antisemitic hate acts and a primary target for white supremacist groups.

Nativists viewed Roman Catholics as politically dangerous and potentially seditious because of their relationship to their priests, bishops, and ultimately the pope. The verbiage of the Naturalization Act of 1795 reflects this fear in its stipulation that any person naturalizing must declare an oath "to renounce forever all allegiance and fidelity to any foreign prince, potentate, state, or sovereignty whatever." "Potentate" serves as code for the pope, who had, in American Protestant imagination, long been associated with the Antichrist. As the immigration of Catholic Irish and Germans increased in the mid-nineteenth century, the Know Nothing political party, with anti-Catholicism at its core, rose to prominence. The party argued that the influx of Catholic immigrants posed a seditious threat, and that Irish Catholics in the U.S. military were not American patriots but an unholy army that would "rally at the call of the Bishop and the Priest. They are the soldiers of the Church of Rome, bound to defend its interests at whatever peril."[13]

Thus, one prominent demand in the Know Nothing platform was that the United States should lengthen mandatory residency for naturalization from two to twenty-one years, in essence the number of years from birth to voting age. Hence, an immigrant had to be "born again" as an American. The idea also implied an American *religious* identity, since being "born again" denoted Protestant conversion then as it does now. Though the notion of religious naturalization may appear to contradict the separation of church and state, it does so only in the popular understanding of the principle. In fact, requiring an Irish Catholic to be "born again" as a Protestant does *not* contradict the separation of church and state as originally conceived, that is, to prevent one's religious salvation from affecting one's civic status. Just as a Black enslaved person's status as a "born-again" Christian could not affect their personal status as enslaved and ineligible for citizenship, an Irish Catholic's devotion did not, under U.S. law, negate their legal right to citizenship and enfranchisement. The rhetorical force of the Know Nothings' anti-Catholicism was not that civic and religious status should be joined together but rather that Catholics *did not respect their separation.* They thus concluded that all Catholics posed a political and military threat because of their *political* allegiance to Rome.[14]

This understanding of the (non)separation of church and state is illustrated in a Know Nothing political cartoon circulating in 1855 titled "The Propagation Society—More Free Than Welcome" (figure 11). The title itself reflects the status of the Irish as "legally white": "The Propagation Society" refers to the growing numbers of Catholics coming to America, particularly Irish Catholics, as signaled by the bishop anchoring the incoming boat to the United States by means of a shamrock. This "society" is free: its peoples are not enslaved and can legally naturalize and vote, but they are not welcome. The words of the arriving bishops and the pope himself indicate the threat the Irish immigrants pose: the takeover of American lands and wealth and the transformation of America into a degraded European

Fig. 11. "The Propagation Society—More Free Than Welcome," probably by Louis Maurer, New York: Nathaniel Currier, 1855. (Library of Congress, Prints & Photographs Division, LC-DIG-pga-04985.)

Catholic nation. The pope says, "My friend we have concluded to take charge of your spiritual welfare, and your temporal estate," suggesting the Vatican's interest in taking charge of American wealth. And the bishop furthest left says, "We'll . . . elevate this Country to the Same degree of happiness and prosperity, to which we have brought Italy, Spain, Ireland and many other lands," an obviously sarcastic statement that assumes these countries are impoverished because of Catholicism.

The words spoken by the pope and bishop warn the reader that Catholic religious power encompasses political power and ambition. Even more damning are the words of Brother Jonathan, an Uncle Sam–type character representative of New England and America. Brother Jonathan says, "No you don't, Mr. Pope! you're altogether too willing; but you can't put the 'mark of the Beast' on Americans." This statement not only references the long tradition of identifying the papacy as the Antichrist and the Beast of the Sea of Revelation 13, it also shows the specific danger that English and American Protestants feared from Catholic immigration: Catholic political and economic domination and the corruption of Protestant faith.[15]

The passage in Revelation reads: "And all the inhabitants of the earth will worship [the Beast of the sea], everyone whose name has not been written from the foundation of the world in the book of life of the Lamb that was slaughtered. . . . [The Beast of the earth] causes all, both rich and poor, both free and slave, to be given a brand on the right hand or forehead, so that no one can buy or sell who does not have the brand, that is, the name of the beast [of the sea] or the number for its name" (13:8, 16–17). Through the words of Brother Jonathan, the Know Nothings argue that Catholic immigrants would enact a scenario similar to (if not the same as) that of Revelation by flooding the voting booths and acquiring American land and wealth, thus claiming the U.S. nation for the pope. The heresy of Catholicism would thereby destroy America the New Jerusalem in two ways: on a spiritual level by the increase of Catholics through immigration and conversion; and on a political level by infiltrating the nation and seizing its wealth and military.

The Know Nothing party dissolved into irrelevancy in the 1860s as the nation plunged into civil war. Nevertheless, nativist sentiment against Catholics and the Irish continued through the nineteenth century. And yet, despite hateful discourse against the Irish, southern and eastern Europeans, and Jews, none of these groups lost the right to immigrate to the United States, naturalize as citizens, vote, or marry freely. That is not to say they did not face discrimination in society at large or in immigration policy: the literacy test introduced by the Immigration Act of 1917 was intended to reduce the numbers of these groups coming into the country. And the immigration quota laws of the 1920s, embracing eugenicist arguments, heavily favored northern European immigration over and against southern and eastern. These restrictions required that newcomers who were "legally white" or "white other" satisfy the requirements of the Book of Deeds, even if their status in the Book of White Life was secure if they gained entry through the gates. This stability of being white within the law was not the privilege of people who were "sometimes permissible," who could be erased from the Book of White Life.

## Blotted out from the Book of White Life

In 1955, after a stint in the U.S. Army, Carlos Corella began work in Socorro, Texas, for the U.S. Department of Labor. His job at Rio Vista, a processing center for braceros (manual laborers) entering and exiting the country, was to guide men through the immigration process at the border. In a recorded interview, he describes what first happened to braceros when they arrived at the center:

> So, first order of business was to disinfect them. They would go through, they were formed in about four or five lines, they were placed through a Quonset hut, and they were asked to strip, and they were sprayed with a white powder all over their body, including their hair, facial hair, the hair on their head, and even around the low area. Some of the braceros that experienced that for the first time were embarrassed, and some thought it was kind of cute, it was a laughing matter. When they would come out of the Quonset hut, they would look at each other, and they were all white, and they'd say, "Well, I guess we're gringos now."[16]

The grim humor expresses the core truth of U.S. immigration: entry and inclusion belong to those who are white. But who qualified as white? Entering from Mexico, the braceros were required at the entrance of the New Jerusalem to "wash their robes" (Rev 22:14) and to be powdered white with pesticide (figure 12), although their identity remained non-white, and they could not stay in the country. Meanwhile, Corella, the gatekeeper who oversaw the process, was a Mexican American born in Clint, Texas, who had served in the U.S. military and was an American citizen. Did his citizenship afford him the identity and belonging of whiteness?

The different identities and statuses that the braceros and Corella held in 1955 were the result of over a century of U.S. racialization of Mexicans, the

Fig. 12. A masked worker fumigates a bracero with DDT at the Hidalgo Processing Center, Texas, while others wait in line, 1956. (Leonard Nadel Photographs and Scrapbooks, Archives Center, National Museum of American History, Smithsonian Institution.)

construction of an identity rife with contradictions and contingent on underlying political and economic motivations. The history of the American construction of the category of "Mexican" and subsequently of "Hispanic" and "Latino" is the history of a category of people who were and are only "sometimes permissible." In this section, I highlight key moments of this long history, intertwining the histories of other "sometimes permissible" peoples whose names were tentatively added, then blotted out of the American Book of White Life.

At the end of the U.S. War with Mexico in 1848, the two nations signed the Treaty of Guadalupe Hidalgo, which ceded huge tracts of Mexican land to the United States. This land was the home of people who found themselves suddenly residing in a different nation. Senate debate leading up to the treaty focused in part on the identity and racialization of such Mexicans. "The Mexicans are no better than Indians," Senator Sam Houston (D-TX) declared, "and I see no reason why we should not go on in the same course now and take their land." Senator John C. Calhoun (D-SC) argued against seizing all of Mexico while using the same understanding of Mexican identity to make the opposite argument: "To incorporate Mexico, would be the very first instance of the kind of incorporating an Indian race. . . . Ours, sir, is the Government of a white race. . . . Are they fit to be connected with us?"[17]

In the end, the Treaty of Guadalupe Hidalgo did not force the removal of Mexicans from annexed territory or demand the rest of Mexico as a province. The Mexican government, moreover, successfully secured the right of Mexicans who stayed on the ceded lands to naturalize as U.S. citizens. In this way, Mexicans were "sometimes permissible" as citizens, which was exceptional at the time since only whites were eligible for American naturalization. This arrangement is similar to the terms of the Treaty of Dancing Rabbit Creek that was offered to the Choctaw Nation in 1830 and signed after President Jackson passed the Indian Removal Act earlier that year. The Treaty of Dancing Rabbit Creek offered Choctaw people who wished to stay on the land the ability to naturalize as citizens after a period of five years.[18] Up until this treaty, Native peoples had not been able to become citizens because they were not white and the U.S. government considered them citizens of their own nations, even as the United States was taking lands away from those very nations.

Both the Treaty of Dancing Rabbit Creek and the Treaty of Guadalupe Hidalgo were the result of negotiations in which the category of "sometimes permissible," and eligibility for citizenship, was offered as a bargaining chip while the United States seized land and assumed the right to adjudicate the belonging, property, and rights of peoples already living and belonging to those lands. The seeming olive branch of citizenship served the purposes of the United States, not the other party: it increased the likelihood that the leaders and elite of those groups would agree to cede their land, and it assuaged the moral qualms of those in Congress concerned for those "beleaguered Indians."[19]

In reality, the promises of these treaties—land grants and property rights, citizenship and civil rights—were neglected or denied. White squatters and speculators took over the land while U.S. officials in scattered field offices denied citizenship or refused to explain and enact procedures. Native Americans, moreover, were never legally or socially racialized as "white" after the Choctaw treaty. Citizenship for indigenous peoples was sometimes possible through the nineteenth century (until the Indian Citizenship Act of 1924, when it was granted to all Native people), but the qualifications for citizenship entailed a "whitening" of one's identity. Citizenship was *not* granted by birthright (even under the Fourteenth Amendment) but through naturalization and the forsaking of tribal membership, or through marrying a white person, paying taxes, and serving the military of the white government.[20]

In the racial categories of the United States at its founding, "Indian" identity can be understood as a "third pole" alongside the racial categories of white and Black. Paul Spickard writes that there was "a tripolar system at work in the eastern United States from the beginning: White, Black, and Red. In Texas and New Mexico in the nineteenth century, the racial system grew a fourth pole and so was White, Red, Black, and Brown. California added a fifth pole: Yellow."[21] The equivalence of Mexican identity with Native identity (see Senators Houston and Calhoun's comments above), combined with Mexican Catholicism and a history of "mixed" racial origins, culminated in a "Brown" identity. Thus, while Mexicans were technically qualified to obtain citizenship, they remained on a lower tier or were denied citizenship altogether because of their racialization as Indian and as Brown.

Following the Treaty of Guadalupe Hidalgo, Mexicans in California whom officials marked as having indigenous ancestry were not allowed to vote because they were not "white." In the Texas federal district court case *In re Ricardo Rodríguez* (1897), in which Ricardo Rodríguez sought the right to naturalize, the court concluded that although by "the scientific classification of the anthropologist," Rodríguez "would probably not be classed as white," he could legally still naturalize. Despite this ruling, however, but using similar racial reasoning, officers of the Bureau of Immigration and Naturalization often denied Mexicans citizenship because they "looked Indian," were not "a white man, or an African," or their "color would preclude association with whites."[22]

So although various treaties, acts, and amendments throughout the nineteenth century technically expanded citizenship to include non-whites

(Black peoples, Mexicans, certain Native Americans), this expansion also meant the increase of legal opinions, laws, policies, rules, and regulations to police this expansion, which in effect multiplied the ways non-whites could be disqualified. Texts proliferate interpretation, leading to more texts. In the world of U.S. immigration, the growing variety of legal ways to qualify for citizenship also meant a proportionally growing variety of ways to be found *illegal*.[23] In as many ways as one could "merit" citizenship, one could also be stricken from the record, blotted out from the Book of White Life. The U.S. Immigration Book of Deeds, understood as recording years of residency, lands ceded, military service, marriages to citizens, good behavior, documents obtained, and on and on, cannot be understood without the U.S. Book of White Life: the Book of Deeds exists to protect the Book of White Life. Prima facie, the Book of Deeds offers ways to earn and merit citizenship that go beyond the predestination of birth. In reality, it creates barriers to registering in the Book of White Life and increases the threat of erasure for those whose names were not written in it as "white" from the foundation of the nation.

In the ancient text of Revelation, the Son of Man tells the church of Sardis: "If you conquer . . . I will not erase your name from the book of life" (3:5). The introduction of this condition, "if you conquer," creates its negative counterpart, "if you do not conquer" and the subsequent possibility of erasure from the Book of Life. This condition also introduces the necessity of judgment: what qualifies as "conquering"? What deeds meet the standard? Conquer what or whom? The text proliferates interpretations, every one of which creates new ways to be disqualified. This implicitly explains why "the dead were judged according to their works, as recorded in the books," and how this guarantees nothing if one's "name was not found written in the book of life"; one could still be "thrown into the lake of fire" (Rev 20:12, 15). As a text of deeds, qualifications, and standards, the Book of Deeds may actually function to erase names from the Book of Life rather than result in the registry of them.

Likewise, the opportunity to qualify for citizenship in the United States has meant the proliferation of new qualifications, set by the United States for U.S. interests, whether for land, labor, the military, or international relations.

Qualifications for citizenship based on these interests have been fragilely taped to the bedrock understanding of the United States as an originally white nation, and this type of contingent citizenship can be, and has been, taken away. Furthermore, the maintenance of procedures that guarantee (or appear to guarantee) that qualifications are met has created ever-growing racial categorization and documentation.

## Racial Categorization

In terms of racial categorization, the above discussion has covered how Mexicans were marked as partly Native American and racialized as Brown so that many were ruled ineligible for citizenship. The Treaty of Guadalupe Hidalgo and the ambiguity of Mexican identity in part led to the major question "What is white?" and the subsequent crystallization of that category. Ian Haney López states that, from 1878 to 1952, fifty-two lawsuits were filed in which plaintiffs of various nations (Canada, Japan, Mexico, and Syria, for example) argued that their race was eligible for naturalization. In each of these cases, the petitioner had to qualify either as "white" or as "Black" to become a citizen. In fifty-one of the fifty-two cases, the plaintiffs wished to establish their identity as "white." The immigrants knew the score: the only secure identity in American citizenship was a white one, the permanent default identity, never to be stricken from the Book of White Life. Black people, regardless of the Fourteenth and Fifteenth Amendments, faced violence and disenfranchisement that continually blotted their names out of the registry each time they were written in.[24]

During the 1920s, two Supreme Court cases brought the debate about whiteness to a sharp point at a moment when new restrictions on immigration and naturalization abounded. In 1922, the case of Takao Ozawa reached the U.S. Supreme Court. Ozawa had sought to naturalize after twenty years of residence in the United States. He had gone to U.S. schools in Berkeley, California, attended Christian churches, and maintained English as the language spoken in his household—all markers both political parties cited as significant, not to mention the actual color of Ozawa's skin: a pale hue. Thus by color, education, language, and creed, Ozawa could arguably be deemed "white" and eligible for citizenship. The Supreme Court, however, rejected this reasoning. Although white, Ozawa was not white in the court's opinion. The court ruled that to determine race "by the mere color of the skin of each individual is impracticable, as that differs greatly among persons of the same race, even among Anglo-Saxons." "Anglo-Saxons," it should be noted, are mentioned here as implicitly the exemplar of "white." Color is not determinative after all, the court stated, but "the federal and state courts, in an almost unbroken line, have held that the words 'white person' were meant to indicate only a person of what is *popularly known as the Caucasian race.*" However, even the label "Caucasian race" did not demarcate the category sharply, the court said, but rather established "a zone of more or less debatable ground outside of which, upon the one hand, are those clearly eligible, and outside of which, upon the other hand, are those clearly ineligible." The court thus strategically and contradictorily argued for both clarity ("clearly eligible," "clearly ineligible") and vagueness ("a zone"), reserving for itself interpretation of the people "popularly known as the Caucasian race."[25]

This strategic precedent was immediately significant in the Supreme Court case *United States v. Bhagat Singh Thind* the next year. An immigrant from India, Thind, like Ozawa, had attended the University of California and had furthermore served in the U.S. Army during World War I. And although he was not Christian but Sikh, Thind claimed that according to scientific classification, the same as that cited by the courts in *In re Ricardo Rodríguez* and *Ozawa v. United States*, he was "Caucasian." But here the vague, contradictory construction of "white" laid down in *Ozawa* provided the rationale whereby the court denied Thind's claim to whiteness. "What we hold now," the court argued, "is that the words 'free white persons' [of the Naturalization Act of 1790] are words of common speech," and thus one can qualify for citizenship as a Caucasian "only as that word is popularly understood."[26] By this circular reasoning, people of Indian ancestry were not Caucasian because they were not white, and therefore not white (and eligible to naturalize) because they were not Caucasian.

Who, then, was white? Who could not be stricken from the Book of White Life? The argument made by the court appealed to the original intended meaning, arguing that the words of the Naturalization Act of 1790 "were intended to include only the type of man whom [Congress then] knew as white. The immigration of that day was almost exclusively from the British Isles and Northwestern Europe." This definition was further expanded in the court opinion to include those "legally white," as discussed above: "The succeeding years brought immigrants from Eastern, Southern and Middle Europe, among them the Slavs and the dark-eyed, swarthy people of Alpine and Mediterranean stock, and these were received as unquestionably akin to those already here and readily amalgamated with them."[27] In short, peoples who could claim European origin could claim whiteness. It was the expansion of immigration that led to the explicit creation and demarcation of racial categories. Vice versa, this expansion also multiplied the ways in which people could be *denied* whiteness by virtue of scientific classification and "popular understanding" despite residency, education, language, creed, and military service. Immigrants who believed they might merit a place in America in light of their record in the Book of Deeds discovered that they still fell short of the proliferating qualifications for citizenship. Their names could not be written into the Book of White Life after all—or they could be stricken from it even after having been registered.

## Documentation

Like racial categorization, documentation also proliferated as a means of policing the entries in the Book of White Life. Some documentation was necessary as early as the colonial period in order to prove years of residency and oath swearing. As paths to citizenship multiplied, so did the documentation needed to provide evidence of the fulfillment of requirements. Documentation also included the counting of people and the reporting and recording of those numbers—that is, the census. Keeping track of group populations and their growth from time to time (which is related in essence and in practice to surveillance) is intimately tied to ideas of national identity and fears about changes to it, especially via immigration.[28]

As the U.S. government created more and more restrictions on immigration from the end of the nineteenth century onward, the census became a tool for constructing further restrictions. The Emergency Quota Act of 1921 and the Immigration Act of 1924 (the Johnson-Reed Act) capped immigration from different nations according to a National Origins Formula. The number of immigrants allowed from each nation was based on a percentage of their existing population in the United States. This formula did not consider the United States *itself* as a location of origin, a significant exclusionary and apocalyptic conceptualization of the country: the United States itself was constructed as an empty destination that came into being ex nihilo and was subsequently populated, like the utopia of the New Jerusalem. This conceptualization discounted first and foremost indigenous populations (who did not immigrate in this epoch). Similarly, the National Origins Formula did not include U.S. nationality as a nationality. It also defined people of "native stock" *not* to mean indigenous people but the descendants of white people at the founding of the nation. "Native stock" is one example of the many racial categories created and codified in policy at this juncture of restriction. These categories also included "mulatto," "Indian," "Chinese," "Japanese," and "Hindu."[29]

The Quota Board (one of many bureaus created to produce, maintain, and oversee immigration restrictions) concluded that the National Origins Formula, which was supposedly based on the "inhabitants in the continental United States in 1920" would not include: "(1) immigrants from the [Western Hemisphere] or their descendants, (2) aliens ineligible for citizenship or their descendants, (3) descendants of slave immigrants, or (4) the descendants of the American aborigines."[30] This meant the formula would not include in the total population of the United States any populations of Hawai'i, Alaska, Puerto Rico, people from Mexico and other countries in the Western Hemisphere or their descendants, people of Asian descent (ineligible for citizenship or descendants of those ineligible for citizenship), and anyone of African descent (which the board conflated with Black Americans, whether descended from those enslaved or born free). This exclusion skewed the *countable* population of the United States, resulting in larger quotas for European nations. In terms of who was legally countable, Mae Ngai writes, "the law excised all nonwhite, non-European peoples from that vision, *erasing them* from the American nationality."[31]

The 1924 act did not impose quotas on Mexico or Latin America, and since Mexicans could technically naturalize as citizens, this meant that the quota acts did not impose any limits on Mexican immigration. This lack of restriction in the law reflected the enormous need for agricultural and manual labor in the West and Southwest up through the 1920s. But nativist reaction to what seemed to be limitless immigration from south of the border was fierce, especially at the onset of the Great Depression in 1929, when nativists viewed Mexicans as a threat to American employment. At this point, Mexicans were being reconceptualized as an immigrant group and not as native, as they had been under the Treaty of Guadalupe Hidalgo. In reaction to the 1920s quota laws, white nativists and eugenicists campaigned to identify Mexicans not only as foreign and immigrants but as quintessentially illegal. This was in part a consequence of the increase in procedures and documentation for immigration, from which "the undocumented Mexican laborer who crossed the border to work . . . emerged as the prototypical illegal alien."[32]

Working toward reducing Mexican populations outside of the quotas, the U.S. State Department in 1928 instructed its consular offices in Mexico to reduce the number of visas they issued. In 1929, Congress approved Public Law 1018, which made crossing the border into the United States without a visa a misdemeanor punishable by up to a year in prison.[33] Visa documentation and the notion of being "undocumented" became an essential part of U.S. racialization of Mexican laborers.

The demand for documentation from immigrants and its utilization to record immigration had begun in earnest after the first enforced federal immigration restriction law, the Page Act of 1875, effectively barred Chinese women from immigration. To prove that they were not entering the country for "lewd and immoral purposes," immigrant Chinese women had to provide photographic identification and documentation of their upstanding character. A spate of subsequent Chinese restriction and exclusion laws multiplied the documentation required, especially the Geary Act of 1892, which required Chinese immigrants to carry and be able to provide a certificate proving their legal entry into the country. These measures led directly to a corresponding demand for documentation at the U.S.-Mexico border, where the U.S. government was afraid that Chinese immigrants might enter illegally. This scrutiny of papers then shifted to Mexicans crossing the border, and the Immigration Bureau began requiring visas, photo identification, and other papers demonstrating employment at entry. The enforcement was lax enough to allow as great an influx of cheap labor as needed, but it could be strengthened at any point to intimidate, frighten, and force Mexicans to leave.[34]

This was exactly what happened during the 1930s, when over four hundred thousand Mexicans, including Mexican American citizens, many of them children with birthright citizenship, were forcibly deported or intimidated into repatriating voluntarily. Campaigns to frighten people into leaving the United States were accomplished by demanding documentation, that is, by rounding up groups of people and demanding to see passports or other immigration documents. In this way, the same papers purportedly required for entry and naturalization became the tools for denial and expulsion. In apocalyptic terms, the documents of the Book of Deeds—papers showing marriages, births, military service, visa applications—guarded the registry of the Book of White Life from the addition of names by creating innumerable difficulties. This documentation-based Book of Deeds simultaneously created an illusion of opportunity, of reaching naturalization by navigating paper trails, while creating a bewildering labyrinth of paper barriers, both of which could go up in flames when the overruling authority of the Book of White Life was invoked.[35]

This is what happened again and again to immigrants from Mexico. When the U.S. economy needed agricultural labor in the 1910s and 1920s, entry was encouraged, with documentation loosely required. But as the Great Depression began, the same documentation requirements were used to justify the removal of hundreds of thousands. Then, as World War II depleted the number of workers at home, the U.S. government implemented the Bracero Program to bring laborers from Mexico back in, where they worked under threat of deportation if they protested unfair wages or poor working conditions. Twelve years into the Bracero Program in 1954, however, the Immigration and Naturalization Service (INS) launched Operation Wetback with the goal of capturing a million undocumented Mexican workers and deporting them.[36] The history of Mexicans in America, first as indigenous to the land, then reformulated and racialized as foreign and illegal, shows that, for those whose names were not in the Book of White Life at the founding of the nation, the addition of their names through qualification in the Book of Deeds could easily be blotted out.

## Betrayal by the Book of Deeds

One year after the launch of Operation Wetback is where the story of the previous section began: with Carlos Corella at Rio Vista in 1955, overseeing the dusting of braceros with white pesticide. The braceros who joked they were now "gringos" thanks to the white dusting hit on the essential truth of U.S. immigration: to belong, be protected, and have permanent rights in the nation was to be white. Their entry and belonging in the country were, like the powder on their skin, temporary and removable. What was permanent was the suffering, trauma, and generations of racialization as illegal, lazy, and criminal, as permanent as the sickness and cancers caused by being "washed" in DDT for entry into America the New Jerusalem.

Immigration can be apocalyptic under any circumstances: it presents a shift of worlds, imbued with promise and with fear. Like the narrative journey in Revelation, immigration can be a moving of heaven and earth, a traveling through frightening terrain beset by war, disasters, and disease, filled with hopes of a glorious destination and fears of a calamitous ending. For those hoping to gain entry and become citizens of the United States, assurance belongs to people whose names were written in the Book of White Life at the foundation of the nation. For all others, the Book of Deeds offers the faint chance of being added to the Book of White Life, always with the threat of being blotted out.

U.S. history is full of the betrayal of being blotted out of the Book of White Life, especially through the manipulation of the Book of Deeds to create shifting requirements and definitions. The establishment of birthright citizenship in the case *United States v. Wong Kim Ark* (1898) may have seemed like a victory, especially for Chinese immigrants. But this success was eroded by the Page Act, which prevented Chinese women from immigrating, and by existing anti-miscegenation laws and subsequent greater restrictions on immigration. So when the United States granted Chinese birthright citizenship, it simultaneously made it as difficult as possible to form families for further births. The full rights of citizens were also disregarded in the removal of Japanese Americans from their homes and their incarceration during World War II. And when the United States acquired the Philippines as a territory, it did not grant Filipinos citizenship but rather categorized them as "nationals," people who had free movement but did not hold citizenship rights. Yet the U.S. government had no qualms in enlisting Filipino soldiers for World War II and promising them veteran benefits, only to strip them of their status as U.S. veterans after the war through the Rescission Act of 1946. Most recently, immigrants from predominantly Muslim nations in Africa and the Middle East, which have had the same quota allowed as other nations in the Eastern Hemisphere since 1965, were banned from entering the United States in a series of executive orders, nicknamed the "Muslim Ban," signed by Donald Trump.[37] Time and again, people have been added to the registry of the nation in response to its temporary needs, only to be removed when their non-white presence becomes feared, unwanted, and expendable.

When Lyndon B. Johnson signed the Immigration and Nationality Act of 1965 into law, the National Origins Formula of the 1920s was abolished. This was a victory for certain Euro-American ethnic groups against whom the quota acts of 1921 and 1924 were aimed in order to favor northern European nations. But the 1965 law also introduced a numerical cap on immigration where there was none before, namely on Western Hemisphere nations. By 1976, the quota for these nations was set at twenty thousand each, an extreme and severe reduction of immigration from Mexico, from which two hundred thousand braceros had entered the United States annually during the 1960s. So while the Immigration and Nationality Act of 1965 was touted as a move toward numerical equality, it continued the normalizing of number caps, which then placed greater reliance on documentation and qualifications for entry in accordance with the Book of Deeds. The more ways one may qualify or be disqualified by entries in the Book of Deeds, the more the illusion is created that the *individual* is responsible for entry or exclusion and not the overriding Book of White Life. As Ngai states, "Narrating Western Hemispheric restriction as an expression of the liberal principle of fairness reinforced the notion that illegal immigration was a problem that could be blamed on the Mexican migrant (or on Mexico) and, moreover, one that could be solved with enforcement."[38]

The hardening of the racialization of Mexican and Latin American immigrants as illegal, legitimated only through the enforcement of documentation, has greatly increased since 1965. Arizona passed state law SB 1070 in 2010, requiring law enforcement to check citizenship or immigration papers based on "reasonable suspicion." Under the Trump administration, Immigration and Customs Enforcement (ICE) sharply increased the number of raids it conducted to arrest undocumented persons. Governor Greg Abbott of Texas recently referred to victims killed in a mass shooting simply as "illegal immigrants." And Florida governor Ron DeSantis signed SB 1718 into law on May 10, 2023, to enact penalties against employing "illegal aliens" and to require hospitals to report expenses of care for "illegal aliens." The governor's office proclaims the law triumphantly as the most severe in "[combatting] the dangerous effects of illegal immigration caused by the federal government's reckless border policies."[39]

The history of the proliferation of immigration laws and policies in the United States is the history of the expansion of the American Book of Deeds. Its role in the national narrative is to proclaim that the United States is a "nation of immigrants," that anyone "with the will and the heart to get there" can merit entry and citizenship. The Books of Deeds is supposed to demonstrate that the nation belongs to more than those written in the Book of White Life and predestined for inclusion at the foundation of the nation. But the Book of Deeds, which began with the recording of residency and oath-taking, has grown to near incomprehensible size. Its qualifications can be met or subverted, as they have been by generations of determined immigrants, but its guarantees of registration in the U.S. Book of White Life are dangerously impermanent.

# PART FOUR

# The Construction of Crisis

# SEVEN

# "Even Heaven Is Going to Have a Wall around It"

## Borders, Walls, and the New Jerusalem

Wide open and unguarded stand our gates,
Named of the four winds, North, South, East, and West;
Portals that lead to an enchanted land
Of cities, forests, fields of living gold . . .

Wide open and unguarded stand our gates,
And through them presses a wild motley throng
Men from the Volga and the Tartar steppes,
Featureless figures of the Hoang-Ho

—*Thomas Bailey Aldrich, "The Unguarded Gate" (1892)*

And I am convinced that when we get to heaven, we'll find the
streets are guarded by United States Marines.

—*Ronald Reagan (1982)*

## An Exceptional Wall

The drive to the Border Patrol Museum takes around fifteen minutes from downtown El Paso. The rectangular cement building sits off Highway 375 opposite the slopes of Castner Range National Monument. The surrounding landscape is brown, shrubby, and empty except for the building's neighbor, the El Paso Museum of Archaeology. A plaque at the entrance to the Border Patrol Museum declares that it was founded in 1978 by "the Fraternal Order of Retired Border Patrol Officers . . . in order to preserve the unique spirit of the Border Patrol and to perpetuate the loyalties and friendships which accrued to us during our active service." As it began, so the museum continues: privately funded through donations and preserving the "unique spirit" of a brotherhood.[1]

The building houses memorial rooms dedicated to fallen agents, an exhibit of the agency's history, and historical artifacts including vehicles, helicopters, seized ladders, boats, and weapons, including weapons carried by agents in the field. Weapons form an important part of agent identity: a display shelf dedicated to Jefferson Milton, the first agent appointed in 1924, bears the rifle he carried. Other shelves in the same case display a "Colt Inspectors Special .357 magnum" commemorating the INS "Diamond Jubilee," and a "Border Patrol 50th Anniversary Commemorative Smith & Wesson .357 Magnum." At the time of writing, the website of the museum, in anticipation of the hundredth anniversary of the agency's founding, is offering a "Centennial Commemorative Pistol," with a link to preorder a special Glock 47, made to U.S. Border Patrol recommendations and featuring night sights.[2]

That the chosen symbol commemorating the U.S. Customs and Border Protection (CBP) agency should be a gun is unsurprising. In the early days of the Border Patrol, agents were given a ".45 single action revolver in a web belt—and that was it." Active training took place on the job in the field, and the vast majority of evidence and testimony from the history of the CBP reveals that, from the beginning, the Border Patrol assumed its responsibilities as a criminal enforcement agency, although its supposed task was enforcing civil law.[3]

Congress created the Border Patrol with the Labor Appropriations Act of 1924, which gave funding for "enforcement of laws regulating immigration of aliens into the United States, including the contract labor laws." There had already been patrols along the U.S.-Mexico border, especially after Chinese exclusion, to prevent the illegal entry of Chinese immigrants. The 1924 act formally organized the agency and approved "at least $1,000,000 . . . expended for additional land-border patrol." The establishment of the Border Patrol came only two days after the enactment of the Immigration Act of 1924, which controversially did not cap immigration from Mexico. While strident nativists had protested the lack of a quota on immigrants from Mexico and other Western Hemisphere nations, the need for cheap labor (particularly after the dwindling of Chinese laborers) ruled the day in Congress. Thus, the Border Patrol was in part a white nativist response to the increasing influx of Mexican workers. It was also a continuation of organized white Texan brutality against Native and Mexican peoples dating back to the 1830s with the formation of the Texas Rangers, a vigilante group that has become a paramilitary organization.[4]

Many Texas Rangers became members of the Border Patrol, even some who had been dismissed by the Rangers following investigations of violence against Mexicans.[5] Members of the Border Patrol also came from the National Guard in El Paso, of which one witness states, "Practically every other member was in the Klan."[6] It is therefore unsurprising that the Border Patrol put into practice the violent vigilante and intimidation tactics of the Texas Rangers and the Ku Klux Klan, such as torture, lynching, and "revenge by proxy," whereby a crime committed by one Mexican person is repaid by the torture and murder of many others. Within the first six years of the patrol, a total of twenty-two charges of murder were brought against officers, twelve of whom were convicted, two acquitted, and eight cases were dismissed or not processed. These numbers only reflect incidents that were reported and duly prosecuted, whereas testimonies point to a much higher number of vigilante killings, especially revenge killings in response to the death of officers on duty, and these crimes were overlooked or their perpetrators easily exonerated.[7]

But from the perspective of the CBP and the Border Patrol Museum, whatever actions were taken by officers in the field were taken in the spirit of the agency's motto, "Honor First." In that spirit, the many risks and dangers faced by agents in the field constitute part of a noble calling and sacrifice to defend the United States from terrible enemies. As ever-vigilant guardians and sentinels, they could justify whatever actions they took. The ethos, aesthetic, and impunity of the agency weave together the macho romance of the

Lone Ranger and the passion of religious martyrdom, as evident in this description of the agency submitted to Congress in 1927:

> The border patrol is a young man's organization; it appeals strongly to the lover of the big outdoors—the primeval forests, the sunparched deserts, the mountains, and the plains; the business upon which it is engaged calls for manhood, stamina, versatility, and resourcefulness in the highest degree. "Honor first" is its watchword; privations and danger but serve as a challenge which none refuses. . . . Its members *must be left largely to their own devices* and upon their honor. . . . The uniform is *sacred*; it not only symbolizes authority, the law's majesty, and all the power of the Federal Government, but it entails obligations upon the wearer in the way of deportment which are intuitively recognized and scrupulously observed . . . they are charged with a serious responsibility and keenly realize it. In the vast majority of cases their work is a *religion*.

This description promotes the necessity for the Border Patrol to operate without oversight, and indeed in 1925 Congress had already granted the agency the power to search and seize without warrant, and to arrest without warrant "any alien who in his presence or view is entering or attempting to enter the United States in violation of any law or regulation made in pursuance of law regulating the admission of aliens."[8]

Thus, from the Border Patrol's founding, and through unfettered vigilante activity even before its establishment, the U.S.-Mexico border was a zone of exception, that is, an exceptional space in which laws and oversight are waived.[9] As with times of siege and emergency, the greater the pronounced threat along the border, the greater the exceptions made in regard to constitutional law and civil and human rights. Mexican immigrants had, like Chinese immigrants, been deemed a growing threat to white American labor in the 1910s and 1920s. With the Undesirable Aliens Act of 1929, unauthorized entry into the United States became illegal, and Mexicans were transformed in American imagination from competitors for labor to criminals. This perception, in addition to identification of Mexicans and migrants south of the border as diseased, has only solidified throughout the last century.

The degree of exceptionalism at the border has kept pace with the criminalization of Mexican identity and, more recently, other Latin American identities. From the Treaty of Guadalupe Hidalgo (1848) and the granting of citizenship to Mexicans native to the land to the instability caused by the Mexican Revolution (1910–17) to the scarcity of the Depression, the renewed need for labor during World War II, and the beginnings of the "war on drugs" in the 1960s to the repercussions of the North American Free Trade Agreement (1994), the "war on terror" post-9/11, continued arms deals between Latin American countries and the United States and other countries, and increased migration of refugees fleeing violence and government corruption, each decade has seen mounting criminalization of immigrants south of the border and a corresponding waiving of laws and human rights in policing the boundary. This has also hardened the border, literally, from an invisible line to a few border markers to a few feet of fencing and finally to steel barrier walls.[10]

The hard materialization of a border wall has gone hand in hand with the violent dehumanization of immigrants wishing to cross it. The increase in bestializing discourse matches an increased clamoring for a wall, as demonstrated in a small sampling of xenophobic public statements against migrants in the last twenty years: "More than a decade before Trump's election, congressman Steve King of Iowa suggested that the United States build a concrete border wall topped with wire to keep out migrants, stating, 'We could also electrify this wire. . . . We do that with livestock all the time.' Six years later, King gave a speech comparing immigrants to dogs. In 2010, Tennessee Republican Curry Todd likened undocumented immigrants to 'rats [who] multiply.' The next year, Kansas state representative Virgil Peck suggested that migrants be shot like 'feral hogs' as a solution to America's 'illegal immigration problem.' "[11] The demonization of immigrants, the transformation of the border into a zone of exception, and the demand for a physical barrier wall grew synchronously at an increasing rate from the end of the twentieth century into the beginning of the twenty-first.

Following the attacks of 9/11, the founding of the Department of Homeland Security, and the passing of the Patriot Act in 2001, all U.S. borders (and certain regions within the nation) became zones of exception, and this further increased the insistence on a physical wall at the U.S.-Mexico border. The Real ID Act, signed by George W. Bush in 2005, declared the secretary of Homeland Security authorized "to waive all legal requirements as necessary to ensure expeditious construction of certain barriers and roads at the U.S. border." This measure expanded previous militarization of the border and the waiving of rights authorized by the Illegal Immigration Reform and Immigrant Responsibility Act of 1996; and the Real ID Act itself was subsequently expanded by the Secure Fence Act of 2006. All these acts operate on the assumption of a crisis of illegal immigration that purportedly justifies the overruling of laws that protect the environment, endangered species, indigenous groups, and residents along the border.[12]

But less than two decades earlier, the concept of border walls was largely spoken of as a political embarrassment, as an unseemly, undiplomatic concept, as something to rally against as un-American. The shining example of this is of course Ronald Reagan's "Tear Down This Wall" speech at the Brandenburg Gate in June 1987. Jimmy Carter, in 1978, was quick to distance himself from any physical wall at the U.S.-Mexico border, saying, "[The steel wall border] was a serious mistake. . . . But any sort of fencing device that would injure people is certainly contrary to my own inclinations." Eight years before that, Richard Nixon claimed in a speech in Puerto Vallarta, Mexico, that the "border we can say today is not a wall that divides us, but a bridge of friendship which unites us." Franklin Roosevelt, at the Canadian border in 1938, told his audience, "It is a pleasure to me to meet you here, where a boundary is a gateway and not a wall. . . . There will be no challenge at the border and no guard to ask a countersign. Where the boundary is crossed the only word must be, 'Pass, friend.' "[13]

And even up to the very month before 9/11, George W. Bush insisted that walls (physical and otherwise) should be torn down: "We want our neighbors to be successful. . . . And that's why it's so important for us to tear down barriers and walls that might separate Mexico from the United States. . . . Oh, I know there's some voices who want to wall us off from Mexico. They want to build a wall. I say to them, they want to condemn our neighbors to the south in poverty, and I refuse to accept that type of isolationist and protectionist attitude."[14] But after the apocalyptic events of 9/11, a U.S.-Mexico border wall became an acceptable and necessary desideratum in American politics. Following a long history of alienating, incriminating, exploitative, and dehumanizing policies and actions at the border came the solidification of them into steel walls.

The border wall is a physical manifestation of the anti-immigrant discourse using the themes and images of Revelation. The rhetoric arguing for the construction of barrier walls continues the conceptualization of America as the heavenly New Jerusalem in literal terms, with walls and gates like the New Jerusalem. This pro-wall language and the legal exceptions made for wall-building reflect a culminating understanding of America as God's city in the most extreme mode, relying on biblical justification that apocalyptic times call for apocalyptic measures.

One such example of this extremism comes from Lara Logan, once a chief foreign affairs correspondent for CBS, now a strident critic of "mainstream media." Appearing on the right-wing cable news show *Newsmax* in October 2022, Logan stated as a matter of fact that "[God] knows that the open border is Satan's way of taking control of the world through all these people who are his stooges and his servants."[15] Logan went on to spout QAnon conspiracy theories, which caused *Newsmax* to condemn her statements after the broadcast and bar her from reappearing. Nevertheless, her comments casting America as God's country and closing the border as God's will, as part of a cosmic struggle of good against evil, are no different than pro-wall and anti-immigration rhetoric coming from other political and religious leaders.

A month after Donald Trump's inauguration, in February 2017, the Conservative Political Action Conference (CPAC) hosted a panel titled, "If Heaven Has a Gate, a Wall, and Extreme Vetting, Why Can't America?" In 2019, Steve King, who was a congressman of Iowa at the time, tweeted: "Heaven has a wall, a gate and a strict immigration policy. Hell has open borders." In 2022, U.S. congresswoman Marjorie Taylor Greene (R-GA) stated that Catholic charities helping immigrants demonstrate that "Satan's controlling the church." And after Florida governor Ron DeSantis in 2023 signed SB 1718 into law, a highly restrictive immigration bill, Florida congresswoman

Kiyan Michael proclaimed before the state House of Representatives: "Heaven has borders, hell has none."[16]

This equation of the United States with heaven manifests most obviously now among far-right politicians and Christian nationalists, but it has its roots and foundation in centuries-long ideations of America as the New Jerusalem. And the claims that "heaven has a gate, a wall, and extreme vetting" are based on the description of the Judgment of the Dead and the New Jerusalem in Revelation 20–21. What more extreme vetting is there than having the entirety of one's deeds analyzed and an ultimate registry of names consulted, the result of which could be entry to eternal glory or being thrown into the lake of fire? As for walls and gates, those of the New Jerusalem serve as the border wall par excellence upon which the majority of frenzied "Build the Wall" language in the United States is currently based.

The walls of the New Jerusalem in Revelation 21 are themselves a zone of exception in the theology and architectural metaphors of the New Testament. Like presidential rhetoric up until 9/11, all other mentions of walls in the New Testament involve their being torn down or passed through. Most pointedly, in a verse proclaiming racial-ethnic reconciliation, the Letter to the Ephesians states, "[Christ] has broken down the dividing wall, that is, the hostility between us" (Eph 2:14). But the walls of the New Jerusalem mark an absolute and permanent division. There, at the heavenly customs and immigration bureau before the gates, the policy of forgiveness of sins has expired: one is either written in the Book of Life or not, with no further changes allowed. The border walls of the New Jerusalem comprise a space of exception where all theological laws are waived: although diseases had in the past been healed (Matt 8:1–4), the unclean and filthy now are barred (Rev 21:27; 22:11); though once even the faith of a "dog" was recognized (Mark 7:24–29), dogs are shut outside the walls (Rev 22:15); though sexual immorality and sin used to be met with compassion (John 8:3–11; Luke 7:36–50), here they condemn a person to beyond the gates (Rev 22:15); when once even idolaters (1 Thess 1:9) and those accused of murder (Acts 2:36–38) could receive forgiveness, at the gates of the New Jerusalem there is no such possibility (Rev 22:15).[17]

## Heaven Has a Wall

The Frontier Thesis of historian Frederick Jackson Turner (1861–1932) has been well criticized and deconstructed for its erasure of indigenous peoples and oversimplified account of western expansion and the rugged American pioneer. Nevertheless, Turner's sweeping and romantic thesis of American identity and character as driven by the frontier has captured intellectual and political imagination well into the twentieth century. "Since the days when the fleet of Columbus sailed into the waters of the New World," said Turner, "America has been another name for opportunity, and the people of the United States have taken their tone from . . . incessant expansion." According to Turner, addressing the American Historical Association in 1893, the dominant characteristic of American history and national identity had been movement and expansion, ever pushing the frontier away from the East Coast and away from the Old World. *Had been*, but it could be so no longer. "And now," Turner concludes, "four centuries from the discovery of America, at the end of a hundred years of life under the Constitution, the frontier has gone, and with its going has closed the first period of American history."[18]

The disappearance of the frontier did not, however, mean the end of frontier mentality and spirit, Turner argues, only that Americans no longer had "gifts of free land" and the limitless West toward which to reach and on which to struggle, build, and fight in cathartic transformation. In *The End of the Myth: From the Frontier to the Border Wall in the Mind of America*, Greg Grandin points to other, more abstract frontiers that have served American desires for expansion, and that have also served as release valves for violence. These abstract frontiers have been social "frontiers" for internal progress or against government restraint, and also, perhaps most significant, the "frontier" of war. American military occupation and war, from Mexico to the Caribbean to Central America, in the Philippines, through the world wars, in Korea, then Vietnam, from the Cold War to the War against Terror, have fed an incessant American need to extend a frontier, whether at home or abroad, literal or figurative.[19]

But the myth of the frontier, the most powerful and most invoked of American myths, Grandin argues, came to an end with Donald Trump. The shattering of the myth was signaled most clearly when Trump announced during his 2015 presidential campaign, "I will build a great, great wall." There have been border markers and some scattered structures delimiting U.S. territory since the nineteenth century, but Grandin argues that Trump's declaration of a great, continuous, physical border wall marks the end of the boundless frontier and the beginning of a new symbol of America: the wall. And the wall signaled the end to any pretense of exceptional American abundance and welcome. The wall, in Grandin's words, "stands for a nation that still thinks 'freedom' means freedom from restraint, but no longer pretends, in a world of limits, that everyone can be free—and enforces that reality through cruelty, domination, and racism."[20]

In Grandin's interpretation, this new symbol represents a startling shift in political rhetoric and imagination, but one long in the making. Now, instead of the limitless beyond of golden prairies, the vision of the wall "refashion[s] the country into a besieged medieval fortress, complete with its own revered martyrs' cult."[21] America, Grandin argues, is leaving the myth of the frontier for the new myth of the wall.

But as the last six chapters have shown, there is another enduring myth of American identity. That myth was also present at the sailing of Columbus and foundational to the identity of America, and it is one that has not ended with the loss of the frontier but continues to the present, spanning the eras of Columbus, colonies, frontiers, wars, and now the wall. It is the myth of America as the New Jerusalem, part of God's new heaven and new earth from the book of Revelation. Like the frontier myth, the myth of the New Jerusalem promoted American exceptionalism and powered westward expansion. But unlike the frontier myth, which changed and hardened into the myth of the wall, the myth of the holy city promises both infinite possibility in the eternity of heaven *and* guarded walls protecting God's people from the outer darkness. The New Jerusalem myth can house, so to speak, all the other American identity myths, regardless of their contradictions: the myth of the shining city on a hill, since it is the radiant city of the righteous; the frontier myth, since it symbolizes eternity and infinity; and the myth of the wall, since its walls are divinely impenetrable and glorious.

Ancient apocalyptic texts like Revelation offer extraordinarily malleable narratives and images, capable of being used and reused without signs of wear and tear, as illustrated by the hundreds of expired end-time predictions and millenarian cults of the last two thousand years. Revelation stretches with amazing elasticity to encompass an apocalyptic "discovery" myth for Columbus, searching for Paradise; the promise of a New Jerusalem for the Puritans establishing a new church order; the divine fiat to expand God's kingdom through Manifest Destiny; and the language and imagery to justify a pure, clean, and, especially, white heavenly population. Political and religious leaders, journalists and missionaries have used and recycled Revelation's myth, and now a vocal political faction uses its visions to clamor for a wall and, failing a literal wall, all the barriers possible to exclude the unwanted at America's borders.

There is no doubt that the language surrounding Trump's wall is the language of the Bible and of Revelation. On the day of his inauguration, January 20, 2017, Trump sat in St. John's Episcopal Church across the street from the White House for a religious service before the inaugural ceremony. The Reverend Robert Jeffress, a Southern Baptist pastor and Trump campaigner, delivered the sermon, the main theme of which likened Trump to a hero of the Bible: Nehemiah. This is what Jeffress preached:

> When I think of you, President-elect Trump, I am reminded of another great leader God chose thousands of years ago in Israel. The nation had been in bondage for decades, the infrastructure of the country was in shambles, and God raised up a powerful leader to restore the nation. And the man God chose was neither a politician nor a priest. Instead, God chose a builder whose name was Nehemiah.
>
> And the first step of rebuilding the nation was the building of a great wall. God instructed Nehemiah to build a wall around Jerusalem to protect its citizens from enemy attack. You see, God is NOT against building walls![22]

To Jeffress and to thousands of Trump supporters, Nehemiah perfectly prefigures the role they believed Trump would play. They believed Trump, like

Nehemiah, was chosen by God yet not confined by the restraints of an official religious role, not a "politician" but a builder (never mind that Nehemiah was assuredly a politician as the royal cupbearer and later governor of Judea [Neh 1:11b, 8:9]).[23]

Trump appeared to his loyalists as divinely destined to "rebuild" America, to "make it great again," just as Nehemiah did by repairing and rebuilding Jerusalem's walls. Jeffress's words implicitly condemn the Obama administration and those before it for letting the nation decay into ruin. The sermon also promises that Trump will both figuratively and literally rebuild and build anew an impenetrable wall, as he promised throughout his campaign. He said in May 2015: "I would build a wall like nobody can build a wall," and again in August 2015: "I'm a great builder. What do I do best in life, I build. Your infrastructure is crumbling. Isn't it nice to have a builder? A real builder."[24]

In using Nehemiah's story, Jeffress not only emphasizes Trump's wall-building promises but also, implicitly, Trump's white nativist promise to "take our country back." When Nehemiah completes the wall and gathers the people in Jerusalem, his next order of business is to condemn the men who had married foreign women, whose children "could not speak the language of Judah," and thus he "cleansed them from everything foreign" (Neh 13:23–30). Thus Nehemiah not only repaired and built the walls of the old Jerusalem but also "cleansed" the city and its people of foreigners. Trump is thus set up as the builder of the border wall and also as the one to cleanse America of what is "foreign."[25]

The border wall is of course inextricably linked with immigration, "foreigners," and the crossing of national boundaries. Jeffress's elaboration of the Nehemiah analogy in a later interview shows that Trump's wall is also apocalyptic in its exceptional exclusion of the dirty and sinful. Trump is not building just any wall, he is building the Wall of America the New Jerusalem, the shining city on a hill. As Jeffress said on *Fox and Friends*: "I said [in the inaugural sermon], 'Mr. President, God is not against walls!' Walls are not un-Christian. The Bible says even heaven is going to have a wall around it! Not everyone's going to be allowed in."[26]

Jeffress does not equate the United States and heaven, but he assumes that America is modeled on it. And the heaven he invokes clearly comes from the description of the New Jerusalem in Revelation 21, the walled-in destination of the holy saints after the final judgment.[27] Historically, America's boundary discourse, cordoning the nation off from the foreigner, had always been tinged with the language of Revelation. But the use of Revelation's New Jerusalem was never as clear or explicit as in the touting of the Trump border wall, capitalizing on centuries of the myth of America the New Jerusalem.

## Big and Beautiful

But can concrete slabs or steel fencing along the U.S.-Mexico border resemble the bejeweled walls of the New Jerusalem? The language that wall proponents and especially Trump have used echoes several main themes of the description we find in Revelation 21, which describes the city thus:

> It has the glory of God and a radiance like a very rare jewel, like jasper, clear as crystal. It has a great, high wall with twelve gates, and at the gates twelve angels, and on the gates are inscribed the names of the twelve tribes of the Israelites. . . . The angel who talked to me had a measuring rod of gold to measure the city and its gates and walls. The city lies foursquare, its length the same as its width; and he measured the city with his rod, fifteen hundred miles [Greek: twelve thousand stadia]; its length and width and height are equal. He also measured its wall, one hundred forty-four cubits by human measurement, which the angel was using. The wall is built of jasper, while the city is pure gold, clear as glass. The foundations of the wall of the city are adorned with every jewel. . . . And the twelve gates are twelve pearls, each of the gates is a single pearl, and the street of the city is pure gold, transparent as glass. . . . And the city has no need of sun or moon to shine on it, for the glory of God is its light, and its lamp is the Lamb. The nations will walk by its light, and the kings of the earth will bring their glory into it. Its gates will never be shut by day— and there will be no night there. People will bring into it the glory

and the honor of the nations. But nothing unclean will enter it, nor anyone who practices abomination or falsehood, but only those who are written in the Lamb's book of life. (21:11–12, 15–19, 21, 23–27)

This description in Revelation is one of the most detailed ekphrastic passages in the New Testament, but four major themes regarding the wall stand out: it is big, it is beautiful, it is clear, and it has gates.

The measurements of the New Jerusalem are *massive*: 12,000 stadia by 12,000 stadia—or, in U.S. measurements, 1,500 miles by 1,500 miles, making the city larger than India and almost two-thirds the geographic area of the United States. Even more bizarre is the mention that the angel also measures the *height* of the city at 1,500 miles, indicating an otherworldly type of wall, which would stretch beyond Earth's atmosphere. The angel also measures the thickness of the wall: it is 144 cubits or roughly 216 feet. It is hard to imagine such a city wall, just as many of Revelation's descriptions confound the imagination.[28]

But the bizarre measurements imply that a literal comprehension and coherent visualization of the wall are not the point. More important, and typical of apocalyptic description, is the focus on the perfect numbers of Jewish numerology (all divisible by twelve) and the overwhelming awesomeness conjured by such a description. The 12,000 stadia sides of the city encompass an area of 144,000 stadia square, recalling the 144,000 chosen of Israel from Revelation 7. The city also forms a square, a perfect shape in ancient Jewish and Greek conception and similar to other legendary cities, such as its vilified counterpart, Babylon. And the New Jerusalem's shape as a perfect cube outdoes all other powerful ancient cities, symbolizing its preeminence. But the incredible length, height, and thickness of the walls are simply that: not credible. These walls are not practical or even functional in human imagination. Their description is not a blueprint with practicable architectural details but rather an ekphrastic passage using architectural rhetoric. The passage is a description of a built space whose measurements, configuration, and ornamentation form and frame belief and reality. The gigantic, impenetrable, 1,500-mile-high walls of the New

Jerusalem communicate not only infinite security and protection but also, theologically, politically, and ideologically, the omnipotence of the God who created these walls, and the absolute inclusion and exclusion effected by God's judgment.[29]

In similar and repetitive ekphrastic speech, Trump has described his wall throughout his campaign and presidency, consistently dwelling on just how big the wall would be by using specific numbers. Over and over again, Trump claimed during his campaign and into the first half of his presidency that the wall would stretch one thousand miles long. He also stressed how high the wall would stand: sometimes fifty feet tall, sometimes thirty feet. The inconsistency of the proclaimed measurements did not matter; neither did the fact that Trump's imagined wall was structurally and economically ridiculous. The measurements were and are symbolic, just as they are for the New Jerusalem. The numbers are vast and whole and repeated, drummed into the ears of the faithful so they believe Trump's authority and ability to build the wall, sealing off America as the New Jerusalem.[30]

Again, Trump's border wall does not need to be practical or possible: its endlessly repeated descriptions build an imaginary monument, a gigantic one, and, in the words of Lloyd Barba, "the physical dimensions of any monument speak to intent of ideological shaping." The hugeness of the touted border wall, like the walls of the New Jerusalem, "exude leadership, dominance, and a sense of permanency." Even the promise of quarrying and transporting such vast amounts of metal, earth, and rock is "a show of power."[31]

In a further show of power, Trump claimed over a hundred times that he would "have Mexico pay" for the border wall, another incredible promise not kept.[32] This package of promises—a huge wall that keeps out enemies, yet is paid for by a subjugated power—echoes the promises of the New Jerusalem wall. What funds the economy of the holy city? The "kings of the earth" who "bring their glory into it," kings over whom the Whore of Babylon had ruled (Rev 17:18), but who now are subject to the New Jerusalem. The "Mexico will pay" promise aligns even more closely with the description of the New Jerusalem in Isaiah, from which Revelation borrows. The prophecy in Isaiah states, "Nations shall bring you their wealth, with their kings led in procession," and, most significant for Trump's bombastic claims, "Foreigners shall build your walls, and their kings shall minister to you" (60:10–11). The promise of "foreigners" building the walls has not materialized—but the marvelous thing about both Revelation's New Jerusalem and Trump's border wall is that these promises never *have* to materialize—their repeated description is enough to generate faith, money, and power.

Beyond "big," "a thousand miles long," and "fifty feet high," the other main descriptor Trump used to describe the wall was "beautiful." Again and again, Trump referred to a "big, beautiful wall." Perhaps his vocabulary is limited, or perhaps he enjoyed the alliteration, or perhaps he just likes the word, but Trump's emphasis on *beautiful* went beyond slapping a pretty veneer on an ugly dividing line. For one thing, Trump felt that anything that bore his name should be beautiful. "I want it to be beautiful," he said, "because maybe someday they'll call it The Trump Wall. Maybe. So I have to make sure it's beautiful, right?" Of course, Trump may have somewhat idiosyncratic ideas of beauty given that he once said, "Barbed wire used properly can be a beautiful sight."[33]

Be that as it may, Trump's language of a beautiful wall made its way into the wider discourse, even affecting the language of the U.S. Customs and Border Protection when they commissioned eight companies to build prototypes for the border wall. "We'll be looking at aesthetics," stated CBP acting deputy commissioner Ronald D. Vitiello, leading with the *beauty* of each prototype, and then adding, "how penetrable they are, how resistant they are to tampering and then scaling or anti-climb features." Commissioner Vitiello did not speak idle words: seventy-six personnel evaluated the wall using an "aesthetics test" comprising scores for "attractiveness" followed by "effectiveness." And once the eight prototypes had been revealed to the general public, a nonprofit organization named, simply, MAGA petitioned to preserve the prototypes as a national monument, stating that they "have significant cultural value and are historical land art." The organization titled the land art exhibition *Prototypes* and offered guided tours of these structures.[34]

Revelation's narrator John of Patmos also receives a guided tour, on which he beholds the big, beautiful walls of the New Jerusalem. As the city descends from heaven, the twelve foundations of its wall gleam with precious jewels, significant to Israelite history and representing opulence and power. And just as Trump imagined his name to be attached to his big, beautiful wall, there are names inscribed on the wall and its foundations— the twelve tribes written at each gate, and the twelve apostles on each foundation. These inscriptions convey status, power, and legacy to all those entering the city and to those shut out.[35]

People love a spectacle. The walls of the New Jerusalem and in Trump's speeches stand big and beautiful, no matter their immateriality and their existence solely in discourse. The words describing them, gleaming with jewels or barbed wire stretching out thousands of miles, awe, provoke, inspire, and simply entertain. More important for the faithful audience of Revelation and Trump's speeches, the awesomeness of the walls stokes fervor and zeal, inspiring emotions of triumph, vindication, and exultant pride. Trump knew this. During the run-up to the election, he told the *New York Times* about his strategy for working up his audience at campaign rallies: "You know, if it gets a little boring, if I see people starting to sort of, maybe thinking about leaving, I can sort of tell the audience, I just say, 'We will build a wall!' And they go nuts."[36]

## Clear as Crystal

Adding to the spectacle of the New Jerusalem is the incredible light that emanates from it. The entire city glows with the glory of God, who dwells within, and this radiance shines not just outward from the city but *through* the city walls. Revelation 21:11 reads, "[The city] has the glory of God and a radiance like a very rare jewel, like jasper, clear as crystal."[37] This clear stone (which is not modern jasper) also forms the gigantic wall resting on top of the foundation of jewels, so the reader can imagine the New Jerusalem not just as formidable, enormous, and beautiful, but also as luminously transparent, with the brilliance of the Divine shining through the entire edifice.

Incredibly, this detail *also* figures prominently in Trump's description of his border wall. After receiving border patrol feedback regarding his giant concrete wall, Trump added that his wall would not only be big and beautiful but also "see-through":

One of the things with the wall is you need transparency. You have to be able to see through it . . . so it could be a steel wall with openings, but you have to have openings because you have to see what's on the other side of the wall . . . when they throw the large sacks of drugs over, and if you have people on the other side of the wall, you don't see them—they hit you on the head with 60 pounds of stuff? It's over. As cray [sic] as that sounds, you need transparency through that wall. But we have some incredible designs.

Again, he explained, "They need see-through. So, we need a form of fence or window. . . . If you have a wall this thick and it's solid concrete from ground to 32 feet high, which is a high wall, much higher than people planned. You go 32 feet up and you don't know who's over here. . . . If you don't know who's there, you've got a problem."[38]

Of course, Trump and the border patrol required a "transparent" or "see-through" wall not to magnify the divine radiance of America, the shining city on a hill, but for purposes of surveillance. Trump made sure to characterize those hoping to climb the wall as drug lords or smugglers—somehow launching sixty-pound bags of drugs over an imagined thirty-two-foot-high barrier. These criminals, he argued, must be watched; these are the "bad hombres" he focused on when promoting "strong borders" and the wall to his listeners, without mention of refugees, families, and certainly not children.[39]

Radiant light, however, really does shine from the United States at the border wall: it is the light of vigilantes and guards and the light of surveillance. In fact, lighting the wall began long before Trump's political career. In 1990, a California group calling itself the Alliance for Border Control organized a monthly protest called Light Up the Border. In order to deter border-crossing immigrants, members of the group parked hundreds of cars along the border to shine their headlights together into Mexico. A few years later, in order to surveil a surge of immigration at the border due to the North American Free Trade Agreement (NAFTA), the Clinton administration set up stadium lights along the wall, shining them into Tijuana, as part of Operation Gatekeeper. And these are not the only lights shining at the border. Sensor lights, infrared, and backscatter lights also beam their rays, creating a barrier of watchfulness against intruders.[40]

Naturally, guards also watch the borders and gates, like the twelve angels at the twelve gates of the New Jerusalem. This is not just a fanciful and extended comparison: in 1986, the organization Civilian Material Assistance, a group including Vietnam veterans, Ku Klux Klan members, and ultraconservative "Birchers," dispatched twenty vigilantes to the border, calling them "border angels." The heavenly language of Revelation creeps into every corner of immigration, borders, and walls.[41]

Vice versa, the language of immigration, borders, and walls may also be said to creep into every corner of Revelation. That is to say, reading the Revelation of John through the lens of American immigration history suggests interpretations that surprise and subvert expectations. Is the light of the New Jerusalem simply a glorious, divine radiance, illuminating the city for the sake of its citizens?[42] Or is it also the light of surveillance? On a related note, why does the city have walls? Why does it not simply span the whole of existence without a boundary wall? Why does it have an enclosure with definite measurements, impossibly high and impossibly thick? Certainly the presence of angels at the gates, high walls, and beaming lights denote something more than just opulent glory, something more sinister, like omnipotent surveillance and exclusion.

Weren't all of God's enemies—those who worshiped the Beast, the Devil, and Death and Hades themselves—thrown into the lake of fire before the descent of the New Jerusalem? If they were, why would the city need to display such prominent defensive architecture and watchfulness? But Revelation, again, as is typical of the apocalyptic, offers neither consistency nor chronological continuity. Revelation 22:14 states, "Blessed are those who wash their robes, so that they will have the right to the tree of life and may enter the city by the gates." Yet immediately afterward the narrator says, "Outside are the dogs and sorcerers and sexually immoral and murderers and idolaters, and everyone who loves and practices falsehood" (22:15). This latter verse appears at the end of Revelation, after the descent of the heavenly city. Still lurking outside the gates are the beasts, the sexually depraved, and the violent, that is, the "animals," "bad hombres," the "drug dealers, criminals, and rapists" envisioned by Trump and his allies.[43]

## The Open Gate

Despite the dangers lurking outside the walls, the New Jerusalem wall has gates, twelve in number, each of them made from a single enormous pearl (Rev 21:21). Although the city is encircled by an impossibly imposing wall, it is not hermetically sealed from the outside. In fact, these twelve gates remain open at all times because they "will never be shut by day, and there will be no night there" (Rev 21:25). Whether bathed in the glow of the Divine or pierced by the surveilling searchlights of the Almighty, the gates do not shut while there is light. And even Trump conceded that there must be a gate in his wall. In fact, he stated that the border wall would have "a very big, very beautiful door."[44]

Trump is not the first or only person to imagine America with such walls and gates. As discussed in the first chapter of this book, Ronald Reagan also envisioned America as a walled New Jerusalem, albeit in far more eloquent terms, in his farewell speech to the nation in January 1989:

> I've spoken of the shining city all my political life, but I don't know if I ever quite communicated what I saw when I said it. But in my mind it was a tall proud city built on rocks stronger than oceans, wind-swept, God-blessed, and teeming with people of all kinds living in harmony and peace, a city with free ports that hummed with commerce and creativity. And if there had to be city walls, the walls had doors and the doors were open to anyone with the will and the heart to get here. That's how I saw it and see it still.[45]

Reagan takes imagery from Revelation 21, down to the detail of city walls and open gates. Unlike Trump, Reagan mentions these structures in a reluctant tone, regretting that such things need be.

But besides walls and open gates, both Reagan and Trump (and many others) pick up on another aspect of Revelation's New Jerusalem: the description of those allowed and actively entering the gates. Reagan, Trump, and the U.S. government, for as long as borders have been enforced in its history, agree with Revelation that those who may enter the open gates without question are those who bring tribute to enrich the city, whether as individual immigrants or as nations through trade agreements.[46]

Trump states, "This will be a wall with a very big, very beautiful door, because we want the legals to come back into the country." The type of "legals" to whom Trump and his administration want to open that beautiful door are "people of talent." In the same vein, former ICE director Tom Homan writes that the Trump administration's vision of desirable immigrants would be those of "Extraordinary talent; Professional and specialized vocations; Exceptional academic track records." This would "[prioritize] merit over chance." Reagan, ever playing the benevolent host, softens the language to say that anyone "with the will and the heart" may enter America as the New Jerusalem. But with what kind of populace does Reagan people his shining city? "All kinds living in harmony and peace," yes, but with an emphasis on "free ports that [hum] with commerce and creativity." Clearly the gates to America open for those outside so long as they bring with them prosperity, privilege, and the promise of wealth.[47]

This was certainly the type of immigrant to whom the Immigration and Nationality Act of 1965 gave preference for entry to the United States, resulting in the "brain drain" of Asian countries. The act favored granting visas to, after family members of U.S. citizens, those "qualified immigrants who are members of the professions, or who because of their exceptional ability in the sciences or the arts will substantially benefit prospectively the national economy, cultural interests, or welfare of the United States." The "professions" include "architects, engineers, lawyers, physicians, surgeons, and teachers."[48]

Revelation's gates stand open for the same reason: the city admits those carrying in riches and tribute. Revelation 21:24 and 26 read: "The kings of the earth will bring their glory into it. . . . People will bring into it the glory and the honor of the nations."[49] These are the *only* people described as actively entering the city: those bringing wealth to enrich the New Jerusalem. Immediately following these verses, as is typical in immigration discourse, is the description of those who may *not* enter: "But nothing unclean will enter it, nor anyone who practices abomination or falsehood, but only those who are written in the Lamb's book of life."

Curiously, the "kings of the earth" who bring wealth into the New Jerusalem have somehow passed through the immigration process of the angelic bureau of the Book of Life and the Book of Deeds. The "kings of the earth" last appeared with the Beast, preparing for war against the Rider on the White Horse (Rev 19:19). Before that, they watched the smoke rise from the burning Whore of Babylon, whom they had exploited sexually and economically (Rev 18:3, 9). But the walls of the New Jerusalem are a zone of exception: the rules of entry can be waived for kings, specifically for those who can benefit the kingdom.[50]

Like the entry policy of the New Jerusalem in Revelation, American policy at the U.S.-Mexico border and at virtually every point of contact internationally opens the gates for wealth and commerce. Just as kings with tribute may enter freely at the walls of the New Jerusalem, so the barrier between the United States and Mexico dissolves when it comes to individuals with the greatest wealth and power. This presents an apt analogy for NAFTA, and now its successor, the U.S.-Mexico-Canada Agreement, which enables multinational corporations to cross borders at will and manufacture, drill, frack, and refine with impunity with regard to the environment, local laws, and each nation's workforce. While the Border Patrol continues to track, surveil, capture, and detain the migrant at the border, corporations, who are the new kings of the earth, can freely exploit, privatize, and profit with little thought for national boundaries.[51]

## Within the Walls

The Trump wall and the barrier fencing in place before it have never been effective, and their primary utility has not been to serve as a physical deterrence. Just as celestial walls that are fifteen hundred miles high serve no physical purpose in a truly post-apocalyptic, post-lake-of-fire landscape, the U.S.-Mexico border wall does not provide a real defense against drug smugglers and human traffickers. Instead, it has harmed workers, refugees, and families, not to mention migrating wildlife and the surrounding natural environment. The wall's utility lies in its symbolic power to rally votes and fire up a cult of personality and political extremism, to stir up white supremacist hatred based on myths of scarcity within and violence without.

The vast majority of drugs traveling from Mexico into the United States go through normal ports of entry in cars, trucks, and ships, not over the border wall. Yet the Biden administration has continued work on the wall, filling in some of its gaps, even when experts agree that drug cartels have and will find other points of entry. The source of the problem does not lie outside the U.S. walls but inside. "It goes back to the demand side in the U.S.," stated Homeland Security Investigations' David Shaw in 2017. "If demand wasn't so high, then you wouldn't have the supply problem." And the current fentanyl crisis in the United States has its roots within the walls as well, going back to prescription opioids, U.S. pharmaceutical companies, and the exploitation of those in need of pain medication. Additionally, over 80 percent of those convicted of fentanyl trafficking in the United States from 2018 to 2021 have been U.S. citizens. In truth, drug trafficking has nearly nothing to do with immigrants seeking entry at the border.[52]

The same can be said about human trafficking and the ways it has been falsely linked with border crossing, when in fact the majority of human trafficking victims are born in the United States, and what drives this criminal activity comes from demand within the country. Human trafficking may also mistakenly be equated with human smuggling, the illegal transportation of people across the border, which usually involves the exploitation of those seeking work and safety and sometimes ends in violence and horrific death. The irony is that government officials point to such happenings as talking points for "securing the border," when securing the border with walls, laws, policing, and vigilantism creates the very illegality and desperation that result in such deaths. Meanwhile, political leaders such as Governors Ron DeSantis (FL) and Greg Abbott (TX) lure migrants onto vehicles with false promises of housing and employment, transport them to a faraway location (usually politically left-leaning), and abandon them. This cruel exploitation of human lives for political gain by scoring points with white nationalists, all in the name of being tough on illegal immigration, is itself human trafficking.[53]

America as the New Jerusalem does not need walls, let alone a barrier that has been climbed, breached, and tunneled under. The United States enforces borders everywhere without a single concrete slab or steel slat through its military, surveillance, and corporate interests in territories and markets around the globe. It has effectively set up borders all over in the interest of intelligence and finances, joining other walls, physical and otherwise, erected by other nations, so that, as Grandin notes, "[the world] looks more like a maze than a shared planet."[54]

The imagery and vision helping to promote this American empire of borders is the apocalyptic conceptualization of the nation as God's heavenly city, justifying both American exceptionalism and an American right to power. In each stage of American expansion, from "discovery" to global economy, the New Jerusalem metaphor has morphed to be used anew. Politicians throughout American history have borrowed Revelation's discourse—wittingly or unwittingly—from the beginning, when it so well captured European imagination in the fifteenth and sixteenth centuries, and the idea has proved pliable and expedient in every age thereafter.

Even when the frontier ends with the wall, or the shining city of American exceptionalism seems snuffed out in the selfishness and cruelty of "America First," the New Jerusalem myth endures. It can be both Reagan's shining city on a hill and Trump's heaven with a wall around it.[55] The city on a hill may no longer glow with self-righteous American exceptionalism, but it still shines with the search lights of constant surveillance.

The utility of the New Jerusalem metaphor lies chiefly in its recyclability, so that what once convinced colonists that indigenous genocide was "clearing the land" for their heavenly dwelling can be repurposed to forbid the Yellow Peril from entering as a swarm of locusts. America as the New Jerusalem continues to be used and reused for its political expediency to both inspire and incite. The border wall and its discourse likewise recycle racist, white supremacist hatred and violence from throughout American history—and they recycle such actions not only figuratively but also materially. The first real barrier that went up along the U.S.-Mexico border in 1945, after World War II, was made of chain-link fencing recycled from the camps used to imprison Japanese Americans. Almost fifty years later, the

Clinton administration put up fifteen miles of wall manufactured from steel helicopter landing pads used in the Vietnam War. They were so sharp that those attempting to climb over "often severed their fingers."[56]

The term *apocalypse* rarely evokes visions of comfort in popular culture. Still, many people, past and present, have derived comfort from the promises offered within the New Jerusalem walls, where death is no more, where every tear is wiped away, where one can find healing and eternal life in the light of God. But in the architectural vision of the seer, God's city is not a free and borderless habitation, and its demarcations are disturbingly defensive. The New Jerusalem's walls are powerful, authoritative, and calculated to intimidate. The walls surround the entire city, dividing those inside from those outside absolutely.

# Conclusion
## The Myth, the Spectacle, and the Prophecy

Woe, woe, woe to the inhabitants of the earth.

—*Revelation 8:13*

### The Myth

The abiding myth of the book of Revelation is one of destination. Before the gates of the ultimate destination, the New Jerusalem, all journeys meet their conclusion, all travelers receive their just reward. The warnings, disaster, plagues, and battle of the narrative end with the Book of Life and the Book of Deeds, dividing all people into two: those predestined to enter the city and those destroyed in the lake of fire or shut out forever beyond the walls. Inside dwell the righteous, chosen, pure, and rich. Outside lurk the criminal, bestial, diseased, and filthy. The walls of the city separate inside from outside with splendid and awful beauty, in a show of strength eclipsing any human construction with its blinding radiance.

This myth shapes the discourse of immigration in America, imparting to the history of the country the same ideas of destination, judgment, belonging, and division. As the inhabitants of a place conceived from its European discovery as an apocalyptic land, the fulfillment of divine promise, the first immigrants understood themselves as exceptional and chosen, whether in establishing God's church or God's nation. From the beginning, entry and belonging to this America were dictated by predestination in the Book of White Life. As subsequent laws, policies, bureaus, and borders multiplied, they further articulated, justified, and separated those inside from those out-side, both in discourse and in the realities experienced by those seeking en-try. Whether guided by the ethos of American exceptionalism or America First, white nativist discourse identifies those within the United States as righteous, chosen, pure, and rich. The unwanted immigrants, to be kept outside, are criminal, bestial, diseased, and filthy. This narrative spans the American political spectrum; any politician with a fighting chance of being elected will say that the United States must have strong borders. A strong border has become the symbol of America's power and might.

The America-as-New-Jerusalem myth has been used to incite hate and fear against any number of unwanted peoples, whether the Antichrist-serving Irish, the locust horde of Chinese, the criminal Mexican, or the infidel Mus-lim. But though the New Jerusalem myth has been a one-size-fits-all narra-tive for fearmongering and racist protectionism, the story no longer so neatly fits the new realities of American immigration and national life.

The first signs of the crumbling myth is the U.S. border wall, which is cut through, climbed over, dug under, and most often of all simply ignored by those passing through official ports of entry. Trump used the wall as the key symbol of his presidency, and the Biden administration has continued to build it, also as a symbolic act—symbolic because the wall does not work. Other politicians, such as Texas governor Greg Abbott, have created other kinds of physical barriers, such as a "floating wall," to prevent swimming across river borders. But these serve as political rallying cries and have very little practical purpose.[1]

Border walls and physical barriers to entry are the descendants of city walls, like the walls of the New Jerusalem. They are relics of ancient and medieval times and are outdated in a world of digitization, air travel, global trade, and capitalism. Border walls do not stop incoming criminal activity or the spread of disease, when these can and do travel easily into the country via sanctioned pathways. Border walls do not matter to the rich and the priv-ileged around the globe, and they especially do not matter to corporations. Those most harmed by physical barriers are the poor and refugees, who have no other recourse than to scale them, and the communities split by the border wall, migrating animals, and the environment.

But besides being technologically outdated, border walls represent a xenophobic defense against an "immigration crisis" that does not exist—at least not in the way nativists claim. *Net* immigration to the United States has gradually slowed for much of the past decade, not all of which is due to Trump's policies (many of which have been reversed) or to pandemic restrictions.[2] When Title 42, which restricted immigration on account of COVID-19, was lifted in May 2023, unauthorized entries did not surge as anticipated but actually dropped by 70 percent. The United States also accepted historically low numbers of refugees under Trump, and even with a significant increase under Biden the figures remain low in comparison to the three prior decades.[3] And while migrant encounters are picking up again at the time of writing, this does not represent the crisis of invasion imagined by anti-immigrant politicians. Rather, crises are caused by anti-immigrant laws like Florida's SB 1718, which promises to worsen the state's already serious worker shortage.[4]

Meanwhile, the United States has experienced a decline in birth rate, which may eventually lead to an even greater shortage of labor and a disproportionately large elderly population. American cities are also losing population density, and American citizens are showing greater than ever interest in leaving the country in the current moment of extreme political division, unrelenting gun violence, and the emboldened rise of far-right groups and leaders.[5]

Experts see immigrant and refugee populations as a solution to the sustainability problems caused by these changes in the U.S. workforce and population.[6] And yet major political discourse about immigration has not moved on from the mythical New Jerusalem narrative, where America is the ultimate destination that must be protected from hordes of invading outsiders. In June 2023, Greg Abbott retweeted a video praising Texas national guardsmen installing razor wire at the Rio Grande, saying, "They have one goal—deny illegal entry into Texas." On the other side of the political divide, the Biden administration's policy of "asylum ineligibility" has drastically reduced the numbers of asylum-seekers allowed entry—from 83 percent in 2014–19 to 43 percent in 2023.[7]

A statement from the Biden White House in March 2023 repeats the same key points of the traditional American New Jerusalem myth, touting a secure border and militant policing against criminals while maintaining a stance of righteous, judicious hospitality:

> President Biden has taken historic steps to secure our border and rebuild a safe, orderly, and humane immigration system that was gutted by the previous Administration. Over the past two years, the Biden-Harris Administration has secured more resources for border security than any of the presidents who preceded him, deployed the most agents ever—more than 23,000—to address the situation at the border, prevented record levels of illicit fentanyl from entering our country, and brought together world leaders on a framework to deal with changing migration patterns that are impacting the entire Western Hemisphere. ... The President's Budget includes billions of dollars to keep America's borders secure and enforce our immigration laws, while expanding legal pathways for migrants seeking asylum.[8]

The one significant note of difference sounded here is the mention of bringing together leaders to address changing migration patterns, which shows awareness of the shifting story. But the underlying narrative of the shining city on a hill, barring evildoers at the walls while graciously offering entry to those seeking refuge (while actually cutting asylum eligibility), remains the same.

It has become obligatory to say one is "strong on the border" to win political office, even though the modern American reality no longer fits the traditional New Jerusalem myth. This is not to say, of course, that America ever truly embodied the New Jerusalem, but the aspirations and fears of American leaders had once neatly fit the contours of Revelation's story in popular discourse and imagination. Now, however, the population appears headed toward decline, other nations advise caution when visiting the United States, legal immigration is increasingly difficult, and labor shortages occur across industries.[9] The outlines of the myth versus reality have diverged to a breaking point. And yet government officials and public leaders continue to legislate, write, preach, build, surveil, deport, and imprison while invoking the New Jerusalem myth, so powerful is the rallying cry around chosenness and exclusion.

Fueling the obsession for "strong borders" and a barricaded America is the continual spectacle made of immigrants at the border. Again and again, politicians and pundits fixate on the wall, perceived scarcity, and alleged threats from outside. And as long as news media are obligated to report on and draw the nation's focus to that spectacle, and public discourse continues to retell the myth of America the New Jerusalem, the realities of the country more and more fulfill Revelation's prophecies of catastrophe rather than that of the Celestial City.

## The Spectacle

Colonists, expansionists, and nativists have used the vocabulary of Revelation to describe and justify the wiping out of indigenous peoples by disease and genocide as the work of the "sword of the Lord," the denying of self-possession and humanity to enslaved Black people whom they proselytized for God's plantation, the exclusion and exploitation of the Chinese as idolaters, and the barring of supposedly violent and bestial Mexicans at the wall. It has let in the kings of the earth and their riches by the gate while excluding and criminalizing those of the Global South, often exploited to produce those same riches.

In the last few decades, however, a new element of public discourse has changed the way the nation's populace receives and understands immigration events. The major change is not in the exclusion, violence, and white supremacy experienced by those seeking entry and naturalization—those experiences remain relatively the same, whether cloaked in legitimating policy-speak or out in the open in unvarnished hate speech. The difference lies in the greater—sometimes incessant—reporting of immigration stories through hundreds of online and televised venues, made immediately and widely available, with accompanying pictures and videos. Photographs of the border wall, of migrant caravans, and of lines at customs accompany every news story, editorial, and statistical report, creating a visual and textual spectacle that reinforces—whether intentionally or not—the story of a besieged nation confronting an immigration crisis.

One of the most significant factors driving public sentiment during Trump's 2018 "zero tolerance" policy, which led to a sharp increase in the number of children separated from their parents at the U.S.-Mexico border, was a photograph. Photographer John Moore captured the image of a Honduran two-year-old girl in a pink long-sleeved shirt standing by her mother and crying; the camera is brought down to her level, so the viewer sees her terrorized sobbing face next to the legs of her mother and a border agent. The girl's face became the image of fundraisers, news stories, and social media posts, creating outrage against the policy and the Trump administration while helping to raise millions of dollars for those facing separation and detention at the border.[10]

This powerful photograph and its influence are an example of the way an image can inspire empathy and call for compassion. But such images are part of a larger dynamic that perpetually props up the cycle of declared crisis, defensive action, attendant (and necessary) journalism, and consequent spectacle and discourse, which reignites the declaration of an immigration crisis. Thus, a political figure with an eye toward elections declares that they will solve America's immigration crisis; they roll out razor wire or visit the wall or deny asylum; reporters and photographers file their stories and images; the nation's populace sees the Black and Brown faces at the borders and shakes their heads (or fists) at the awful problem of immigration and looks for a leader who will solve the immigration crisis.

Certainly empathy and compassion may be the response to the crisis, especially when viewers focus on the story of an individual, of a child, of the bond between child and mother. But the suffering of those at the border can also spark glee and celebration. In 2021, Border Patrol agents on horseback chased after Black Haitian migrants, stooping down from their saddles to grab a man by his shirt and waving reins in the air as they ran travelers down into the Rio Grande. These images outraged many, but some were exultant and embraced these images as an iconic show of American strength against invaders. Unofficial U.S. Border Patrol "challenge coins," commemorative and collectable medallions celebrating the event, showed up for sale on eBay. They depicted an agent on horseback, catching a migrant by his shirt, with mottos such as "Honor will always be first," "You will be returned," "Reining it in since May 28, 1924," and "Whipping ass since 1924." According to one seller, the coins were "flying off the shelf," selling for as much as $500 apiece.[11]

Although U.S. Customs and Border Protection has condemned these coins, the agency's iconography commemorates the traditional vigilante ethos of the CBP and a white American aesthetic of protecting the border.[12] Nearly the same image greets visitors at the U.S. Border Patrol Museum in El Paso: a larger-than-life metal sculpture of a border agent on horseback, standing up with one foot in a stirrup, ready for action. The statue, the museum, and the challenge coin share an aesthetic handed down from the Texas Rangers and white American colonization of the West. They all celebrate a group whose membership is dedicated to the exclusion of the outsider and memorialize a sainthood of individuals martyred in that task.

The spectacle of immigrant suffering and its celebration unite white nativists, a group that has been regaining strength and boldness in the clamor to Make America Great Again. The selling of the challenge coin commemorating violence against Haitian migrants is emblematic of exactly the phenomenon Cristina Beltrán describes in *Cruelty as Citizenship*: "For nativists who yearn for the freedom to police, punish, and exclude, targeting migrants makes them feel stronger, freer, more agentic, transforming acts of racialized violence—whether people are committing, *witnessing,* or *merely describing* such acts—into feats of heroism, democratic redemption, civic engagement, and virtuous sovereignty."[13]

And the celebratory spectating of the guarding of the walls and purity of the New Jerusalem furthermore produces a unity and sense of membership in a group that nostalgically valorizes the civic world of the Founding Fathers, when only white, free men were citizens. Beltrán states: "While critics like Adam Serwer have rightly argued that when it comes to the bond between Trump and his supporters, 'the cruelty is the point,' my claim is that such cruelty is not only an experience of community and delight; it's fundamentally a return to a particular *civic* experience. ... For those invested in an ideology of whiteness, racial exclusion, violence, and domination *produce* a sense of membership, creating a commonsense understanding of community, opportunity, futurity, and possibility."[14] And in the American environment of immigration spectacle, people—sympathetic or not—are drawn together as viewers within, watching calamity unfold without.

This is also a part of the New Jerusalem in Revelation, where John of Patmos "sees" and describes the suffering of those on earth in ekphrastic speech, where kings and merchants watch from afar the smoke rise from the burning of the Whore of Babylon (18:9–10, 17–18). It is an echo of the Book of Isaiah, where the people of the New Jerusalem "go out and look at the dead bodies of the people who have rebelled against [God]" (66:24). And the voyeurism of Revelation continues through early Christian texts in tours of hell, where sinners suffer their deserved torment. And it continues in Christian theological treatises through the ages—from Augustine to Aquinas to Jonathan Edwards to James I. Packer—arguing that those in the New Jerusalem will see the agonies of those in hell.[15]

The voyeurism of punishment and suffering unites the citizens of the New Jerusalem and imparts to them—and readers who identify with them—membership in an exclusive city and vindication of their righteousness. In long and diverse Christian traditions, the saints watching from heaven will exult in their victory and, as they cannot be wrung with pity since that is a theological impossibility in heaven, they will glorify God's justice. So Jonathan Edwards preached in New England in 1739: "Every time [the saints] look upon the damned, it will excite in them a lively and admiring sense of the grace of God. . . . The view of the misery of the damned will double the ardor of the love and gratitude of the saints of heaven." Indeed, this is why the walls of the New Jerusalem, according to some theologians, must be transparent: so that the saints can view the punishment of the damned, and the damned see the glories enjoyed by the citizens of heaven.[16]

The Trump wall was also supposed to be "see-through," primarily for surveillance. But the view from within America to outside the border is afforded not only through the steel bollards of the border wall but also in the constant feed of texts and images of travelers at the border, immigrants being chased, apprehended, separated, reunited, and flown and bussed about. Like the citizens of the New Jerusalem tradition, the U.S. populace is a captive audience to the spectacle of immigration at its borders. Just as theologians imagined different reactions to the spectacle of hell, the American population experiences varying reactions of anger, compassion, pity, joy, and exultation in the rule of law. But all are witnesses to those punished beyond the walls; they watch a crisis exacerbated and in part created by political grandstanding and fearmongering that ignore or shunt to the side how little America now fits the story of the New Jerusalem. With the nation's attention, political power, and resources focused on the border and the enemy beyond, the scene inside the walls comes to resemble more and more the imagined dangers outside.

## The Prophecy

Three major desiderata of American immigration under the New Jerusalem myth have been the exclusion of criminal activity, the exclusion of disease and plagues, and the creation of borders, physical and bureaucratic, to enact such exclusions. U.S. immigration policy has operated under the logic that if people groups identified as criminal, diseased, and subhuman can be kept out by a strong border, then the laws and guarding of the country have succeeded. In fact, the pursuit of these objectives has produced the opposite effect within and around the walls of America. In the mission to fulfill the prophecy of the New Jerusalem, the United States has instead been fulfilling Revelation's prophecies of disaster, which is more apparent now than ever.

The primary weapon used to exclude people groups from entry and naturalization has been xenophobia, particularly in the form of white supremacy. But xenophobic discourse and constructions of racial identity affect not only those outside the borders but those living within the walls as well. Even as the language of "keeping criminals out" vilifies the immigrant at the gate, the centuries-long association of Black and Native peoples and other peoples of color with violence has in turn produced violence against these identities and across communities within the country. In 2021, the United States saw its highest gun death rate in thirty years. Meanwhile, gun purchases have accelerated in volume, and those who are buying guns are more diverse than ever.[7]

Studies have shown that racist xenophobia and reactions to it have driven the ownership of guns, and increasing access to weapons has led to further violence and death. White gun ownership today is tied to anti-Black and racist motivations. One study shows that the higher the percentage of enslaved Black people in a county in 1860, the higher the rate of gun ownership today. Another study shows that white racist attitudes drive both gun ownership and resistance to gun control legislation. Furthermore, non-white groups are also making more gun purchases, specifically in response to racism and violence. This trend includes Black people motivated for self-protection after anti-Black violence and hate speech, and Asian Americans in response to anti-Asian crimes and hate speech during the COVID-19 pandemic. Rather than keeping the murderer outside the wall, the centuries-old discourse painting non-white peoples as outsiders, as dangerous and diseased, has only driven rates of gun ownership and gun violence within the United States ever higher. So much for the exclusion of violence.[18]

One of the earliest immigration restrictions of America was a law passed in the Massachusetts Colony in 1700 barring the "infirm," the beginnings of prohibiting ill or diseased immigrants from entering. Sickness has been associated with unwanted ethnic groups in American immigration ever since. In recent years, Trump and right-wing conservatives placed blame for COVID-19 primarily on two groups: on China, and by association Chinese people, and on immigrants at the U.S.-Mexico border. This scapegoating of "foreigners" was as effective as the previous barring of "diseased" groups in the past: not at all. The focus of attention on immigration bans, accusations, and public vitriol against China, Chinese, and immigrants not only led to an increase in hate crimes against Asian Americans, it also stalled public health action, politicized preventative measures, and severed U.S. ties with the World Health Organization. The blaming of the foreign for disease did nothing to mitigate the pandemic; in fact, it worsened the catastrophe. So much for the exclusion of diseases and plagues.[19]

Finally, the focus on the border wall and guarding the boundaries of the United States should supposedly prevent the entry of the criminal and the diseased, and discourage migrants from seeking a home in America. But as the United States focuses on guarding its borders, creating restrictive policies, expanding the military, and building the wall, it directs toward its boundaries money, resources, and human attention that could otherwise be invested in preventing environmental damage and counteracting climate change, which is poised to become the biggest driver of global migration. From 2013 to 2018, the United States spent $19.6 billion on militarizing the border compared to only $1.8 billion toward climate finance and action, almost eleven times more. The United States joins six other countries that are the greatest emitters of greenhouse gases in collectively spending 2.3 times more on securing their borders than on fighting climate change. In short, the wealthiest countries that are the most to blame for greenhouse gas emissions are doing as much as they can to wall themselves off from the rest of the world, while damaging the environment as they do so.[20]

But climate knows no borders. The hurricanes, droughts, flooding, and wildfires driving unwanted migrants to U.S. borders are also already wreaking havoc within the country's walls. The prioritization of strengthening and militarizing its borders will only increase migration, both internationally and domestically, when this deprioritizes alternative immigration and refugee policies and combating climate change. And if nothing changes the investment priorities of U.S. political power and money, America will eventually find itself in the lake of fire rather than the New Jerusalem.

Revelation's apocalyptic prophecies may seem the stuff of religious fanatics and doomsday predictors. But its language nevertheless makes its way onto America's largest political stages. Upon the unsealing of Trump's indictment charges regarding classified documents in June 2023, the former president posted on social media:

> NOW THAT THE "SEAL" IS BROKEN, IN ADDITION TO CLOSING THE BORDER & REMOVING ALL OF THE "CRIMINAL" ELEMENTS THAT HAVE ILLEGALLY ENTERED THE COUNTRY . . . I WILL APPOINT A REAL SPECIAL "PROSECUTOR" TO GO AFTER THE MOST CORRUPT PRESIDENT IN THE HISTORY OF THE USA . . . AND ALL OTHERS INVOLVED WITH THE DESTRUCTION OF OUR ELECTIONS, BORDERS, & COUNTRY ITSELF![21]

On the surface, the broken "seal" refers to the unsealed criminal charges. But of course Bible readers and believers across the nation understand the "seal" as one of the seven seals on a heavenly scroll, each of which is broken in Revelation 6–8. Perhaps Trump understands himself as the hero on a white horse, riding out at the breaking of the first seal (Rev 6:1–2). He certainly announces that he will accomplish what his followers believe to be heroic: closing the borders, purging the country of criminals, and destroying his enemies.

Myriad possibilities await the nation at this time of writing, a phrase that feels more precarious now than ever. But if the country's leaders and many of its people pursue the fulfillment of "closing borders" and "removing all criminal elements" as their foremost goal, while insisting on America First, on America the walled-in golden city, then it may soon seem in the United States that Revelation's other seals are being broken and the trumpets of God are sounding, as people slaughter one another (6:4) and die of famine and pestilence (6:8), as trees and grass burn (8:7), as the sea is polluted and its creatures die (8:9), and as the water of the land is poisoned so that many die drinking it (8:11).

## Remembering

Nothing is a foregone conclusion—yet. Popular interpretation of Revelation understands the text as a set of mysterious predictions concerned with final destinies and the fulfillment of prophecy. And this is, in part, why the appropriation of Revelation in immigration discourse must end, because the language of prophetic eschatology casts ideas of American identity, ways of being, and principles of exclusion and membership as the fulfillment of destiny, as always already existent and essentially true. The country needs to forget Revelation, erase it from its national imagination and discourse. What we must do instead is remember history.

This is not a call to remember history lest it be repeated, since history cannot be repeated nor catastrophe averted simply by recollection. This is also not a reminder that America is "a nation of immigrants," since indigenous peoples still live in the land, and all immigrants benefit from settler colonialism. This is furthermore not a reminder that immigrants boost the U.S. economy, which is an argument that evaluates human beings in terms of capital.

What must be remembered is that every law, policy, wall, documentation, and office of the U.S. government did not always exist but are the constructions of human judgments and principles that are neither eternal nor essential. None of the elements of U.S. immigration is a given, and remembering history demonstrates this. Thirty years ago, in the early 1990s, bar hoppers could walk across the border from Juárez into El Paso without a passport. In the 1960s, students and workers could cross that border for a lunch break. Less than a hundred years ago, U.S. citizens were not required to carry passports to travel. Just over a hundred years ago, the Border Patrol did not exist. Less than 150 years ago, immigrants did not carry documentation certifying their "lawful" entry. The category and construction of the illegal alien did not exist, had not yet happened. Documentation, surveillance, borders, being legal or illegal are not natural aspects of the human condition. They have been normalized over time as given and fixed.[22]

This is not a call to remember "simpler times." Remembering immigration history in America should never be an exercise in nostalgia. Memory of this history must recall the cruelty of a place taken and made to be a nation where only free white men unquestionably belonged, where every subsequently created category, boundary, and rule governing immigration and naturalization hinged on that founding principle.

And therefore, every category, boundary, and law can be questioned. The country's imagination of itself, of migration, and of belonging must finally escape its prison in the New Jerusalem.

# Timeline of Immigration History[a]

| | |
|---|---|
| 1350–51 | Under Edward III, those born to English parents outside of England can inherit English citizenship. |
| 1492 | Christopher Columbus makes landfall in the Bahamas. |
| 1607 | The English settlement Jamestown is founded in Virginia. |
| 1610 | Under James I, a foreigner can naturalize as English by the "mere Grace and Favour" of the king, but this is limited to Protestant Anglicans. |
| 1698–99 | Those born in the "King's Dominion" can inherit from alien parents or ancestors. |
| 1700 | The Massachusetts Bay Colony passes a law barring the "infirm" from entering. |
| 1709 | The Foreign Protestants Naturalization Act requires foreign (for example, German) Protestants to swear an oath and take the Lord's Supper to naturalize as English citizens. |
| 1712 | The Foreign Protestants Naturalization Act is repealed. |
| 1740 | The Plantation Act permits Protestant aliens to become "his Majesty's natural-born subjects of this Kingdom" after seven years' residency in the American colonies. |
| 1776 | Founding of the United States of America. |

1790      The Naturalization Act permits any "free white person" who has resided for two or more years in the United States to naturalize.

1795      The Naturalization Act extends the residency requirement for naturalization to five years.

1798      The Alien and Sedition Acts give the president the authority to imprison and deport noncitizens during wartime. Mandatory residency for naturalization is extended to fourteen years.

1802      The Naturalization Law lowers mandatory residency again to five years.

1830      Indian Removal Act gives the president authority to grant lands west of the Mississippi River to Native peoples living east of it; Native peoples are incentivized and coerced into leaving their homelands.

                 The Treaty of Dancing Rabbit Creek, the first Indian removal treaty, allows Choctaw who wish to stay on their land in modern Mississippi the ability to naturalize after five years. The rest relocate to Oklahoma.

1840s      California gold rush attracts immigrants to California, including Chinese immigrants.

1845–52      The Great Famine of Ireland causes mass migration of Irish to the United States.

1846–48      U.S. War with Mexico (also known as the Mexican-American War).

1848      The Treaty of Guadalupe Hidalgo ratifies the cession of Mexico's northern territories to the United States; Mexicans living on ceded land who wish to remain may naturalize as U.S. citizens or relocate to Mexico.

1854      First documented identification of Chinese with pestilence.

1855      New York's Emigration Landing Depot opens at Castle Garden.

                 Congress adopts the principle of derivative citizenship: a woman's citizenship status is determined by that of her husband or father; a woman marrying a U.S. citizen gains citizenship.

1857     The Supreme Court decision in *Dred Scott v. Sanford* rules that people of African descent cannot be citizens.

1865     The Thirteenth Amendment abolishes slavery.

1868     The Fourteenth Amendment establishes the principle of birthright citizenship, nullifying the Supreme Court decision in *Dred Scott v. Sanford.*

        The Burlingame Treaty eases U.S.-China relations, lifting restrictions on immigration from China.

1869     Completion of the transcontinental railroad, built in large part by Chinese laborers.

1870     The Fifteenth Amendment forbids the states to limit citizenship "on account of race, color, or previous condition of servitude."

        The Naturalization Act permits people born in Africa or of African descent to naturalize, but excludes those of Chinese descent.

1875     The Page Act effectively prohibits Chinese women from entering the United States.

1880     Pierton Dooner publishes *Last Days of the Republic*, possibly the first "Yellow Peril" novel.

1882     Chinese Exclusion Act bans the immigration of Chinese laborers.

1884     Amendments to the Exclusion Act of 1882 deny entry to Chinese from any place of origin (not just China), with the exception of teachers, students, diplomats, and merchants.

1888     The Scott Act prohibits resident Chinese laborers from returning to the United States, canceling their certificates for reentry.

1891     The Immigration Act establishes the Office of the Superintendent of Immigration within the Treasury Department, marking the creation of federal immigration inspection.

1892    The Geary Act enhances the Chinese Exclusion Act by requiring all Chinese laborers in the United States to carry a resident permit, the first such federal requirement of documentation.

Ellis Island opens as an immigrant-processing station.

1893    The National Quarantine Act prohibits foreign vessels departing from ports deemed infected to enter U.S. seaports and maritime waters.

1895    The Office of the Superintendent of Immigration becomes the Bureau of Immigration, which is subsequently moved to the Department of Commerce and Labor in 1903.

1897    *In re Ricardo Rodríguez*: a civil rights case in which the federal district court in Texas affirms the citizenship of Mexicans, but notes that Mexicans are not white by "scientific classification."

1898    *United States v. Wong Kim Ark*: the Supreme Court affirms birthright citizenship regardless of race.

1898–1902    The Philippine-American War.

1903    U.S. Public Health Service defines Class A diseases as preventing immigrant entry and Class B as marking an immigrant "likely to become a public charge."

1904    The Geary Act is made permanent.

1906    The Naturalization Act requires immigrants to learn English to qualify for naturalization.

1907    The Gentleman's Agreement between Japan and the United States results in the curtailment of immigration from Japan, while allowing Japanese family migration.

The Expatriation Act determines that women lose citizenship when marrying noncitizens.

1910    Angel Island Immigration Station opens; health inspection measures include the bacteriological examination of Asian immigrants' feces.

1912   The Public Health Service is created from the reorganization of the Marine Hospital Service.

1913   The California Alien Land Law prohibits "aliens ineligible for citizenship" from owning farmland in order to discourage Japanese immigration.

1917   The Immigration Act, also called the Asiatic Barred Zone Act, bans immigration from much of Asia and the Pacific islands (excepting Japan and the Philippines) and bans illiterate immigrants from entry.

1921   The Emergency Quota Act, subsequently known as the National Origins Formula, introduces the use of quotas to set numerical limits on immigration.

1922   *Takao Ozawa v. United States:* the Supreme Court finds Takao Ozawa, who was born in Japan, ineligible for naturalization, which, the Court argues, was open only to "free white persons" under all naturalization acts from 1790 to 1906 and, since 1870, persons of African origin or descent. The Court finds Ozawa not white, despite his skin color, because he is not "Caucasian."

1923   *United States v. Bhagat Thind Singh:* the Supreme Court finds Bhagat Thind Singh, who was born in India and who had served in the U.S. Army, ineligible for naturalization. The court rules that while Thind might be scientifically categorized as "Caucasian," he is not Caucasian in the "popular understanding" of that term.

1924   The Immigration Act, also known as the Johnson-Reed Act, bans immigration from Asia and numerically caps immigration based on the National Origins Formula, which favored immigration from the British Isles and western Europe.

    The Labor Appropriations Act establishes the U.S. Border Patrol in the Immigration Bureau, housed in the Department of Labor.

1928   U.S. State Department instructs its consular offices in Mexico to reduce the number of visas they issue.

1929     The Undesirable Aliens Act criminalizes unauthorized entry into the United States.

1930s     Over 400,000 Mexicans, including Mexican American citizens, are forcibly deported or intimidated into repatriating.

1933     The Bureaus of Immigration and Naturalization become the Immigration and Naturalization Service (INS), which is moved in 1940 from the Department of Labor to the Department of Justice.

1940     The Nationality Act extends citizenship "only to white persons, persons of African nativity or descent, and descendants of races indigenous to the Western Hemisphere."

Angel Island detention center closes.

1942     The Bracero Program begins, regulating the immigration of migrant laborers from Mexico.

1943     The Chinese Exclusion Repeal Act, also known as the Magnuson Act, allows limited immigration from China for the first time since 1882.

1945     The first real barriers are erected on the U.S.-Mexico border.

1946     The Rescission Act rescinds military benefits to Filipino veterans who fought for the United States in World War II.

1952     The Immigration and Nationality Act, or the McCarran-Walter Act, upholds the national origins quotas system. It also rescinds all restrictions on Asian immigrations and naturalization. However, it allows only 100 visas per year per Asian nation, based on race (that is, nation of ancestry) and not nationality.

1954     Operation Wetback is launched by the U.S. Immigration and Naturalization Services with the goal of capturing and deporting 1 million undocumented Mexican workers.

Ellis Island closes as an immigrant-processing station.

1964     The Bracero Program ends.

1965    The Immigration and Nationality Act abolishes the National Origins Formula, relaxing restrictions on immigration from eastern and southern Europe and Asia. A cap of 170,000 immigrants, and no more than 20,000 from each country, is set for the Eastern Hemisphere, effective in 1968; a cap of 120,000 is set for the Western Hemisphere.

1976    A cap on immigration from the Western Hemisphere nations is set at 20,000 per country.

1989    President Ronald Reagan delivers his "Farewell Address to the Nation," invoking the "shining city on a hill."

1994    The North American Free Trade Agreement (NAFTA) is ratified, leading to a significant rise in undocumented migrant workers from Mexico.

1996    The Illegal Immigration Reform and Immigrant Responsibility Act imposes harsh penalties on noncitizens who are undocumented or in violation of their visas, extending to deportation.

2001    The Patriot Act, passed in the wake of 9/11, authorizes the indefinite detention of immigrants without trial.

2002    The Homeland Security Act is passed, creating the Department of Homeland Security and the position of the secretary of Homeland Security.

2003    Dissolution of the INS and creation of Customs and Border Protection (CBP), Immigration and Customs Enforcement (ICE), and U.S. Citizenship and Immigration Services under the Department of Homeland Security.

2005    The Real ID Act imposes a heavier burden of proof on asylum seekers, waives laws that impede the construction of a border fence in the San Diego area, and expands grounds for the inadmissibility and deportation of immigrants.

2006    The Secure Fence Act authorizes the construction of 700 miles of fencing along the U.S.-Mexico border.

2010    Arizona passes state law SB 1070, requiring law enforcement to check citizenship or immigration papers based on "reasonable suspicion."

2012     The Deferred Action for Childhood Arrivals (DACA) program is created to allow undocumented immigrants brought as children to defer deportation and obtain work permits.

2017     President Donald Trump imposes a self-styled "Muslim Ban" in a series of executive acts, banning travel from majority-Muslim countries; Trump also rescinds the planned expansion of DACA.

2018     The Trump administration adopts a "zero tolerance" policy of family separation to deter illegal immigration; over 5,500 children are separated from their parents at the U.S.-Mexico border.

Construction of new barriers, authorized by executive order in 2017, begins on the U.S.-Mexico border.

2019     The U.S.-Mexico-Canada Agreement replaces NAFTA, creating a free-trade zone among the signatories.

2020     "Title 42," referring to the section of U.S. Code that authorizes the expulsion of immigrants on account of communicable disease, is utilized by the Trump administration to prevent the entry of migrants during the COVID-19 pandemic.

2021–22     President Joe Biden halts construction of the border wall in 2021, but resumes construction at four busy corridors in Arizona in 2022.

2023     Florida governor Ron DeSantis signs SB 1718 into law on May 10, enacting penalties for employing "illegal aliens" and requiring hospitals to report expenses of care for "illegal aliens." An exodus of migrant workers leaves Florida.

The expulsion policy under Title 42 is repealed.

---

a. This is not a comprehensive timeline of immigration and naturalization events and policies. It instead lists the events that are most closely related to the happenings, phenomena, and issues discussed in this book. For a more comprehensive timeline up to 2019, see Immigration and Ethnic History Society, "Timeline," *Immigration History*, 2019, https://immigrationhistory.org/timeline/.

# *Structural Outline of the Book of Revelation*

Prologue and Greeting (1:1–8)

   I. Vision of the Son of Man (1:9–20)

      A. Letter to the Seven Churches

         1. Ephesus (2:1–7)

         2. Smyrna (2:8–11)

         3. Pergamum (2:12–17)

         4. Thyatira (2:18–29)

         5. Sardis (3:1–6)

         6. Philadelphia (3:7–13)

         7. Laodicea (3:14–22)

  II. Vision of the Throne Room (4–5)

      A. Opening of the Seven Seals

         1. The White Horse and the Conqueror (6:1–2)

         2. The Red Horse and the Warrior (6:3–4)

         3. The Black Horse and the Rider with the Scales (6:5–6)

         4. The Pale Green Horse and the Rider Death, with Hades (6:7–8)

         5. The Righteous Slaughtered Are Robed (6:9–11)

         6. An Earthquake and Darkness (6:12–17)

         7. Silence in Heaven (8:1–2)

III. Vision of the 144,000 of Israel (7)

    A. Blowing of the Seven Trumpets

        1. Hail and Fire, the Earth Burns (8:7)

        2. A Mountain Is Thrown in the Sea, the Sea Becomes Blood (8:8–9)

        3. A Great Star Falls, the Waters Are Poisoned (8:10–11)

        4. The Sun Is Stricken, Darkness Falls (8:12)

        5. A Plague of Locusts (9:1–12)

        6. War upon the Earth (9:13–21)

        7. The Praise of God in the Temple of Heaven (11:15–19)

IV. Vision of Slaughter in Jerusalem and the Two Witnesses

    A. Seven Times the Seer Sees

        1. The Woman Clothed with the Sun and War in Heaven (12:1–18)

        2. The Beast of the Sea (13:1–10)

        3. The Beast out of the Earth (13:11–18)

        4. The Lamb on Mount Zion (14:1–5)

        5. The Angels Flying in Heaven (14:6–13)

        6. The Son of Man on a Cloud and the Winepress of God (14:14–20)

        7. The Seven Angels with Seven Plagues

V. Vision of the Sea of Glass (15)

    A. Pouring out of the Seven Bowls of God's Wrath

        1. Foul and Painful Sores (16:2)

        2. Sea Becomes Blood (16:3)

        3. Rivers and Springs Become Blood (16:4–6)

        4. Sun Scorches (16:8–9)

        5. Kingdom of the Beast Plunged into Darkness (16:10–11)

        6. Euphrates Dries up, Demonic Spirits Assemble at Harmagedon (16:12–16)

        7. A Violent Earthquake, the Great City Splits into Three (16:17–21)

VI. Vision of the Whore of Babylon (17–18)

    A. Seven Times the Seer Sees

        1. The White Horse Ridden by the Word of God (19:11–16)

        2. Angel Standing in the Sun (19:17–18)

## Introduction

Epigraph 1: Katharine Lee Bates, "America," *Congregationalist*, July 4, 1895, 17. This is the original poem, later set to music and popularized, with amended lyrics. Epigraph 2: Wong Chin Foo, "Why Am I a Heathen?" *North American Review* 145.369 (1887): 171.

1. All biblical quotations are from the New Revised Standard Version translation unless otherwise noted.

2. See, for example, Roberto Mata, "The Deportation of Juan: Migration Rhetoric as Decolonial Strategy in Revelation," *Open Theology* 7 (2021): 654–69; Roberto Mata, "Border Crossing into the Promised Land: The Eschatological Migration of God's People in Revelation 2:1–3:22," in *Latinxs, the Bible, and Migration*, ed. Efraín Agosto and Jacqueline M. Hidalgo, Bible and Cultural Studies (Cham: Palgrave Macmillan, 2018), 171–90. Related are Jacqueline M. Hidalgo, *Revelation in Aztlán: Scriptures, Utopias, and the Chicano Movement*, Bible and Cultural Studies (Cham: Palgrave Macmillan, 2016); and David A. Sánchez, *From Patmos to the Barrio: Subverting Imperial Myths* (Minneapolis: Fortress, 2008).

3. Brandon C. Martinez, Joshua C. Tom, and Joseph O. Baker, "Flowing across with Demonic Hate: Belief in Supernatural Evil and Support for Stricter Immigration Policy," *Journal for the Scientific Study of Religion* 61.2 (2022): 409–10.

4. See Natalia Molina, "Understanding Race as a Relational Concept," *Modern American History* 1 (2018): 101–5.

5. Paul Spickard, *Almost All Aliens: Immigration, Race, and Colonialism in American History and Identity* (New York: Routledge, 2007), 25.

## Chapter 1. America the New Jerusalem

Epigraph: "Quadruplex sensus Sacre Scripture aperte insinuatur in hac dictione Ierusalem. Hystorice enim significat, civitatem illam terrestrem ad quam peregrini petunt. Allegorice significat Ecclesiam militantem. Tropologice significat quamlibet fidelem animam. Anagogice significat celestem Ierusalem, sive patriam, vel regnum celorum." Primary text and translation from Christopher Columbus, *The*

*"Libro de las profecías" of Christopher Columbus,* ed. and trans. Delno C. West and August Kling (Gainesville: University Press of Florida, 1991), 100–101. This is a quotation of Guillaume Durand's *Rationale Divinorum Officiorum* 1.12, and this excerpt is collected by Columbus in his "notebook" of prophecies.

1. See David Woodward, "Medieval *Mappaemundi*," in *The History of Cartography,* ed. J. Brian Harley and David Woodward (Chicago: University of Chicago Press, 1987), 341: "The strengthening of the idea of Jerusalem as the spiritual center, a natural outcome of the Crusades, may have been responsible for the noticeable shift in the structure of mappaemundi from 1100 to 1300, toward centering maps on Jerusalem." See also John Kirtland Wright, *The Geographical Lore of the Time of the Crusades: A Study in the History of Medieval Science and Tradition in Western Europe* (New York: American Geographical Society, 1927), 259–60. While other types of maps, such as portolan (navigational) and topographical maps, were certainly in use during Columbus's time, symbolic T-O maps were also important in that time period for understanding and *interpreting* the world, with T-O maps accounting for over 50 percent of the extant mappaeumundi from the fifteenth century (around 330 maps). See Woodward, "Medieval *Mappaemundi*," 286–370, especially fig. 18.8 and 18.9 on 298.

2. The other points of the compass here are *Arthos* [*sic*] for *Arctos* (north) to the left, *Mesembria* (south) to the right, and *Disis* (Greek: δύσις, west, "sunset") at the bottom. The place name on the lower left-hand side is *Anglia* (England).

3. Jonathan T. Lanman, "The Religious Symbolism of the T in T-O Maps," *Cartographica* 18.4 (1981): 18–22. See also Woodward, "Medieval *Mappaemundi*," 334.

4. This is categorizable as an Orosian-Isidoran map as it uses elements based on both Orosius's *Historiae adversus paganos* and Isidore of Seville's *Etymologiae.* See Woodward, "Medieval *Mappaemundi*," 347–348. See also Gary Pischke, "The Ebstorf Map: Tradition and Contents of a Medieval Picture of the World," *History of Geo- and Space Sciences* 5 (2014): 155–61.

5. Woodward, "Medieval *Mappaemundi*," 340, 340–341.

6. For evidence that Columbus referred to T-O maps, see Paolo Revelli, *Cristoforo Colombo e la scuola cartografica genovese* (Genova: Consiglio Nazionale delle Richerche, 1937), 226, cited in Margarita Zamora, *Reading Columbus* (Berkeley: University of California Press, 1993), 115; quotation from Zamora, *Reading Columbus,* 115.

7. See John Leddy Phelan, "The Apocalypse in the Age of Discovery," in *The Millennial Kingdom of the Franciscans in the New World,* 2nd ed. (Berkeley: University of California Press, 1970), 17–28; Abbas Hamdani, "Columbus and the Recovery of Jerusalem," *Journal of the American Oriental Society* 99.1 (1979): 39–48; and Carol Delaney, "Columbus's Ultimate Goal: Jerusalem," *Comparative Studies in Society and History* 48.2 (2006): 260–92.

8. Columbus, *The "Libro de las profecías,"* 109, 101; emphasis added.

9. Columbus, *The "Libro de las profecías,"* 111. On this claim about Joachimite prediction, see Phelan, "Apocalypse in the Age of Discovery," 22: "It is difficult to determine with any satisfactory degree of exactitude what pseudo-Joachimite work, if
   any, Columbus had in mind when he twice quoted that prophet to the effect that
   the man who is to rebuild the temple of Mount Sion is to come from Spain. The
   decisive fact to stress, however, is that Columbus consciously sought to surround
   himself with the magic aura that over the centuries had enveloped the name of
   Joachim by proclaiming himself the Joachimite Messiah."

10. Christopher Columbus [Cristóbal Colón], letter to Doña Juana de la Torre, in
    Christopher Columbus, *Textos y documentos completos : Relaciones de viajes, cartas
    y memorials,* ed. Consuelo Varela (Madrid: Alianza, 1982), quoted and translated in
    Zamora, *Reading Columbus,* 141.

11. On documentary evidence, West and Kling state in their introduction to Colum-
    bus, *The "Libro de las profecías,"* 86: "Among the handwritten notes, or postilles, on
    the margins and blank pages of one of the earliest volumes in the personal library
    of Christopher Columbus, we have found clear evidence of an earlier, smaller ver-
    sion of the *Libro de las profecías* bearing the date 1481. Columbus was at that time
    thirty years old, and both his use of the Bible and his plan for a voyage of discovery
    are already discernible in the notes. The volume bearing these notes, preserved
    today in the Biblioteca Colombina at Seville, was printed in Venice in 1477. It is his
    copy of Aeneas Sylvius Piccolomini (Pope Pius II), *Historia rerum ubique gestarum.*
    Four postilles written in the clear hand of Columbus on the blank pages at the end
    of Piccolomini's treatise form the essence of the later *Libro de las profecías.*" Quota-
    tion from Christopher Columbus, *The "Diario" of Christopher Columbus's First
    Voyage to America, 1492–1493,* abstracted by Fray Bartolomé de las Casas, trans. and
    ed. Oliver Dunn and James E. Kelley Jr. (Norman: University of Oklahoma Press,
    1989), entry for Wednesday, December 26, 1492, folio 48v, 291.

12. Columbus, *Diario,* entry for Wednesday, November 14, folio 24v, 153–55.

13. Zamora, *Reading Columbus,* 143, eloquently states: "The Indies is not only on the
    figurative way to Jerusalem, it is also in the vicinity of Paradise. Such a geography
    makes sense only in the context of a paradigmatic cartographic discourse in which
    spatiotemporal coordinates are determined ideologically rather than empirically.
    Columbus describes the voyage's trajectory from west (Spain) to far east (the pre-
    sumed Asiatic mainland) as an ascent up the slope of a pear-shaped southern hemi-
    sphere toward a Terrestrial Paradise, situated at the very top, on the spot closest to
    heaven."

14. See Phelan, *Millennial Kingdom of the Franciscans;* also Leisa Kauffman, "The
    Indian Church and the Age of the Spirit: Joachimist Millennialism and Fray Tori-
    bio de Motolinía's *Historia de los indios de la Nueva España," Acontracorriente:
    Una revista de estudios latinoamericanos* 7.2 (2010): 119–36, esp. 123, summarizing
    the work of Motolinía (one of the Twelve Apostles of Mexico) thus: "The three-part

structure of *Historia de los indios de la Nueva España* can be seen as a rough super-imposition of Joachim's three stages of history onto Mexican reality. The Age of God or the Old Testament (the time of Israelite's [*sic*] darkness and wandering, their idolatry) corresponds to the description of Aztec religious practices in Treatise One, the vision of Mexico as a world of darkness and deception in servitude to the 'Prince of Darkness.' The Age of Christ or the New Testament (salvation of mankind through the coming of a Messiah—Jesus) corresponds to the descriptions of the Franciscans' establishment of the sacraments of baptism, marriage, and penitence in Treatise Two. Finally, the Age of the Spirit, the millennial reign of the saints, corresponds to the extolling of the Mexican landscape and the faithful Indian Christians in Treatise Three."

15. On the subsiding of "apocalyptic optimism," see Phelan, *Millennial Kingdom of the Franciscans*, 107–9. On the Peruvian friars, see Lucero de Vivanco-Roca Rey, "Un profeta criollo: Francisco de la Cruz y la Declaración del Apocalipsi," *Persona y sociedad* 20.2 (2006): 25–40; Antonio Eguiluz, "Father Gonzalo Tenorio, O.F.M., and His Providentialist Eschatological Theories on the Spanish Indies," *Americas* 16.4 (1960): 329–56; Ana de Zaballa Beascoechea, "La discusión conceptual sobre el milenarismo y mesianismo en Latinoamérica," *Anuario de historia de la Iglesia* 10 (2001): 353–62. Francisco de la Cruz held extreme views and was executed as a heretic. Gonzalo Tenorio avoided such a fate—but his massive sixteen-volume work was not published in his time. See Phelan, *Millennial Kingdom of the Franciscans*, 122–25.

16. Quotation from Phelan, *Millennial Kingdom of the Franciscans*, 24: "Only after the equation 'the New World equals the end of the world' is understood can some new light be thrown on the origins of one of the most celebrated New World myths; namely, that the Indians were the descendants of the ten lost tribes of Israel." The lost tribes are just one aspect of the many apocalyptic beliefs surrounding the New World, and later, America and the United States, that should be understood in light of this equation.

17. Allan Appel, "At Rapture Runway, Pair Passed Over," *New Haven Independent*, May 21, 2011, https://www.newhavenindependent.org/index.php/article/city_misses_out_in_race_for/. Note that Revelation does not describe the "rapture" of the faithful, which actually comes from 1 Thessalonians 4:16–17. The reporter conflates the 144,000 of Revelation with the rapture of 1 Thessalonians.

18. In private correspondence with Nicholas F. Bellantoni, emeritus Connecticut state archaeologist, May 2, 2022; Eric D. Lehman, Connecticut historian, January 28, 2020; Edward Surato, the Whitney Library, New Haven Museum, March 17, 2020; and in conversation with Michelle Reynard Georgevich, church historian of the Center Church on the Green, April 5, 2022. See also Eric D. Lehman, *Connecticut Town Greens: History of the State's Centers* (Guilford, CT: Globe Pequot, 2015), xii: "The New Haven Green is the most impressive example [of town greens serving as

cemeteries]; in 1638 it was built to hold the exact number of people the Puritan settlers thought would ascend to heaven during the rapture: 144,000." No source is cited.

19. On the discovery of remains, see Thomas Macmillan and Melissa Bailey, "Skeletal Remains Found in Upended Tree; the Death Investigator Exhumes Skull," *New Haven Independent,* October 30, 2012, https://www.newhavenindependent.org/index.php/article/skeleton_found_in_upended_tree_on_green/#.UJA88p1w2y4.twitter. Estimations of the number of bodies buried in the New Haven Green range from three thousand to more than five thousand: Henry Taylor Blake, *Chronicles of the New Haven Green from 1638 to 1862* (New Haven: Tuttle, Morehouse & Taylor, 1898), 255; and "The Crypt," *Center Church on the Green,* https://www.centerchurchonthegreen.org/history/crypt/, accessed May 5, 2022. Quotation from Dan Corcoran, "Hidden in Plain Sight: New Haven's Secret Crypt," *NBC Connecticut,* January 30, 2022, https://www.nbcconnecticut.com/investigations/hidden-in-plain-sight/hidden-in-plain-sight-new-havens-secret-crypt/2704643/, at 3:12 with historian Harold Peck.

20. John Archer, "Puritan Town Planning in New Haven," *Journal of the Society of Architectural Historians* 34.2 (1975): 140.

21. On measurements, see Norris C. Andrews, "Davenport-Eaton and 52 Rods," *Journal of the New Haven Colony History Society* 33.1 (1986): 3–14; and Archer, "Puritan Town Planning," 142. This is not the standard cubit but the long or "royal" cubit, as explicitly stated in Ezekiel 40:5; see Walther Zimmerli, *Ezekiel 2: A Commentary on the Book of the Prophet Ezekiel, Chapters 25–48,* trans. James D. Martin, ed. Paul D. Hanson with Leonard Jay Greenspoon, Hermeneia (Philadelphia: Fortress, 1983), 349. For utopian schemas, see Johann Valentin Andreä, *Christianopolis: An Ideal State of the Seventeenth Century,* trans. Felix Emil Held (New York: Oxford University Press, 1916); originally published as *Reipublicae Christianopolitanae descriptio* (Strasbourg: Zetzner, 1619); John Drury, "An Epistolical Discourse," in *Clavis Apocalyptica: A Prophetical Key by Which the Great Mysteries in the Revellation of St. John and the Prophet Daniel Are Opened,* trans. Samuel Hartlib (London: William Du-Gard, 1651), 37f. For the ties between these men, along with Johann Amos Comenius (the Protestant Czech theologian) and Davenport, see Archer, "Puritan Town Planning," 144–45. Castalion's visual representation of Ezekiel's temple can be found in the English translation of Iacopo Aconcio [Iacobus Acontius], *Satan's Stratagems; or, The Devil's Cabinet Councel Discovered,* trans. John Goodwin with John Drury (London: J. Macock, 1648); Cornelius à Lapide, *Commentaria in quatuor Prophetas Maiores* (Antwerp: Martin Nuyts, 1634); Juan Bautista Villalpando [Ioannes Baptista Villalpandus] and Jerome Prado [Hieronymus Pradus], *In Ezechielem explanationes et apparatus urbis ac Templi Hierosolimitani,* 3 vols. (Rome: Carolus Vulliettus, 1596–1604). See also Archer, "Puritan Town Planning," 147–49; and Sergey R. Kravtsov, "Juan Bautista

Villalpando and Sacred Architecture in the Seventeenth Century," *Journal of the Society of Architectural Historians* 64.3 (2005): 312–39.

22. See Erik Vogt, "A New Heaven and a New Earth: The Origin and Meaning of the Nine-Square Plan," in *Yale in New Haven: Architecture and Urbanism*, ed. Vincent Scully, Catherin Lynn, Erik Vogt, and Paul Goldberger (New Haven: Yale University Press, 2004), 37–52, esp. 44–49.

23. John Davenport, *The Power of the Congregational Churches Asserted and Vindicated* (London: n.p., 1672 [written ca. 1648]), 57.

24. On Puritan colonists' intention to merge state and church governance, see Michael P. Winship, *Godly Republicanism: Puritans, Pilgrims, and a City on a Hill* (Cambridge, MA: Harvard University Press, 2012); on Davenport's hopes for New Haven and surrounding regions specifically, see Francis J. Bremer, *Building a New Jerusalem: John Davenport, a Puritan in Three Worlds* (New Haven: Yale University Press, 2012), 181–219; these quotations are from John Cotton, recorded by his grandson: Cotton Mather, *Magnalia Christi Americana; or, The Ecclesiastical History of New-England from Its First Planting in the Year 1620 unto the Year of Our Lord, 1698* (London: Thomas Parkhurst, 1702), book 3.53, 3.55.

25. On naming New Haven, see Blake, *Chronicles of the New Haven Green*, 46: "The community tired its jaws and rasped its vocal organs over these conflicting aboriginal cognomens until September 1, 1640, when a town meeting, in evident desperation, cut the gordian knot by curtly voting, 'This town now called New Haven.' None of the early settlers, so far as known, came from New Haven in England and the reason for selecting this name is unexplained. A contemporary document informs us that 'London' was talked of and was rejected 'only least it should seem too high.' This cautious self-restraint suggests that possibly 'New Heaven' may have been under consideration and that it was modified into 'New Haven' from motives of modest forbearance." Colonizer John Smith of the Virginia Company of London named the region stretching from current-day Connecticut to Maine "New England" in 1616: John Smith, *A Description of New England; or, The Observations, and Discoveries, of Captain John Smith (Admirall of That Country) in the North of America in the Year of Our Lord 1614* (London: Humfrey Lownes for Robert Clerke, 1616). At the time, the name "New England" was not charged with any overtly apocalyptic themes, but it nevertheless came to fit conceptions of a new heaven and new earth. On longing for the past and the future, see Mircea Eliade, "Paradise and Utopia: Mythical Geography and Eschatology," in *Utopias and Utopian Thought*, ed. Frank E. Manuel (Boston: Houghton Mifflin, 1966), 268: "*New* England, *New* York, *New* Haven—all these names express not only nostalgia for the native land left behind, but above all the hope that in these lands and these new cities life will know new dimensions. And not only life: everything in this continent that was considered an earthly paradise must be greater, more beautiful, stronger."

26. On the memory of the earthly Jerusalem, see Dereck Daschke, *City of Ruins: Mourning the Destruction of Jerusalem through Jewish Apocalypse*, Biblical Interpretation Series 99 (Leiden: Brill, 2010). For other ancient mentions of the New Jerusalem, see, for example, Ezekiel 40–48; Isaiah 65:16–19; 1 Enoch 24–26, 28–36, 90:28–29; 2 Baruch 4:2–7, 32:1–4. On the many meanings of the New Jerusalem, see Pilchan Lee, *The New Jerusalem in the Book of Revelation: A Study of Revelation 21–22 in Light of Its Background in Jewish Tradition* (Mohr Siebeck: Tübingen, 2001); Jan A. du Rand, "The New Jerusalem as Pinnacle of Salvation: Text (Rev 21:1–22:5) and Intertext," *Neotestamentica* 38.2 (2004): 275–302; and Michael J. Chan, "Apocalyptic Innovations: A Meditation on the New Jerusalem," *Word & World* 41.4 (2021): 315–24.

27. On Puritan discourse: it should be noted that "dominant Puritan discourse" generally means the words left to us by religious and political leaders and not necessarily the beliefs and hopes of their congregants, townspeople, and fellow immigrants. For an exploration of lesser known perspectives of travelers to America at the time, see David Cressy, *Coming Over: Migration and Communication between England and New England in the Seventeenth Century* (Cambridge: Cambridge University Press, 1987); for a deconstruction of the persistent narrative that the Puritans held fully consistent apocalyptic beliefs cojoined with American exceptionalism and a "journey into the wilderness," see Sarah Rivett and Abram Van Engen, "Postexceptionalist Puritanism," *American Literature* 90.4 (2018); and more on this below. On the Puritan belief that Jews would convert to Christianity at the eschaton and have Israel returned to them, see Reiner Smolinski, "Israel Redivivus: The Eschatological Limits of Puritan Typology in New England," *New England Quarterly* 63.3 (1990): 357–95, esp. 361–67. Quotation from Increase Mather, "A Discourse concerning the Glorious State of the Church on Earth under the New Jerusalem," in *Increase Mather's 'New Jerusalem': Millennialism in Late Seventeenth Century New England*, ed. Mason I. Lowance Jr. and David Watters (Worcester, MA: American Antiquarian Society, 1978), 395–97; emphasis in original, quoted in Smolinski, "Israel Redivivus," 375; on this dual New Jerusalem see also Smolinski, "Israel Redivivus," 376–77.

28. On Puritan understanding of New England and the New Jerusalem, I disagree in part with Smolinski, "Israel Redivivus," 389, who argues against American historians Perry Miller, Sacvan Bercovitch, et al. who "trace the origin of the American sense of mission and manifest destiny to the typological identification of New England as the New Jerusalem" and have "misunderstood the Puritan position on such crucial issues as the restoration of the Jews, America's millennial role, and the function and location of the New Jerusalem." While nuance is needed, I also note the important point made by Christopher J. Richmann, "America as New Jerusalem," *Word & World* 40.2 (2020): 152: "But theological movements are rarely fully consistent, and 'doctrine' should not necessarily trump rhetoric." More will be said

below about this and the trend of the last thirty years to deconstruct American exceptionalism.

29. John Davenport, "Epistle to the Reader," preface to Increase Mather, *Israel's Salvation Explained and Applyed* (London: n.p., 1669). It is important to underline Davenport's phrase "as is attainable," that is, neither he nor any other Puritan leader or believer necessarily thought perfection was *possible*, but that striving for such a goal was. See Joy Gilsdorf, *Puritan Apocalypse: New England Eschatology in the Seventeenth Century* (New York: Garland, 1989), 90–91: "That regenerate men could be fallible, New Englanders would have been the first to admit. There would be no time before the end when the church upon earth would be so pure, that not a hypocrite would be in it. Yet this inability to attain perfection was no warrant for including within the Kingdom men patently unregenerate." This adds nuance to wholesale rejections of Perry Miller's "city on a hill" thesis, such as found in Winship, *Godly Republicanism*, 233: "One of the most durable fictions built on Perry Miller's 'city on a hill' argument was that the immigrants to Massachusetts anticipated that they would build the millennial New Jerusalem themselves. Puritans did not think like that; even at their most active, they retained a core of anxious fatalism, for they knew that God disposed as he wished." Regardless of generalizations about how "Puritans think," the discourse left to us speaks of aspirations of church purity and perfection, with the admission that men always fall short.

30. John Cotton, *The Churches Resurrection; or, The Opening of the Fifth and Sixth Verses of the 20th Chap. of the Revelation* (London: R.O. & G.D. for Henry Overton, 1642), 9. See also Gilsdorf, *Puritan Apocalypse*, 65–71.

31. Cotton Mather, *Theopolis Americana: An Essay on the Golden Street of the Holy City*, ed. Reiner Smolinski (Boston: B. Green, 1710), 9–10, Electronic Texts in American Studies 29 (n.d.), https://digitalcommons.unl.edu/etas/29/; emphasis in the original for all quotations from this text.

32. Cotton Mather, *Theopolis Americana*, 28, 29.

33. Cotton Mather, *Theopolis Americana*, 30–31. The passage Mather alludes to is Aelian, *Varia Historia* 3.18, although Aelian writes of *two* islands, actually: Machimos ("Valorous") and Eusebes ("Pious").

34. See James P. Byrd, " 'The Fierceness and Wrath of the Almighty God': Revelation in the Revolution," in *Sacred Scripture, Sacred War: The Bible and the American Revolution* (Oxford: Oxford University Press, 2013), 143–63. Byrd demonstrates that while Revelation was not among the most quoted biblical books during the American Revolution, it still provided rhetorically effective imagery and language to stir up morale, such as the call to martyrdom in the opening seven letters to seven churches (Rev 2–3), the woman fleeing to the wilderness from the dragon (Rev 12), and the militant Christ (Rev 19:11–21). "Through these apocalyptic visions, including the victorious charge of a militant Christ, ministers proclaimed a bellicose Christianity that endowed patriotic sacrifice with sacred martyrdom" (163).

35. On the conflation of America with Zion, see Eran Shalev, *American Zion: The Old Testament as a Political Text from the Revolution to the Civil War* (New Haven: Yale University Press, 2013). For other strands of the New Jerusalem metaphor in American history, see Richmann, "America as New Jerusalem." Conversely, for the use of the punishments of hell in American discourse, see Kathryn Gin Lum, *Damned Nation: Hell in America from the Revolution to Reconstruction* (Oxford: Oxford University Press, 2014). On Joseph Smith, see, for example, Daniel Walker Howe, "Emergent Mormonism in Context," in *The Oxford Handbook of Mormonism*, ed. Terry L. Givens and Philip L. Barlow (New York: Oxford Academic, 2015), 24–37. For more on Julia Ward Howe's writing of "The Battle Hymn of the Republic" (1862) and its use of Revelation, see Ernest Lee Tuveson, *Redeemer Nation: The Idea of America's Millennial Role* (Chicago: University of Chicago Press, 1968), 197–202. The winepress imagery comes not only from Revelation 14:9–10, 18–20, 19:15 but also from Isaiah 63:1–6, Joel 3:13, and Lamentations 1:15.

36. Washington Gladden, "Migrations and Their Lessons: Sermon Preached in the Opera House, Sunday, by Washington Gladden of Columbus," *Ohio Archaeological Historical Society Publications* 3 (1891): 195.

37. See Abram C. Van Engen, *City on a Hill: A History of American Exceptionalism* (New Haven: Yale University Press, 2020), especially the chapters "A White History of America," "The Rise of National History," "The Spread of National Pilgrims," and "The Creation of an Exceptional New England," 88–150. The term *Pilgrims* for the people of Plymouth did not become popular until the nineteenth century, and it was not used by the people of Plymouth Colony itself—except once as a descriptor in William Bradford, *Of Plymouth Plantation, 1620–1647*, ed. Samuel Eliot Morison (New York: Knopf, 1970), 47.

38. See Van Engen, *City on a Hill*, 101–49 on the growing understanding and embrace of the Pilgrims and Puritans as the origin of American identity and character in the eighteenth century.

39. The catalyst for the political use of Winthrop begins with historian Perry Miller, who focused on the sermon and wrote of a Puritan "mission to the wilderness." John F. Kennedy was subsequently the first president to cite Winthrop's sermon. See Van Engen, *City on a Hill*, 241, 256–59. Kennedy's speech was given on January 9, 1961. For a full transcript, see John F. Kennedy Presidential Library and Museum, "Historical Speeches: City upon a Hill Speech," https://www.jfklibrary.org/learn/about-jfk/historic-speeches/the-city-upon-a-hill-speech.

40. Numbers here are based on database searches at the American Presidency Project, *Document Archive*, https://www.presidency.ucsb.edu/, accessed May 27, 2022, which shows thirty-three uses of "city on/upon a hill" by Reagan up through 1989, and ten different mentions of John Winthrop as the source of "city upon a hill." On the significance of Reagan's farewell speech, see Robert C. Rowland and John M. Jones, "Reagan's Farewell Address: Redefining the American Dream," *Rhetoric and Public Affairs*

20.4 (2017): 635–66. For a full transcript of the speech, see Ronald Reagan, "Farewell Address to the Nation," January 11, 1989, Ronald Reagan Presidential Library and Museum, https://www.reaganlibrary.gov/archives/speech/farewell-address-nation.

41. Van Engen, *City on a Hill*, 3.

42. On Reagan's alliance with evangelical leaders, see Steven P. Miller, *The Age of Evangelicalism: America's Born Again Years* (Oxford: Oxford University Press, 2014), 60–86, quoted title from 64. On Reagan's evangelical promises: during his first campaign for the presidency, Reagan famously said to the Religious Roundtable—which included speakers Jerry Falwell, Phyllis Shlafly, Tim LaHaye, and Pat Robinson—"I know this is non-partisan, so you can't endorse me, but I want you to know that I endorse you," which effectively earned the trust of conservative Christians. See William Martin, *With God on Our Side: The Rise of the Religious Right in America* (New York: Broadway Book, 1996), 214–18. On the "Year of the Bible," see Proclamation No. 5018, February 3, 1983, available at https://www.govinfo.gov/content/pkg/STATUTE-97/pdf/STATUTE-97-Pg1545.pdf.

43. See, for example, the Scripture Memory Fellowship, "About SMF," https://scripturememory.com/about-smf, accessed May 31, 2022, which was established in 1977, based on the earlier Bible Memory Association; Thru the Bible with J. Vernon McGee, "About Us," https://www.ttb.org/about/about-thru-the-bible, accessed May 31, 2022; and Back to the Bible, "About," https://www.backtothebible.org/about, accessed May 31, 2022. Church and Sunday school "sword drills" date back at least to 1927—see Susan M. Shaw, "God Speaks to Us, Too: Southern Baptist Women on Church, Home, and Society," *History of Religion* 7 (2008): 64. For description of a sword drill, see John Staper, "The Sword Drill," *Perspectives* 11.9 (1996): 24.

44. Reagan, "Farewell Address to the Nation."

45. Amos Kiewe and Davis W. Houck, *A Shining City on a Hill: Ronald Reagan's Economic Rhetoric, 1951–1989* (New York: Praeger, 1991), 216, point out that Reagan "describe[s] the shining city as an economic entity."

46. The "glory and honor" of Revelation 21:24, 26 is not only homage but also riches and wealth. These verses use Isaiah 60:3–5 and its description of Zion: "Nations shall come to your light, and kings to the brightness of your dawn. . . . The wealth of nations shall come to you." For more on the tradition of the "wealth of nations" in the Hebrew Bible and the ancient Near East, see Michael J. Chan, *The Wealth of Nations: A Tradition Historical Study*, Forschungen zum Alten Testament 93 (Mohr Siebeck: Tübingen, 2017). *Pace* Frederick J. Murphy, *Fallen Is Babylon: The Revelation to John*, New Testament in Context (Harrisburg, PA: Trinity International, 1998), 425–26; and Craig R. Koester, *Revelation: A New Translation with Introduction and Commentary*, Anchor Yale Bible (New Haven: Yale University Press, 2014), 822.

47. On end-times predictions: the best-selling decoding of Revelation's eschatology, Hal Lindsey, *The Late Great Planet Earth* (New York: Bantam Books, 1979) is

representative of this obsession; so also is the 1972 film *A Thief in the Night*, depicting the rapture and apocalyptic "tribulations" unfolding in modern-day America. See Miller, *Age of Evangelicalism*, 27–30, 64, on Reagan's interest in scriptural prophecy and association with predictions of nuclear Armageddon. For the full speech, see Reagan, "Farewell Address."

48. See Gerhard von Rad, "The City on a Hill," in *The Problem of the Hexateuch and Other Essays*, trans. E. W. Trueman Dicken (New York: McGraw-Hill, 1966), 242. Von Rad's association of Matthew 5:14 with Jerusalem, Isaianic prophecy, and Zion and the New Jerusalem is accepted by numerous subsequent interpreters of that verse. See William Barclay, *The Gospel of Matthew*, vol. 1 (Philadelphia: Westminster, 1975), 122–23; Robert H. Mounce, *Matthew, a Good News Commentary* (San Francisco: Harper & Row, 1985), 40; W. D. Davies and Dale C. Allison, *A Critical and Exegetical Commentary on the Gospel According to Matthew*, International Critical Commentary (Edinburgh: T & T Clark, 1988), 475; David E. Garland, *Reading Matthew: A Literary and Theological Commentary on the First Gospel* (New York: Crossroad, 1995), 59; Hans Dieter Betz, *Sermon on the Mount: A Commentary on the Sermon on the Mount, Including the Sermon on the Plain (Matthew 5:3–7:27 and Luke 6:20–49*, ed. Adela Yarbro Collins, Hermeneia (Minneapolis: Fortress, 1995). Strictly evangelical scholars also cited von Rad, for example John A. Kessler, "The Shaking of the Nations: An Eschatological View," *Journal of the Evangelical Theological Society* 30.2 (1987), 164, 165.

49. Reagan, "Farewell Address."

## Chapter 2. On the "Island of Immortals"

Epigraph 1: Huie Kin, *Reminiscences* (Peiping: San Yu, 1932), 24.
Epigraph 2: "Poem 23," in *Island: Poetry and History of Chinese Immigrants on Angel Island, 1910–1940*, ed. Him Mark Lai, Genny Lim, and Judy Yung (San Francisco: Hoc Doi, 1986), 60.

1. "Dead Chinamen," *Elko Independent*, January 5, 1870, 3, cited in CPPR.org, "FAQs: How Many Died Building the Central Pacific Railroad," *Central Pacific Railroad Photographic History Museum*, http://cprr.org/Museum/FAQs.html#died, accessed June 13, 2022. The museum website is run by descendants of Lewis R. Clement, an engineer and surveyor of the Central Pacific Railroad.

2. On the history of Chinese workers and the transcontinental railroad, see Gordon H. Chang, *Ghosts of Gold Mountain: The Epic Story of the Chinese Who Built the Transcontinental Railroad* (Boston: Houghton Mifflin, 2019); Gordon H. Chang and Shelly Fisher Fishkin, eds., *The Chinese and the Iron Road: Building the Transcontinental Railroad* (Stanford: Stanford University Press, 2019); Manu Karuka, *Empire's Tracks: Indigenous Nations, Chinese Workers, and the Transcontinental Railroad* (Oakland: University of California Press, 2019); David R. Roediger and

Elizabeth D. Esch, *Production of Difference: Race and the Management of Labor in U.S. History* (New York: Oxford University Press, 2012). On newspaper reports of the shipment of dead Chinese workers, see "Bones in Transit," *Sacramento Reporter*, June 30, 1870, which notes that the "accumulated bones of perhaps 1,200 Chinamen" weighing "20,000 pounds" were in the train, and observes that Chinese custom requires burial in China; "Bones of Defunct Chinamen," *Sacramento Union*, June 30, 1870, which reports "fifty defunct Chinamen . . . to be interred in Conboie's private cemetery, as have been already the bones of about one hundred others similarly deceased." Whether these reports are describing the same shipment (and, if so, whether the numbers in one or the other story are mistaken or exaggerated) or different cargo trains is unknown. Both articles are cited in response to the question "How many died building the Central Pacific Railroad?" in CPPR.org, "FAQs." CPPR states that the claim of 1,200 dead Chinese workers is highly dubious given the two conflicting reports, although it does not entertain the possibility that the accounts describe two different trains with different destinations (Conboie's cemetery in Sacramento versus China via San Francisco). On the dangers that led to the death of Chinese railroad workers, see Chang, *Ghosts of Gold Mountain*, esp. 225–26.

3. The landowner first unearthed five bodies on his property, which led to the discovery of a total of thirteen bodies on his land and a neighbor's. See Sue Fawn Chung, Fred P. Frampton, and Timothy W. Murphy, "Venerate These Bones: Chinese American Funerary Practices as Seen in Carlin, Elko County, Nevada," in *Chinese American Death Rituals: Respecting the Ancestors*, ed. Sue Fawn Chung and Priscilla Wegars (Lanham, MD: AltaMira, 2005), 107–45, on the discovery of these graves and their analysis. See also Ryan P. Harrod and John J. Crandall, "Rails Built of the Ancestors' Bones: The Bioarchaeology of the Overseas Chinese Experience," *Historical Archaeology* 49.1 (2015): 148–61, on analysis of these remains and the evidence of hard labor in rough environments.

4. The earliest-dated tombstone housed in the crypt of the Center Church on the Green belongs to "Ms. Sarah Trowbridge," who died in 1687. New Haven was "founded" in 1638. See M. Reynard Georgevitch, "Sarah (Rutherford) Trowbridge, 1641–1687," in *Tales from the Crypt: A Cata-Blog of Stones and Stories from the Basement of Center Church*, July 20, 2014, https://ctcryptkeeper.wordpress. com/2014/07/20/sarah-rutherford-trowbridge-1641–1687/. The graves of Chinese discovered in Carlin date from before 1900 through 1924, according to Chung, Frampton, and Murphy, "Venerate These Bones." On Chinese immigrants heading east after working mines in California, see ibid., 108–11.

5. The Naturalization Act of 1870, passed in Congress as H.R. 2201, extended the ability to naturalize to those of African descent, but Congress rejected any amendment that would allow those of Chinese descent to naturalize. Similarly, although birthright naturalization had existed by *jus soli* in the United States and was then codi-

fied in both the Civil Rights Act of 1868 and the Fourteenth Amendment's Citizenship Clause, the children born of Chinese immigrants in the country were not regarded as legal citizens as a matter of course. See, for example, the case *In re Look Tin Sing* (1884) of the California federal circuit court, in which American-born Look Tin Sing's citizenship had to be established in court before he could be legally readmitted in the country. It was not until *United States vs. Wong Kim Ark* (1898) that birthright citizenship was established for all born in the United States— although that has since been questioned in recent decades with regard to the children of "illegal" immigrants. Quotation from the 41st Cong., 2nd sess., *Congressional Globe* 5156, July 4, 1870. Also quoted in Martin B. Gold, *Forbidden Citizens: Chinese Exclusion and the U.S. Congress: A Legislative History* (Alexandria, VA: TheCapitol.Net, 2012), §1.13, p. 17.

6. On "Old" and "New Immigration," see Paul Spickard, *Almost All Aliens: Immigration, Race, and Colonialism in American History and Identity* (New York: Routledge, 2007), 96–98. The numbers cited in Spickard's table include England, Wales, and Scotland; after 1925 they include Northern Ireland. On belief in essential differences between immigrant groups, see, for example, Natalia Molina, *Fit to Be Citizens? Public Health and Race in Los Angeles, 1879–1939* (Berkeley: University of California Press, 2006), 49, a discussion of social Darwinism in America at the turn of the nineteenth to twentieth century and the categorization of the English as the most "fit" and the subsequent conception of "new immigrants" as unfit. Quotation from Spickard, *Almost All Aliens*, 97. For numbers of British and Chinese immigrants to the United States see Spickard, *Almost All Aliens*, 97, table 3.2, and 495, appendix B, table B.16.

7. On the transition of Chinese to other fields of work, see Donald L. Hardesty, "Archaeology and the Chinese Experience in Nevada," *South Dakota History*, Ethnic Oasis: The Chinese in the Black Hills, Special Historic Preservation Issue, 33.4 (2003): 363–79; Chang, *Ghosts of Gold Mountain*, 209–36; D. Michael Bottoms, *An Aristocracy of Color: Race and Reconstruction in California and the West: 1850–1890* (Norman: University of Oklahoma Press), 137–38; Alexander Saxton, *The Indispensable Enemy: Labor and the Anti-Chinese Movement in California* (Berkeley: University of California Press, 1995), 70–71. On the discrimination against Chinese from their first arrival in the United States, see Saxton, *The Indispensable Enemy*, 136–37; and Spickard, *Almost All Aliens*, 161. On the increase of violence with the arrival of more Chinese immigrants, see Bottoms, *An Aristocracy of Color*, 138: The Chinese population in California increased by 50 percent in the 1870s, although their number did not account for more than 10 percent of the total population.

8. *Daily California Chronicle*, April 22, 1854, 2, quoted in Chang, *Ghosts of Gold Mountain*, 44. On the labor of Black Americans who began work on the railroads and especially on their work as Pullman porters and waiters, see Alison Rose Jefferson, "The Transcontinental Railroad, African Americans and the California

Dream," *California Historical Society*, June 17, 2019, https://californiahistoricalsoci ety.org/blog/the-transcontinental-railroad-african-americans-and-the-california- dream/. Quotation from Leland Stanford, *Statement Made to the President of the United States, and Secretary of the Interior, on the Progress of Work, October 10, 1865* (Sacramento: H. S. Crocker 1865), 990, quoted in Chang, *Ghosts of Gold Mountain*, 86.

9. Quotation from the 47th Cong., 1st sess., *Congressional Record*, vol. 13.2, 2616, April 5, 1882. On the numbers of Chinese arriving in the United States during the pe- riod, see Spickard, *Almost All Aliens*, 165. On racially specific immigration laws: Black peoples were the very first racial group explicitly named and targeted in fed- eral immigration law in 1803, but this was applicable only to certain states that banned their immigration. See Gerald L. Neuman, "The Lost Century of Ameri- can Immigration Law (1776–1875)," *Columbia Law Review* 93.8 (1993): 1869ff.

10. On the Exclusion Act: while widely known as the Chinese Exclusion Act, historian Beth Lew-Williams uses the term "Chinese Restriction Act" to capture more accu- rately the phases of legislation against Chinese and Asian immigration: "Historians, with their eyes trained on what Chinese exclusion would become, have overlooked the distinction between the Restriction Period (1882–1888) and Exclusion Period (1888–1943). To understand the radicalism of Chinese exclusion and the contingent history of its rise, we must recognize the period of restriction experimentation, and contestation that preceded it." Beth Lew-Williams, *The Chinese Must Go: Vio- lence, Exclusion, and the Making of the Alien in America* (Cambridge, MA: Har- vard University Press, 2018), 8–9. On the lack of protections for Chinese already living in the United States, see R. Gregory Nokes, *Massacred for Gold: The Chinese in Hells Canyon* (Corvallis: Oregon State University Press, 2009), 76: "But al- though the Exclusion Act effectively blocked new laborers, it failed to protect the estimated 132,300 Chinese who remained. If anything, violence and mistreatment became worse."

11. On expulsions, see Lew-Williams, *The Chinese Must Go*, particularly the map "Sites of Anti-Chinese Expulsion, 1885–1886," 2, and appendix A, "Sites of Anti- Chinese Expulsions and Attempted Expulsions, 1885–1887," 247–51. On Rock Springs, see *U.S. House Report* (1885–86), 49th Cong., 1st sess., no. 2044, 28–32, excerpted in "Memorial of Chinese Laborers: Rock Springs, Wyoming (1885)," in *Chinese American Voices: From the Gold Rush to the Present*, ed. Judy Yung, Gordon Chang, and Him Mark Lai (Berkeley: University of California Press, 2006), 48–54; and Craig Storti, *Incident at Bitter Creek: The Story of the Rock Springs Massacre* (Ames: Iowa State University Press, 1991). On Hells Canyon, see Nokes, *Massacred for Gold*. On the lack of judicial convictions, see Chang, *Ghosts of Gold Mountain*, 231–32; and Lew-Williams, *The Chinese Must Go*, 91–165.

12. Amendments to the Exclusion Act of 1882 were passed in 1884 forbidding Chinese from any place of origin (not just China) from entering, except for teach-

ers, students, diplomats, merchants, and tourists. The Scott Act of 1888 kept Chinese laborers who left the United States from returning, canceling their certificates for reentry. On the beginning of immigrant documentation, see Erika Lee, *At America's Gates: Chinese Immigration during the Exclusion Era, 1882–1943* (Chapel Hill: University of North Carolina Press, 2003), 42.

13. On the committee formed to pass the repeal act in 1943 and their strategies, see Fred W. Riggs, *Pressures on Congress: A Study of the Repeal of Chinese Exclusion* (New York: King's Crown, Columbia University, 1950), esp. 69: "The adoption of the racial quota of 105 [Chinese immigrants admissible per year] met the main objection of labor organizations, namely, that repeal would bring a flood of cheap labor." On Yellow Peril: the essential themes of Yellow Peril date from long before the existence of the United States and can be identified with the conception of the "Mongol" Other in Europe. The use of Yellow Peril in public discourse, art, and entertainment continues to this day. See John Kuo Wei Tchen and Dylan Yeats, eds., *Yellow Peril! An Archive of Anti-Asian Fear* (London: Verso, 2014).

14. Quotation from the 47th Cong., 1st sess., *Congressional Record*, vol. 13.2, 2616, April 5, 1882. I use the Matthean King James Version translation here since it is closest to Bayard's paraphrasing and also most likely the translation with which he (and his fellow senators) were familiar. See also Luke 16:13.

15. 47th Cong., 1st sess., *Congressional Record*, vol. 13.2, 2616, April 5, 1882; emphasis added. On the use of religion and heathenism in particular to racialize in America, see Kathryn Gin Lum, *Heathen: Religion and Race in American History* (Cambridge, MA: Harvard University Press, 2022).

16. 41st Cong., 2nd sess., *Congressional Globe* 5151, July 4, 1870. Also quoted in Gold, *Forbidden Citizens*, §1.30, pp. 14, 18–19, 18; emphasis added.

17. On Chinese luxury goods as status symbols in the eighteenth and nineteenth centuries, see John Kuo Wei Tchen, *New York Before Chinatown: Orientalism and the Shaping of American Culture, 1776–1882* (Baltimore: Johns Hopkins University Press, 1999), 3–59; on the increase of export and trade in tea, silks, porcelain, and other handicrafts from China to America, see Yen-p'ing Hao, *The Commercial Revolution in Nineteenth-Century China: The Rise of Sino-Western Mercantile Capitalism* (Berkeley: University of California Press, 1986).

18. For more on ancient and current interpretations of the misogyny, tragedy, and power of this figure, see Shanell T. Smith, *The Woman Babylon and the Marks of Empire: Reading Revelation with a Postcolonial Womanist Hermeneutics of Ambiveilence* (Minneapolis: Fortress, 2014); Luis Menéndez-Antuña, *Thinking Sex with the Great Whore: Deviant Sexualities and Empire in the Book of Revelation* (New York: Routledge, 2018); Jennifer A. Glancy and Stephen D. Moore, "How Typical a Roman Prostitute Is Revelation's 'Great Whore'?" *Journal of Biblical Literature* 130.3 (2011): 551–60.

19. On Dooner's work as possibly the first Yellow Peril novel, see H. Bruce Franklin, *War Stars: The Superweapon and the American Imagination* (New York: Oxford

University Press, 1988), 33. P. W. Dooner, *The Last Days of the Republic* (San Francisco: Alta California, 1880), 96, 234, 256.

20. For a history of European and later Chinese Christian interpretations of the *long* with regards to biblical dragons and snakes, see Emily Dunn, "The Big Red Dragon and Indigenizations of Christianity in China," *East Asian History* 36 (2008): 73–85. Here I have used the Mandarin transliteration (pinyin) through the body of the text for simplicity and because of the widespread significance of the 龍 across the Sinophone diaspora.

21. G. Tradescant Lay, *The Chinese as They Are: Their Moral, Social, and Literary Character: A New Analysis of the Language with Succinct Views of Their Principal Arts and Sciences* (London: William Ball, 1841), 201, 22; emphasis added. The shorthand reference to China as a dragon continues in American and European news media. Negative associations with the dragon influenced the decision to omit the *long* from signage and mascot characters in the Beijing Olympics of 2008. See "Fiery Debate over China's Dragon," *BBC News*, December 12, 2006, http://news. bbc.co.uk/1/hi/world/asia-pacific/6171963.stm. Compare the centuries-long identification of China and the Chinese with the demonic to the comparatively microscopic controversy of 2014 over the Welsh flag, which displays a bona fide scarlet dragon. See "Christian Group Wants 'Evil' Welsh Flag Changed," *Wales Online*, May 21, 2014, https://www.walesonline.co.uk/news/wales-news/christian-group-wants-evil-welsh-2263878.

22. Robert Woltor ["A Survivor"], *A Short and Truthful History of the Taking of California and Oregon by the Chinese in the Year A.D. 1899* (San Francisco: A. L. Bancroft, 1882).

23. On the Six Companies: the Chinese Consolidated Benevolent Association was formed in the 1850s and formally established in San Francisco in 1882. See Yucheng Qin, *The Diplomacy of Nationalism: The Six Companies and China's Policy toward Exclusion* (Honolulu: University of Hawai'i Press, 2009). Quotation from Woltor, *A Short and Truthful History*, 39.

24. Woltor, *A Short and Truthful History*, 47, 56, 58.

25. Woltor, *A Short and Truthful History*, 58, 79.

26. Woltor, *A Short and Truthful History*, 81, 82.

27. Woltor, *A Short and Truthful History*, 82.

28. W. A. Rogers, "The Dragon's Choice," *Harper's Weekly*, August 18, 1900, cover image.

29. H. Knackfuss, "The Yellow Peril," *Harper's Weekly*, January 22, 1898, 76. The illustration generated many spin-offs and parodies, and even an illustration purporting to show an Asian perspective. See Peter C. Perdue and Ellen Sebring, "The Boxer Uprising I: The Gathering Storm in North China (1860–1900)," in *MIT Visualizing Cultures*, https://visualizingcultures.mit.edu/boxer_uprising/pdf/bx_essay02.pdf, accessed July 15, 2022. The accompanying article in *Harper's Weekly*—an anony-

mously written introduction followed by an essay by painter Jean-François
Raffaëlli—makes fun of the alarmist Emperor Wilhelm while claiming that the
real Yellow Peril is Japan, threatening Asia. It also regurgitates the stereotype that
the Chinese are a nation and race too indolent to accomplish anything. Nevertheless, the image is representative of the alarmist views in America newspapers, literature, and congressional speeches at the time, and the illustration was most likely
more impactful than the accompanying article. On Knackfuss basing the illustration on the kaiser's sketch, see Peter Paret, "The Tschudi Affair," *Journal of Modern
History* 53.4 (1981): 590. On the kaiser's nightmare, see Kuo Wei Tchen and Yeats,
*Yellow Peril!* 12–13.

30. The women may be identified (from right to left) as Marianne (France), Germania
(Germany), Mother Russia (Russia), Austria (Austria-Hungary), Italia (Italy), Great
Britain (Britannia), and Hispania (Spain). See also Asmut Brückmann, *Die Eu-
ropäische Expansion:Kolonialismus und Imperialismus, 1492–1918* (Leipzig: Klett,
2005), 79. The archangel Michael also plays the part of battle commander in other
Jewish apocalyptic sources, for example in Daniel 12:1. See Darrell D. Hannah,
*Michael and Christ: Michael Traditions and Angel Christology in Early Christian-
ity*, Wissenschaftliche Untersuchungen zum Neuen Testament 109 (Tübingen:
Mohr Siebeck, 1999); and James R. Davila, "Melchizedek, Michael, and War in
Heaven," *Society of Biblical Literature Seminar Papers* 35 (1996): 259–72.

31. On "Celestial" as a slur, see, for example, the cartoons "Celestial Occupation in
New York" (depicting a caricatured Chinese man selling cigars on the street) and
"A Promising Applicant: Hibernian Celestial" (depicting a caricatured Irish man
dressed as a Chinese man), both of which appeared in *Yankee Notions*, April 1854,
103, 115. Both cited in Arthur Bonner, *Alas! What Brought Thee Hither? The Chinese in New York, 1800–1850* (Cranbury, NJ: Associated University Presses, 1997),
8–10. "Flowery Kingdom" is a dated term for China, derived from the historical
term and concept of 華夏 (Cantonese: *Wa Ha* / Mandarin: *Hua Xia*). Quotation
from "A Celestial Horde," *Dalles Daily Chronicle*, April 30, 1892, front page,
https://chroniclingamerica.loc.gov/lccn/sn85042448/1892-04-30/ed-1/seq-1/#words=
act+Act+Chinese+exclusion+Exclusion.

32. Kin, *Reminiscences*, 24.

33. Kin, *Reminiscences*, 26–27, 27.

34. Kin, *Reminiscences*, 27.

35. According to J. F. Rose-Soley, "Chinese 'in Bond' on the Mail Dock," *San Francisco Call*, November 6, 1898, 25, some Chinese immigrants were detained on the
Pacific Mail dock for "weeks and months." Quoted in Robert Eric Barde, *Immigration at the Golden Gate: Passenger Ships, Exclusion, and Angel Island* (Westport,
CT: Praeger, 2008), 66–67, who also includes information from a log recording
Chinese detained from August 30, 1908, to January 10, 1909, which shows the
average stay in that short period of time as twenty-three days.

36. "The *Altonower*. Eight Cases of Smallpox Verified Yesterday. Quarantine Hulk Found," *San Francisco Examiner*, May 19, 1882, 3. See Barde, *Immigration at the Golden Gate*, 56–60.

37. "Death trap" quotation comes from Fred Watts, telegram to Immigration Bureau, June 3, 1909, quoted in Barde, *Immigration at the Golden Gate*, 71, see also 60–71. On the Shed, see "To Abandon Old Detention Shed," *San Francisco Call*, August 3, 1908, 12: "During the Denis Kearney agitation a mob attacked the place one night and burned a part of the shed. A riot followed, in which the Chinese and the members of the mob engaged in a general battle. Upon several occasions the Orientals have attempted to break from the place. These attempts became so frequent that a big fire hose was brought into play and used to subdue the immigrants." On conditions in the jail, see Chung Sai Yat Po, "American Newspaper Describes Prison as Inferno," December 18, 1903, quoted in Barde, *Immigration at the Golden Gate*, 58.

38. Mildred Crowl Martin, *Chinatown's Angry Angel: The Story of Donaldina Cameron* (Palo Alto, CA: Pacific Books, 1977), 6, quoting colleague Ethel Higgins. Martin also provides the various names of Cameron throughout the book. Here and elsewhere I provide the Cantonese transliteration for names given by late nineteenth- and early twentieth-century Chinese immigrants who primarily spoke Cantonese.

39. On Cameron's complicated legacy, see Brian Donovan, " 'Yellow Slavery' and Donaldina Cameron's San Francisco Mission," in *White Slave Crusade: Race, Gender, and Anti-vice Activism, 1887–1917* (Urbana: University of Illinois Press, 2006), 110–28, esp. 119–28; and Laurene Wu McClain, "Donaldina Cameron: A Reappraisal," *Pacific Historian* 27.3 (1983): 24–35, esp. 31: "She overlooked the fact that the Chinese Six Companies had attempted to suppress the slave trade earlier; that the Chinese government did not condone the practice; and that but for Chinese who told Cameron where the captive women could be found, she would not have been able to rescue them. She failed to recognize that the slave trade could not have taken place without the collusion of both corrupt San Francisco officials and scheming tong organizations and that the racket was thus promoted by Caucasians as well as Chinese." Quotation from Donaldina Cameron, *The Yellow Slave Traffic* (New York: Board of Foreign Missions of the Presbyterian Church in the U.S.A., 1910), 8. On the home as a spiritually liminal space, see Kirsten Twelbeck, "The Donaldina Cameron Myth and the Rescue of America, 1910–2002," in *Chinatowns in a Transnational World: Myths and Realities of an Urban Phenomenon*, ed. Vanessa Künnemann and Ruth Mayer (New York: Routledge, 2011), 139–40.

40. Sun Yat-sen sent a message to the publisher of the *Chung-hsi jih-pao* ("Chinese-Western Daily") through a newsboy. The publisher was connected not only to a prominent San Francisco Chinese Christian pastor but also to the leader of the San Francisco Chih Kung T'ang ("Chinese Masons"), both of whom worked together to lobby Washington for Sun's release. See Harold Z. Schiffrin, *Sun Yat-sen and the Origins of the Chinese Revolution* (Berkeley: University of California Press, 1968),

328–30. On Sun's immigration file from his entry at San Francisco in 1904, see Neil L. Thomsen, "No Such Sun Yat-Sen: An Archival Success Story," *Chinese America: History and Perspectives* (1997): 16–26.

41. On the desirability of an island detention center, San Francisco commissioner of immigration Hart Hyatt North argued that Angel Island was "ideal" because "it is impossible for anyone to escape by swimming to the mainland." Quoted in Erika Lee and Judy Yung, *Angel Island: Immigrant Gateway to America* (Oxford: Oxford University Press, 2010), 12. Angel Island was named *Isla de Los Angeles* by Juan Manuel de Ayala in 1775. See Erwin G. Gudde, *1,000 California Place Names: Their Origin and Meaning* (Berkeley: University of California Press, 1947), 3–4. The Golden Gate Strait was named by John C. Frémont. See John C. Frémont, *Geographical Memoir upon Upper California, an Illustration of His Map of Oregon and California* (1848; repr., Fairfield, WA: Ye Galleon, 1995), 32: "Called *Chrysopylae* (Golden Gate) on the map, on the same principle that the harbor of *Byzantium* (Constantinople afterwards) was called *Chrysoceras* (golden horn.) The form of the harbor, and its advantages for commerce, (and that before it became an entrepot of eastern commerce,) suggested the name to the Greek founders of Byzantium. The form of the entrance into the bay of San Francisco, and its advantages for commerce, (Asiatic inclusive,) suggest the name which is given to this entrance." Emphasis and punctuation as in original. The now sealed eastern gate of Temple Mount, Sha'ar HaRachamim ("Gate of Mercy") / Bab al-Dhahabi ("Golden Gate") is identified as the Golden Gate where the parents of Mary, mother of Jesus, met and kissed. It is also traditionally understood to be the gate through which Jesus entered Jerusalem from the Mount of Olives. The Golden Gate of Jerusalem is not named as such in the text itself but became a part of its legend. See, for example, Michelle A. Erhardt, "The Immaculate Kiss beneath the Golden Gate: The Influence of John Duns Scotus on Florentine Painting of the 14th Century," *Franciscan Studies* 66 (2008): 269–80; Randall Curb, "The Meeting at the Golden Gate: The Immaculate Conception and Early Renaissance Art," *Arts in Religious and Theological Studies* 10 (1998): 15–19.

42. Gudde, *1,000 California Place Names*, 31.

43. On the contrast with Ellis Island, see Spickard, *Almost All Aliens*, 4–11; and Barde, *Immigration at the Golden Gate*, 4–5: "Angel Island's Immigration Station was not, as some have called it, the 'Ellis Island of the West,' built to facilitate the 'processing' and entry of those welcomed as new Americans. Its role was less benign: to facilitate the exclusion of Asians—first the Chinese, then Japanese, Koreans, Indians, and all other Asians." See also Lee and Yung, *Angel Island*, 22–24. Quotation from Louis Stellmann, "San Francisco to Have the Finest Immigration Station in the World," *San Francisco Chronicle*, August 18, 1907, 4.

44. On the Island of Immortals, or Mount Penglai, see Wai-Ming Ng, *Imagining China in Tokugawa Japan: Legends, Classics, and Historical Terms* (Albany: State University of New York Press, 2019), 190, n. 3.

45. "Poem 23," in Lai, Lim, and Yung, *Island*, 60.
46. "Poem 36,"in Lai, Lim, and Yung, *Island*, 86.
47. On racial separation upon arrival, see Lee and Yung, *Angel Island*, 34. On medical inspection, see Nayan Shah, "Making Medical Borders at Angel Island," in *Contagious Divides: Epidemics and Race in San Francisco's Chinatown* (Berkeley: University of California Press, 2001), 179–203. On the length of detentions, see Robert Barde and Gustavo J. Bobonis, "Detention at Angel Island: First Empirical Evidence," *Social Science History* 30 (2006): 103–36. On the woman detained: Lee Puey You arrived at Angel Island on April 13, 1939, and was deported back to China on November 8, 1940. Lee's case is not straightforward: she had been instructed by her family to claim falsely that she was the daughter of a U.S. citizen. Nevertheless, the conditions, treatment, and immigration policies at work in her case remain reprehensible. See Lee and Yung, *Angel Island*, 93–95. On the case of the boy interrogated, see Lee and Yung, *Angel Island*, 93.
48. Anonymous letter, April 19, 1939, written to and quoted in Wen-Hsien Chen, "Chinese under Both Exclusion and Immigration Laws" (PhD diss., University of Chicago, 1940), 391; reported by H. L. Djang, 1939, to Wen-Hsien Chen and quoted in Chen, "Chinese under Both Exclusion and Immigration Laws," 393.
49. On Katharine Maurer, see Lee and Yung, *Angel Island*, 64–66. On Absalom Sydenstricker, see Pearl S. Buck, *Fighting Angel: Portrait of a Soul* (New York: Reynal & Hitchcock, 1936).
50. See U.S. Customs and Border Protection, "1891: Immigration Inspection Expands," May 23, 2022, https://www.cbp.gov/about/history/1891-imigration-inspection-expands. See also Lee, *At America's Gates*, 40–41.
51. On the proliferation of laws and punishments, see Lee, *At America's Gates*, 41–43. On an "illegal" identity: this notion identifies a person themselves as illegal rather than simply a person who has committed illegal or seditious acts. The ability to imprison and deport "dangerous" aliens formed part of the Alien and Sedition Acts of 1798, which targeted Anti-Federalists. See Library of Congress, "Alien and Sedition Acts: Primary Documents in American History," *Research Guides*, https://guides.loc.gov/alien-and-sedition-acts, accessed July 1, 2023.
52. Quoted in Andrew Gyory, *Closing the Gate: Race, Politics, and the Chinese Exclusion Act* (Chapel Hill: University of North Carolina Press, 1998), 238.
53. Quotation from *Chicago Times*, April 25, 1882, quoted in Gyory, *Closing the Gate*, 254. On the Asiatic Barred Zone: outside the zone were Japan and the Philippines, given U.S. political relationships at the time. Japanese immigrants were barred entirely beginning in 1924, whereas the Philippines remained an American colony until 1948, and Filipinos were thereby not excluded until it was determined that the Philippines would gain independence. For a history of Filipino immigration experience to the United States, see Rick Baldoz, *The Third Asiatic Invasion: Empire and Migration in Filipino America, 1898–1946* (New York: New York University

Press, 2011). For a summary of laws and agreements governing Japanese immigration to the United States up through 1924, including the admission of "picture brides," see Lee and Yung, *Angel Island*, 111–43.

54. King Wallace, *The Next War: A Prediction* (Washington, DC: Martyn, 1892), quoted in Franklin, *War Stars*, 35; William Crane, "The Year 1899," *Overland Monthly*, 2nd ser. 21 (June 1893): 579–89, quoted in Franklin, *War Stars*, 35–36; Jack London, "The Unparalleled Invasion," *McClure's Magazine*, July 1910, 308–16, quotation from 314.

55. On the white-yellow binary, see Lee, *At America's Gates*, 31. Quotation about "Hindu hordes" from *San Francisco Daily News*, September 20, 1910, quoted in Lee, *At America's Gates*, 33. On certain European groups as "Chinese," see Lee, *At America's Gates*, 35. What these anti-Asian and "Chinese-tinged" sentiments meant at Angel Island was that Japanese, Koreans, Russians, and Jews were also engulfed by wave after wave of anti-Chinese policies. They were also segregated and detained on the island. South Asian immigrants at Angel Island suffered in distinct ways as "non-Orientals," and yet also non-white, while leaving homelands colonized by the British. South Asians thus arrived in America without the advocacy of a home government. They were also often scrutinized because of their support for Indian nationalism. They were therefore denied entry at Angel Island at a higher rate than any other group in the station's history. See Lee and Yung, *Angel Island*, 111–14 on Japanese experiences; 177–210 on Korean; 211–46 on Russian and Jewish; 247–73 on Mexican; 145–76 on South Asian.

56. Here and throughout, for "fornication" and "fornicators," I substitute "sexually immoral" (also used in the NRSV updated edition) as a better translation of πόρνοι.

### Chapter 3. "Nothing Unclean Will Enter It"

Epigraph 2: John Smith, *Advertisements for the Unexperienced Planters of New England, or Anywhere; or, The Pathway to Erect a Plantation* (1635; repr., Boston: William Veazie, 1865), 20.

Epigraph 3: Gardiner Spring, *A Sermon Preached August 3, 1832: A Day Set Apart in the City of New York for Public Fasting, Humiliation and Prayer on Account of the Malignant Cholera* (New York: J. Leavitt, 1832), 30.

1. "Attack," "marching," "hijacking," and "front line" are used, for example, in Meredith Wadman, Jennifer Couzin-Frankel, Jocelyn Kaiser, and Catherine Matacic, "How Does Coronavirus Kill? Clinicians Trace a Ferocious Rampage through the Body, from Brain to Toes," *ScienceMag*, April 17, 2020, https://www.sciencemag.org/news/2020/04/how-does-coronavirus-kill-clinicians-trace-ferocious-rampage-through-body-brain-toes; Susan Sontag, *Illness as Metaphor* and *AIDS and Its Metaphors* (New York: Doubleday, 1990), 183.

2. On using the language of domination, see, for example, @realDonaldTrump (Donald J. Trump): "I will be leaving the great Walter Reed Medical Center today at 6:30 P.M. Feeling really good! Don't be afraid of Covid. Don't let it dominate your life. We have developed, under the Trump Administration, some really great drugs & knowledge. I feel better than I did 20 years ago!" posted on Twitter, October 5, 2020, 2:37 p.m., https://twitter.com/realDonaldTrump/status/1313186529058136070.

3. See Thomas L. Long, *AIDS and American Apocalypticism: The Cultural Semiotics of an Epidemic* (New York: State University of New York Press, 2004).

4. On locating the origin of AIDS, see François Clavel, Denise Guétard, Françoise Brun-Vézinet, et al., "Isolation of a New Human Retrovirus from West African Patients with AIDS," *Science* 233.4761 (1986): 243–46. Quotation from Sontag, *Illness as Metaphor*, 140.

5. On blaming Jews for the Black Death, see Samuel K. Cohn, "The Black Death and the Burning of the Jews," *Past and Present* 196 (2007): 3–36. Porphyry as quoted in Eusebius *Praep. Ev.* 5.1.9.

6. For the similar effects of advances in travel in perceptions of race, see Charles Loring Brace, *Race Is a Four-Letter Word: The Genesis of the Concept* (New York: Oxford University Press, 2005), 17–36.

7. Bruce Alberts, Alexander Johnson, Julian Lewis, et al., "Introduction to Pathogens," in *Molecular Biology of the Cell*, 4th ed. (New York: Garland Science, 2002), available online at https://www.ncbi.nlm.nih.gov/books/NBK26917/.

8. On "successful" pathogens that "maximally exploit," see Alberts, Johnson, Lewis, et al., "Introduction to Pathogens." On the destruction of Native populations, see Paul Spickard, *Almost All Aliens: Immigration, Race, and Colonialism in American History and Identity* (New York: Routledge, 2007), 43. For a list of epidemics among Native American populations in Mexico and North America from 1516 to 1901, see 36–37. See also David E. Stannard, "Pestilence and Genocide," in *American Holocaust: The Conquest of the New World* (Oxford: Oxford University Press, 1992), 57–148. On the numbers of Native and colonizing populations, see Russell Thornton, *American Indian Holocaust and Survival: A Population History since 1492* (Norman: University of Oklahoma Press, 1987), 60–90. On diseases suffered by colonists, see Alan M. Kraut, *Silent Travelers: Germs, Genes, and the "Immigrant Menace"* (New York: Harper Collins, 1994), 22.

9. Increase Mather, *An Historical Discourse concerning the Prevalency of Prayer* (Boston: John Foster, 1677), 5–6; Daniel Denton, *A Brief Description of New-York* (London: John Hancock, 1670), 12.

10. Cotton Mather, *Magnalia Christi Americana* (Hartford, CT: Silus Andrus & Son, 1852), 51, 45–46; emphasis in the original.

11. Samuel Danforth, "A Brief Recognition of New-Englands Errand into the Wilderness: An Online Electronic Text Edition" (1670), ed. Paul Royster, *Faculty Publications, UNL Libraries* 35, https://digitalcommons.unl.edu/libraryscience/35. There is

a complex debate over the interpretation of the phrase "errand to the wilderness" and Puritan motivations for sailing to America. The present argument highlights only the rhetorical framing of immigration and colonization in apocalyptic terms and does not engage the debates about details of differences in millenarian understandings or goals behind "modeling" a church order for the rest of the world. For more on these debates, see Jeffrey K. Jue, "Colonial North America: The Puritan Errand Revisited," in *Heaven upon Earth: Joseph Mede (1586–1638) and the Legacy of Millenarianism*, International Archives of the History of Ideas 194 (Dordrecht: Springer, 2006), 175–210; Theodore Dwight Bozeman, "The Puritans' 'Errand into the Wilderness' Reconsidered," *New England Quarterly* 59.2 (1986): 231–51; and the watershed (and subsequently debated) volume, Perry Miller, *Errand into the Wilderness* (Cambridge, MA: Harvard University Press, 1956).

12. On Israel as a rotted or barren vineyard, see, for example, Isaiah 5:3–7, 10:33–34, 18:5 (of Cush); Jeremiah 15:7, 51:2 (of Babylon). On the gathering of useless vegetation to be burned, see, for example, Matthew 3:10 and Luke 3:9; Matthew 3:12, 13:30; John 15:6. On the fruitful seed or vine, see, for example, Mark 4:1–20, 4:30–32, along with synoptic parallels Matthew 13:1–23 / Luke 8:4–15 and Matthew 13:31–32 / Luke 13:18–19, respectively; John 15:5. The winepress in Revelation is an allusion to both Joel 3:13: "Put in the sickle, for the harvest is ripe. Go in, tread for the wine press is full. The vats overflow, for their wickedness is great," and Isaiah 63:2–3: " 'Why are your robes red, and your garments like theirs who tread the wine press?' 'I have trodden the wine press alone. . . . I trod them in my anger and trampled them in my wrath; their juice spattered on my garments, and stained all my robes.' "

13. See, for example, William Bradford, *Of Plymouth Plantation, 1620–1647*, ed. Samuel Eliot Morison (New York: Knopf, 1970); and *Records of the Colony and Plantation of New-Haven, from 1638–1649*, ed. Charles J. Hoadly (Hartford: Case, Tiffany, 1857).

14. On belief in "miasma," see Kraut, *Silent Travelers*, 21–23; see also Martin V. Melosi, *The Sanitary City: Urban Infrastructure in America from Colonial Times to the Present* (Baltimore: Johns Hopkins University Press, 2000), 15–99. In many ways poverty *is* correlated with ill health, not through the fault of the poor but rather because of their exclusion from healthcare, societal benefits, and safety. See Steven Thrasher, *The Viral Underclass: The Human Toll When Inequality and Disease Collide* (New York: Celadon Books, 2022). On the waxing and waning of this theory in the nineteenth century, see Erwin H. Ackerknecht, "Anticontagionism between 1821 and 1867," *International Journal of Epidemiology* 38 (2009): 7–21.

15. Kraut, *Silent Travelers*, 23; emphasis added.

16. Mather, *Magnalia*, 327–28; emphasis in original.

17. Mather, *Magnalia*, 328; emphasis in original.

18. On ancient associations of white clothing, see Candida R. Moss, *Divine Bodies: Resurrecting Perfection in the New Testament and Early Christianity* (New Haven:

Yale University Press, 2019), 100–109. The phrase "high powered detergent" blood comes from Brian K. Blount, *Revelation: A Commentary* (Louisville, KY: Westminster John Knox Press, 2009), 135, 408: Blount understands the washing of robes in the Lamb's blood as symbolic for the act of witnessing. Here I read the metaphor more directly, emphasizing its appeal to cleanliness.

19. See Wilfred G. E. Watson, *Classical Hebrew Poetry,* Journal for the Study of the Old Testament Supplement Series 26 (Sheffield: JSOT Press, 1986), 114–21 on parallelism and structure in Hebrew poetry, 128 on parallel word pairs, and 118 for "proper anti-congruence" as demonstrated in an $a_1$, $a_2$ //-$a_1$,-$a_2$ structure, as in Revelation 22:11. The verse also borrows from Ezekiel 3:27 and Daniel 5:9–10.

20. This is written in the letter to the Church of Laodicea, one of the seven letters to seven churches at the beginning of the book.

21. For the varying distinctions between ritual and moral impurity in ancient Judaism, see Jonathan Klawans, *Impurity and Sin in Ancient Judaism* (Oxford: Oxford University Press, 2000). On the preoccupation of Revelation with cleanliness and purity and its use of the city of Rome and Roman ideas of purification and cleansing, see Yii-Jan Lin, " 'Let the Filthy Still Be Filthy': Revelation as a Text of Dirt and Danger," forthcoming.

22. Massachusetts Colony, *The Acts and Resolves, Public and Private, of the Province of Massachusetts Bay,* 2 vols. (Boston: Wright & Potter, 1869–74), 1:452, 2:336; see also Emberson Edward Proper, *Colonial Immigration Laws: A Study of the Regulations of Immigration by the English Colonies in America* (New York: AMS Press, 1967), 29–30.

23. On the yellow fever epidemic, see Thomas A. Apel, *Feverish Bodies, Enlightened Minds: Science and the Yellow Fever Controversy in the Early American Republic* (Stanford: Stanford University Press, 2016); Molly Caldwell Crosby, *The American Plague: The Untold Story of Yellow Fever, the Epidemic That Shaped Our History* (New York: Berkley, 2006); and John H. Powell, *Bring Out Your Dead: The Great Plague of Yellow Fever in Philadelphia in 1793* (Philadelphia: University of Pennsylvania Press, 1949). On the blaming of foreign groups, see Kraut, *Silent Travelers,* 26–27. The Philadelphia pamphlet quotation comes from *An Earnest Call, Occasioned by the Alarming Pestilential Contagion* (Philadelphia: Jones, Hoff, & Derrick, 1793), 7, quoted in Apel, *Feverish Bodies,* 99. Ashbel Green quotation from *A Pastoral Letter from a Minister in the Country, to Those of His Flock Who Remained in Philadelphia during the Pestilence of 1798* (Philadelphia: John Ormand, 1799), 8, quoted in Apel, *Feverish Bodies,* 99.

24. On the use of classical authors to explain disease, see Apel, *Feverish Bodies,* 47–56. Quotation from Thuc. *Hist.* 2.48; my translation. On scholarly debates of the cause of the plague in Athens, see Robert J. Littman, "The Plague of Athens: Epidemiology and Paleopathology," *Mount Sinai Journal of Medicine* 76 (2009): 456–67.

25. Quotation of Thomas Bond's lecture given December 3, 1766 as quoted in William Currie, *A Sketch of the Rise and Progress of the Yellow Fever* (Philadelphia: Budd &

Bartram, 1800), 40. On Currie's argument for contagion, see Currie, A Sketch, 39–42. On disease as arising from ships from the West Indies, see Currie, A Sketch, 5–9. On the association of Ethiopia and Egypt with extreme remoteness, Blackness, and immorality, see Gay L. Byron, "Egyptians, Ethiopians, Blacks, and Blackness in Greco-Roman Literature," in Symbolic Blackness and Ethnic Difference in Early Christian Literature (New York: Routledge, 2002), 29–51.

26. Elihu H. Smith, "The Plague of Athens," Medical Repository 1 (1797): 17; on Athens's locale as giving rise to disease, 18; on "unity of cause" and similarities between Athens and Philadelphia, 29.

27. On the localists' success, see Apel, Feverish Bodies, 7–8. On Tytler's hypothesis, see James Tytler, Treatise on the Plague and Yellow Fever (Salem, MA: Joshua Cushing for B. B. Macanulty, 1799); on Tytler's censure, see Apel, Feverish Bodies, 36–37, 57–58.

28. On the context of belief in American exceptionalism during these debates, see Apel, Feverish Bodies, 36–37. Quotation about American cities from Samuel Latham Mitchill, excerpted letter to James Hardie, in An Account of the Malignant Fever, Lately Prevalent in the City of New York, ed. James Hardie (New York: Hurtin & M'Farlane, 1799),16, quoted in Apel, Feverish Bodies, 63.

29. "Subscriber," New York Commercial Advertiser, August 2, 1832, quoted and cited in Charles E. Rosenberg, The Cholera Years: The United States in 1832, 1849, and 1866 (Chicago: University of Chicago Press, 1962), 43. American Tract Society, An Appeal on the Subject of the Cholera to the Prepared and Unprepared (1832), 3, quoted and cited in Rosenberg, The Cholera Years, 50. Seizing on this popular belief, Senator Henry Clay of Kentucky proposed a national day of fasting and prayer to score political points against President Andrew Jackson, who had declined to declare such a day. The resolution passed the Senate but not the House. See Rosenberg, The Cholera Years, 48–53; and David Petriello, "Consumption and Compromise: Illness and Its Impact on the Political Career of Henry Clay," Journal of the Southern Association for the History of Medicine and Science 2.1 (2020): 50–51.

30. Spring, A Sermon Preached August 3, 1832, 30, 32 32–33; emphasis in original.

31. Samuel F. B. Morse, Imminent Dangers to the Free Institutions of the United States through Foreign Immigration (1835; repr., New York: Arno, 1969), 13, quoted in Kraut, Silent Travelers, 34.

32. See Kraut, Silent Travelers, 36.

33. Pace Rosenberg, The Cholera Years, 229: "By 1866, however, it was becoming increasingly apparent that the soul could not be made healthy while the body which housed it was diseased. Chloride of lime, not fasting, brought deliverance from cholera; the cure for pauperism lay in education and housing, not prayers and exhortation. Even clergymen were beginning to think habitually in terms of pragmatic goals and environmental causation. It would not be easy to recapture the piety of an earlier generation; preoccupation with material means meant, inevitably, the decreasing reality of spiritual ends."

34. On the use of "objective" science for nativist interests, see Kraut, *Silent Travelers*, 66–68. On the medical inspections at Ellis Island, see Kraut, *Silent Travelers*, 52–64. See also Amy L. Fairchild, *Science at the Borders: Immigrant Medical Inspection and the Shaping of the Modern Industrial Labor Force* (Baltimore: Johns Hopkins University Press, 2003), esp. 119–31.

35. On blaming Italians for tuberculosis, see Kraut, *Silent Travelers*, 105–35. Quotation from Richard Mayo-Smith, *Emigration and Immigration: A Study in Social Science* (New York: Scribner's, 1890), 133, quoted in Kraut, *Silent Travelers*, 109.

36. "Becoming American" quotation from John Foster Carr, *Guide to the United States for the Immigrant Italian* (New York: Doubleday, Page, 1911), 6: "America asks them to take citizenship and become Americans, too—members of this great family of the nation." This is a translation of John Foster Carr, *Guida degli Stati Uniti per l'immigrante italiano* (New York: Doubleday, Page, 1910), 7: "L'America invita tutti gli immigrant ad acquistare la cittadinanza, a divenir membri della grande familiglia della nazione." The English version is quoted with slight variation in Kraut, *Silent Travelers*, 120. "Clean water" quotation from Carr, *Guide*, 46. Carr, *Guida*, 58: "Acqua pura, cibo puro, corpo pulito, abiti netti, casa pulita, strade pulite. Tutto ciò contribuisce a mantenerci sani." "It is the duty" quotation from Carr, *Guide*, 48; bold text in original. Carr, *Guida*, 61: "E' **dovere del cittadino** di fare il possibile per mantenere in buona salute sé stesso ed i propri simili. . . . Dove le condizioni igieniche non sono buone, sia a causa della latrine, sia a causa delle tubature, o del modo con cui si dispone della spazzatura, bisogna liberamente ed immediatamente fare un reclamo all'Ufficio d'Igiene ('Board of Health'). In America tutti fanno così perché questo è l'uso, e voi dovete fare come fanno gli Americani."

37. Carr, *Guide*, 6; emphasis added. Carr, *Guida*, 4: "I Tedeschi e gli Irlandesi di quei tempi, arrivavano poveri come gli Italiani, i Russi o i Greci d'oggi. Come questi, essi pure cominciarono a guadagnarsi la vita col lavoro umile e duro. Oggi essi hanno dimenticato la povertà, gli stenti, l'oppressione che li spinsero a lasciare il vecchio mondo. Molti di essi si sono arricchiti e tutti sono Americani. Essi avevano i loro difetti, come tutti glie esseri umani ne hanno, ma possedevano anche le qualità che hanno contribuito a render questo paese grande e rispettato in tutto il mondo. Come agli Irlandesi ed ai Tedeschi di altri tempi così oggi l'America apre le sue braccia agli Italiani." This understanding of what is possible for Irish, German, Italian, Greek, and Russian immigrants is a main reason to reject the argument in certain studies that such groups "became white," at least on the level of the law. These immigrant groups could legally naturalize, vote, and marry other whites upon arrival and admittance to America. See Philip Q. Yang and Kavitha Koshy, "The 'Becoming White Thesis' Revisited," *Journal of Public and Professional Sociology* 8.1 (2016): article 1, https://digitalcommons.kennesaw.edu/jpps/vol8/iss1/1.

38. The Emergency Quota Act of 1920 did not include Western Hemisphere countries, since cheap agricultural labor was needed. It also did not include Asian countries from where immigration was already barred. The Immigration Act of 1924 was modified in the Immigration Act of 1927 so that numbers were based on the 1920 census, with total immigration capped at 150,000 annually.

39. Quotation from John Higham, *Strangers in the Land: Patterns of American Nativism, 1860–1925* (London: Rutgers University Press, 1983), 309. On blaming Jewish people for disease, see Howard Markel, *Quarantine! East European Jewish Immigrants and the New York City Epidemics of 1892* (Baltimore: Johns Hopkins University Press, 1997); and Kraut, *Silent Travelers*, 136–65.

40. See Michael Dobb, *The Unwanted: America, Auschwitz, and a Village Caught in Between* (New York: Knopf, 2019), 45.

41. Dobb, *The Unwanted*, 21–25.

42. On the history of demonizing Jews, see George M. Fredrickson, *Racism: A Short History* (Princeton: Princeton University Press, 2015), 18–26. On the blood curse, see Fredrickson, *Racism*, 31–35. See also Léon Poliakov, *The History of Anti-Semitism*, vol. 2, *From Mohammed to the Marranos*, trans. Natali Gerardi (Philadelphia: University of Pennsylvania Press, 1973), 328–57.

43. See Eric L. Goldstein, *The Price of Whiteness: Jews, Race, and American Identity* (Princeton: Princeton University Press, 2019).

## Chapter 4. "They Must Go"

1. William Currie, *A Sketch of the Rise and Progress of the Yellow Fever* (Philadelphia: Budd & Bartram, 1800), 38–39, quoting a letter from Isaac Norris, Esq. from 1699 and John Gough, *History of the Friends*, a history of the Quakers published in 1789.

2. John Lining, *A Description of the American Yellow Fever, Which Prevailed at Charleston in South Carolina in the Year 1748* (Philadelphia: Thomas Dobson, 1799), 7; also quoted in Rana Asali Hogarth, "The Myth of Innate Racial Differences between White and Black People's Bodies: Lessons from the 1793 Yellow Fever Epidemic in Philadelphia, Pennsylvania," *American Journal of Public Health* 109.10 (2019): 1339–41, https://ajph.aphapublications.org/doi/full/10.2105/AJPH.2019.305245. Philip Tidyman, "A Sketch of the Most Remarkable Diseases of the Negroes of the Southern States, with an Account of the Method of Treating Them, Accompanied by Physiological Observations," *Philadelphia Journal of the Medical and Physical Sciences* 3.6 (1826): 306.

3. Mathew Carey, *A Short Account of the Malignant Fever Lately Prevalent in Philadelphia: With a Statement of the Proceedings That Took Place on the Subject in Different Parts of the United States*, 3rd ed. (Philadelphia: Printed by the author, 1793), 78.

4. Absalom Jones and Richard Allen, *A Narrative of the Proceedings of the Black People, during the Late Awful Calamity in Philadelphia, in the Year 1793; and a*

*Refutation of Some Censures, Thrown upon Them in Some Late Publications* (Philadelphia: Printed for the Authors by William W. Woodward, 1794), 15; emphasis in
the original. See also Phillip Lapsansky, " 'Abigail, a Negress': The Role and the
Legacy of African Americans in the Yellow Fever Epidemic," in *A Melancholy
Scene of Devastation: The Public Response to the 1798 Philadelphia Yellow Fever Epidemic*, ed. J. Worth Estes and Billy G. Smith (Canton, MA: Science History Publications / USA for The College of Physicians of Philadelphia and the Library
Company of Philadelphia, 1997), 61–78.

5. On sickness suffered by Black soldiers during the Civil War and the refusal to allot
them burial grounds, see Jim Downs, "Emancipation, Sickness, and Death in the
American Civil War," *Lancet*, November 10, 2012, https://doi.org/10.1016/S0140–
6736(12)61937–0; on the belief that Black people were immune to Spanish influenza and their consequent greater suffering, see Elizabeth Schlabach, "The
Influenza Epidemic and Jim Crow Public Health Policies and Practices in Chicago, 1917–1921," *Journal of African American History* 104.1 (2019), https://www.
journals.uchicago.edu/doi/full/10.1086/701105; on the linking of tuberculosis with
African Americans and contradictory constructions of Blackness and health during
segregation, see Samuel Kelton Robert, *Infectious Fear: Politics, Disease, and the
Health Effects of Segregation*, Studies in Social Medicine (Chapel Hill: University
of North Carolina Press, 2009).

6. Quotation of "God's kitchen" from Marie Jenkins Schwartz, *Born in Bondage:
Growing Up Enslaved in the Antebellum South* (Cambridge, MA: Harvard Univer-
sity Press, 2000), 121. Also quoted in Gary Scott Smith, *Heaven in the American Im-
agination* (New York: Oxford University Press, 2011), 89. Quotation of a heavenly
partition from Ella Alford Bastrop quoting Frank Roberson, quoted in John B.
Cade, "Out of the Mouths of Ex-Slaves," *Journal of Negro History* 20.3 (1935): 329.
On Black rejection of heavenly segregation, see Smith, *Heaven in the American
Imagination*, 90–96.

7. Suellen Hoy, *Chasing Dirt: The American Pursuit of Cleanliness* (Oxford: Oxford
University Press, 1997), 87.

8. On leprosaria and isolation of patients from families, see Michelle T. Moran, *Colonizing Leprosy: Imperialism and the Politics of Public Health in the United States*
(Chapel Hill: University of North Carolina Press, 2007); and Warwick Anderson,
*Colonial Pathologies: American Tropical Medicine, Race, and Hygiene in the Philip-
pines* (Durham, NC: Duke University Press: 2006), esp. 158–79. I thank Michael
Libunao-Macalintal for introducing me to these histories. On the identification of
certain diseases as "tropical," see Moran, *Colonizing Leprosy*, 1–16. On different
terms used for the disease and their cultural significance, see Moran, *Colonizing
Leprosy*, 2, 4–5, 20–21. On the name of the disease, see Moran, *Colonizing Leprosy*,
154, where Moran describes white patients at a leprosarium in Carville, Louisiana,
rejecting the term *leprosy*: "Betty Martin, a white Louisiana society woman diag-

nosed with leprosy and incarcerated at Carville in the 1920s . . . refused to accept the news that she had leprosy because her self-image did not match her own conception of a 'leper.' Martin speculated that *leprosy 'might exist in lands far away,* in *India* perhaps, or *China,* but surely leprosy could not exist here, in our own United States, and surely not in me.' . . . Patients [at Carville] sought to alter people's conception of their disease by renaming it. . . . Patients therefore sought to *portray people with Hansen's disease as ordinary, all-American individuals"* (emphasis added). See also Cynthia Ruth Butlin and Diana Nancy Johanna Lockwood, "Why We Should Stop Using the Word Leprosy," *Lancet* 20 (August 2020): 900–901.

9. William Backner, "The Menace of Manila Cigars," *Labor Clarion,* September 17, 1909, 7, quoted in Nayan Shah, *Contagious Divides: Epidemics and Race in San Francisco's Chinatown* (Berkeley: University of California Press, 2001), 173.

10. On the effects of the disease, see David Schollard and Tom Gillis, eds., *International Textbook of Leprosy* (2016), https://internationaltextbookofleprosy.org/. On inaccurate translation: biblical scholars were already cognizant of the inaccuracy of translating צרעת as "leprosy" at the end of the nineteenth century and the beginning of the twentieth. See Jay F. Schamberg, "The Nature of the Leprosy of the Bible from a Medical and Biblical Point of View," *Biblical World* 13.3 (March 1899): 162–69; and J. Dyneley Prince, "Note on Leprosy in the Old Testament," *JBL* 38 (1919): 30–34.

11. For more on the rhetoric of disgust, see, for example, Jaimee Bodtke and George F. McHendry, "Disgusting Rhetorics: 'What's the Warts That Could Happen?' " in *Affect, Emotion, and Rhetorical Persuasion in Mass Communication,* ed. Lei Zhang and Carlton Clark (New York: Routledge, 2019), 143–57; and Thomas Staubli, "Disgusting Deeds and Disgusting Gods: Ethnic and Ethical Constructions of Disgust in the Hebrew Bible," *Hebrew Bible and Ancient Israel* 6.4 (2017): 457–87.

12. On tuberculosis as the more civilized disease, see Moran, *Colonizing Leprosy,* 42. On people, particularly women, purified by suffering tuberculosis, see Katherine Byrne, *Tuberculosis and the Victorian Literary Imagination,* Studies in Nineteenth-Century Literature and Culture Series 74 (Cambridge: Cambridge University Press, 2011); and Carolyn Day, *Consumptive Chic: A History of Beauty, Fashion, and Disease* (London: Bloomsbury Academic, 2017). This was, of course, not the case for associations of Black people with tuberculosis during segregation. See Robert, *Infectious Fear.*

13. See Yii-Jan Lin, "The River of Life and the Cloaca Maxima," forthcoming, on Revelation's River of Life as not just borrowing from Ezekiel and Genesis but also as a critique of the city of Rome's water systems as a point of comparison. For more on the Cloaca Maxima, see John N. N. Hopkins, "The Cloaca Maxima and the Monumental Manipulation of Water in Archaic Rome," *Waters of Rome* 4 (2007), http://www3.iath.virginia.edu/waters/Journal4Hopkins.pdf; and John N. N. Hopkins, "The 'Sacred Sewer': Tradition and Religion in the Cloaca Maxima," in

*Rome, Pollution and Propriety: Dirt Disease and Hygiene in the Eternal City from Antiquity to Modernity*, ed. Mark Bradley (Cambridge: Cambridge University Press, 2012), 81–102; for association of moving waters and sanitation throughout history, see Sanna-Leena Rautanen, Antero Luonsi, Henry Nygård, Heikki S. Vuorinen, and Riikka P. Rajala, "Sanitation, Water and Health," *Environment and History* 16 (2010): 173–94.

14. Loren Gatch, "E. S. Wells Was 'Rough on Rats,' " *Paper Money* 54.6 (2015): 433 on Wells's beginnings; 435 on Wells's rat poison; 436 on Wells's advertisements.

15. The Workingmen's Party meetings in California reportedly began and ended with this slogan in 1878, and Kearney boasted that he ended all his speeches and writings with it. The slogan became nationally known through newspapers, labor meetings, and Kearney's political speeches. See Andrew Gyory, *Closing the Gates: Race, Politics, and the Chinese Exclusion Act* (Chapel Hill: University of North Carolina Press, 1998), 109–10, 116. On the complicated history and political meanings of the queue, see Michael R. Godley, "The End of the Queue: Hair as Symbol in Chinese History," *East Asian History* 8 (1994): 53–72.

16. "Common Council," *Daily Alta California*, August 19, 1854, also cited in Shah, *Contagious Divides*, 20; "Steamer Alta," *Daily Alta California* 5.225, August 15, 1854, also cited in Shah, *Contagious Divides*, 20.

17. *New York Daily Tribune*, September 29, 1854, 4. See Arthur B. Stout, *Chinese Immigration and the Physiological Causes of the Decay of the Nation* (San Francisco: Agnew & Deffebach, 1862); Arthur B. Stout, *Biennial Report of the State Board of Health of California* (Sacramento: California State Board of Health, 1870–71), 55.

18. Shah, *Contagious Divides*, 57–63, 99–100.

19. On rumors of "mouth spray," see, for example, the memoir by Mary McNair Mathews, *Ten Years in Nevada; or, Life on the Pacific Coast* (Lincoln, NV: Buffalo, Baker, Jones, 1880); also the lithograph of a Chinese launderer "mouth spraying" in *Harper's Weekly*, December 29, 1877, cited and depicted in Ronald M. James, Richard D. Adkins, and Rachel J. Hartigan, "Competition and Coexistence in the Laundry: A View of the Comstock," *Western Historical Quarterly* 25.2 (Summer 1994): 165, fig. 1. It is likely that this rumor was sparked by the atomizer Chinese launderers used to spread starch and water onto laundry, which comprised an atomizing tube into which one blew air. See James, Adkins, and Hartigan, "Competition and Coexistence in the Laundry," 170–71. For more on investigations of laundries in San Francisco, see Shah, *Contagious Divides*, 67–69; Hart quotation from editorial "Filthy Chinese Laundries," *Pacific Medical Journal* 40.4 (1897): 232, also quoted in Shah, *Contagious Divides*, 68.

20. On fumigation, quarantine, and deportation, see Shah, *Contagious Divides*, 58–75, 99–100. On facilities at Angel Island, see Shah, *Contagious Divides*, 315, n. 68. On medical examinations and policies of Angel Island during 1910–40, see Shah, *Contagious Divides*, 179–203, esp. 184–85 on the examination for trachoma and

hookworm; see also Angel Island Immigration Museum, "Under the Microscope: Medicine and Immigration: The Role of the Hospital on Angel Island," curated by Russell Nauman, operations manager, and Edward Tepporn, executive director, exhibit online and on site at Angel Island, https://www.aiisf.org/aiimicroscope, accessed June 30, 2023. On bacteriological inspection, see Shah, *Contagious Divides*, 189–97, which also notes that the examination of feces initially targeted immigrants from South Asia to exclude them from entry to the United States. Quotation from Shah, *Contagious Divides*, 196.

21. "Steamer Alta," *Daily Alta California*, August 15, 1854. Also quoted in Shah, *Contagious Divides*, 21.

22. Kathryn Gin Lum, *Heathen: Religion and Race in American History* (Cambridge, MA: Harvard University Press, 2022).

23. Horace F. Page, "Treaty Relations with China," in *Appendix to Congressional Record*, 43rd Cong., 2nd sess., February 10, 1875 (U.S.C.: Washington, DC, 1875), 44, https://memory.loc.gov/cgi-bin/ampage?collId=llcr&fileName=005/llcr005.db&recNum=45.

24. Mary J. Sawtelle, *Medical-Literary Journal* 1.4 (December 1878): 4–7, cited in Shah, *Contagious Divides*, 109. See also California State Legislature, *Chinese Immigration: The Social, Moral, and Political Effect of Chinese Immigration* (Sacramento: State Printing Office, 1876), esp. 102–4, where Dr. Hugh Hugner Toland testifies that he believed "nine tenths" of all cases of syphilis in the city could be traced to Chinese prostitutes, who, he claimed, accepted boys "eight and ten years old." The Whore of Babylon, like the Chinese prostitute in white American imagination, can be both a victim as a lowly brothel prostitute and an imperial decadent power. See Shanell T. Smith, *The Woman Babylon and the Marks of Empire: Reading Revelation with a Postcolonial Womanist Hermeneutics of Ambiveilence* (Minneapolis: Fortress, 2014).

25. Willard B. Farwell and John E. Kunkler, "Report of the Special Committee," in Willard B. Farwell, *The Chinese at Home and Abroad*, part 2 (San Francisco: A. L. Bancroft, 1885), 14; also quoted in Shah, *Contagious Divides*, 80.

26. Mary J. Sawtelle, "The Foul and Contagious Disease: A Phase of the Chinese Question," *Medico-Literary Journal* 1.3 (November 1878): 7, quoted in Shah, *Contagious Divides*, 109. In white women's writings of the nineteenth century, the voice of warning was ever that of the white wife, who was to be a pure moral guide for her husband. See, for example, "Honored Be Woman! She Beams on the Sight, Graceful and Fair, Like a Being of Light," *Daily Alta California*, March 20, 1853, 2; also Sawtelle, "The Foul and Contagious Disease," 1, 8, which instructs mothers to guard their sons against the dangers of syphilitic Chinese prostitutes, cited in Shah, *Contagious Divides*, 108.

27. Emma R. Cable, "Missionary Work among Heathen Women," *Annual Report*, Women's Foreign Missionary Society of the Presbyterian Church, Occidental

Branch (San Francisco: C. W. Gordon, 1881), 40, quoted in Shah, *Contagious Divides*, 112; Emma R. Cable, "House to House Visitation," *Annual Report*, Women's Foreign Missionary Society of the Presbyterian Church, Occidental Branch (San Francisco: C. W. Gordon, 1888), 44–46, quoted in Shah, *Contagious Divides*, 113. For more on Cable, see Shah, *Contagious Divides*, 110–15.

28. Mary H. Field, "Two Homes," *Woman's Work for Woman*, August 1, 1900, 213–14. Is the number of Mrs. Wong Lee's children—seven—used as a holy number in Jewish Christian understanding? Perhaps that is a reach, but the possibility remains.

29. Walter Lindley, "Los Angeles City Annual Health Officer Report to City Council, November 13, 1879," City of Los Angeles, retrieved from the Internet Archive: https://archive.org/details/18791113cityoflosangeleshealthofficerreport/mode/2up, also partially quoted in Natalia Molina, *Fit to Be Citizens? Public Health and Race in Los Angeles, 1879–1939* (Berkeley: University of California Press, 2006), 4; Theodore Roosevelt, "Address at Riverside, California," May 7, 1903, in *The American Presidency Project*, online archive by John Woolley and Gerhard Peters, UC Santa Barbara, https://www.presidency.ucsb.edu/documents/address-riverside-california.

30. Roosevelt, "Address," emphasis added.

31. On classification of diseases, see Amy L. Fairchild, *Science at the Borders: Immigrant Medical Inspection and the Shaping of the Modern Industrial Labor Force* (Baltimore: Johns Hopkins University Press, 2003), 14. On the connections between Los Angeles, sunshine, and Aryan race proponents at the turn of the century, see Molina, *Fit to Be Citizens?* 18–20.

32. Lindley, "Los Angeles City Annual Health Officer Report," 4–5, 2; emphasis added.

33. On anti-Japanese movements and policy, see Roger Daniels, *The Politics of Prejudice: The Anti-Japanese Movement in California and the Struggle for Japanese Exclusion* (Berkeley: University of California Press, 1977). On rumors of Japanese produce, see Molina, *Fit to Be Citizens?* 58. Quotation from John Larabee Pomeroy, "Japanese Evil in California," *Grizzly Bear*, February 1920, 2, quoted in Molina, *Fit to Be Citizens?* 56. On alien land laws: Governor Ron DeSantis and the Florida state legislature recently passed a similar bill, FL SB264, that restricts Chinese citizens and citizens from six other "countries of concern" in the purchase of property. The law took effect July 1, 2023. See Bruce Ritchie, "Justice Department Says New Florida Law Restricting Chinese Land Ownership Unconstitutional," *Politico*, June 28, 2023, https://www.politico.com/news/2023/06/28/justice-department-florida-law-unconstitutional-00104091.

34. On the title of the war: I use the U.S. War with Mexico as the name of the conflict rather than the "Mexican-American War" following Natalia Molina, *How Race Is Made in America: Immigration, Citizenship, and the Historical Power of Racial Scripts* (Berkeley: University of California Press, 2014), and before her, Ernesto Chávez, *The U.S. War with Mexico: A Brief History with Documents*, Bedford Series in History and Culture (Boston: Bedford / St. Martin's, 2008). Article IX, Treaty

of Guadalupe Hidalgo, United States of America and the United Mexican States, signed February 2, 1848, archived at National Archives: Milestone Documents, https://www.archives.gov/milestone-documents/treaty-of-guadalupe-hidalgo. For a clear dissection of this construction of identities in Los Angeles and Southern California in general, see Molina, *Fit to Be Citizens?* 4–11. See also Fairchild, *Science at the Borders*, 157: "At that time [1930s] the U.S. Census would enumerate first- and second-generation Mexicans as an ambiguous yet separate race, 'not definitely white' but also not 'Negro, Indian, Chinese, or Japanese.' " Fairchild quotes this terminology from Joseph Hill, "Composition of the American Population by Race and Country of Origin," *Annals of the American Academy of Political and Social Sciences* 188 (November 1936): 177–84.

35. Molina, *Fit to Be Citizens?* 9.
36. On exploitable labor, see *California State Board of Health Monthly Bulletin*, October 1916, 202: "The Mexican peons are said to be the only available labor for railroad construction." Quoted in Molina, *Fit to Be Citizens?* 61. On the outbreak of typhus, see Molina, *Fit to Be Citizens?* 64–66; and Fairchild, *Science at the Borders*, 153. Quotation from Howard D. King, "Some Sanitary Aspects of the Mexican Revolution," *Southern California Practitioner* 20.3 (1914): 63, quoted in Molina, *Fit to Be Citizens?* 63.
37. *California State Board of Health Monthly Bulletin*, October 1916, 180–81, 185, 182; Molina, *Fit to Be Citizens?* 11.
38. Quotation of "shunned water" from Los Angeles County Health Department, *Progress Report*, 1915–17, 5, quoted in Molina, *Fit to Be Citizens?* 69. On disinfection plants, see Alexandra Minna Stern, "Buildings, Boundaries, and Blood: Medicalization and Nation-Building on the U.S.-Mexico Border, 1910–1930," *Hispanic American Historical Review* 79:1 (1999): 41–43, 70–71. Letter from Dr. Tappan to surgeon general, July 12, 1924, RG 90, General Subject File, 1924–35, Domestic Stations, Texas, El Paso, box 248, file no. 950–56, National Archives and Records Administration, quoted in Fairchild, *Science at the Borders*, 153.
39. *El Paso Herald*, July 21, 1910, 9, quoted in Minna Stern, "Buildings, Boundaries, and Blood," 41. On the building explosion, see Minna Stern, "Buildings, Boundaries, and Blood," 53. Interview with José Cruz Burciaga by Oscar J. Martínez, tape 143, February 16, 1974, UTEP-IOH, quoted in Minna Stern, "Buildings, Boundaries, and Blood," 68–69. On Zyklon B, see David Dorado Romo, *Ringside Seat to a Revolution: An Underground Cultural History of El Paso and Juárez, 1893–1923* (El Paso: Cinco Puntos, 2005), 223, 40–243. On the bath certificate, see Minna Stern, "Buildings, Boundaries, and Blood," 69, 72.
40. On the bubonic and pneumonic plague outbreaks, see Molina, *Fit to Be Citizens?* 83–88. Quotation from "No More Pneumonic Cases," *Los Angeles Times*, November 8, 1924, A1–2, also partially quoted in Molina, *Fit to Be Citizens?* 84.
41. See Molina, *Fit to Be Citizens?* 126–27.

42. On sanitary officers' linking Mexicans to disease at the turn of the century, see Minna Stern, "Buildings, Boundaries, and Blood," 63–64. On associating Mexicans with tuberculosis, see Molina, *Fit to Be Citizens?* 133–36. Quotation from Molina, *Fit to Be Citizens?* 139.

43. On deportations during the 1930s, see Francisco E. Balderrama and Raymond Rodríguez, *Decade of Betrayal: Mexican Repatriation in the 1930s* (Albuquerque: University of New Mexico Press, 2006); and Fernando Saúl Alanís Enciso, *They Should Stay There: The Story of Mexican Migration and Repatriation during the Great Depression*, trans. Russ Davidson (Chapel Hill: University of North Carolina Press, 2017), originally published as *Que se queden allá: El gobierno de México y la repatriación de mexicanos en Estados Unidos (1934–1940)* (Tijuana: El Colegio de la Frontera Norte / San Luis Potosí: El Colegio San Luis and Fernando Saúl Alanís Enciso, 2007). On details of deportations based on sickness and seeking charity executed by the Los Angeles County Department of Charities, see Molina, *Fit to Be Citizens?* 136–41. Governor Ron DeSantis and the Florida state legislature recently passed FL SB 1718, which requires hospitals to check the legal status of patients and report costs of providing healthcare to "illegal aliens." See news release, "Governor Ron DeSantis Signs Strongest Anti-Illegal Immigration Legislation in the Country to Combat Biden's Border Crisis," *Ron DeSantis, 46th Governor of Florida* website, May 10, 2023, https://www.flgov.com/2023/05/10/governor-ron-desantis-signs-strongest-anti-illegal-immigration-legislation-in-the-country-to-combat-bidens-border-crisis/. On the growing list of deportable health conditions, see Molina, *Fit to Be Citizens?* 139.

44. Molina, *Fit to Be Citizens?* 141.

45. On the shift from inspections at Ellis Island to consular inspections, see Fairchild, *Science at the Borders*, 258–76. On fumigation at the border, see Natalia Molina, "Borders, Laborers, and Racialized Medicalization: Mexican Immigration and US Public Health Practices in the 20th Century," *American Journal of Public Health* 101.6 (2011): 1027–29. On current deportations via hospital visit, see Molina, "Borders, Laborers," 1029–30. See also Ethan Blue, *The Deportation Express: A History of America through Forced Removal* (Oakland: University of California Press, 2021).

46. For the current list of inadmissible diseases, see U.S. Citizenship and Immigration Services, "Chapter 6—Communicable Diseases of Public Health Significance," from its *Policy Manual*, https://www.uscis.gov/policy-manual/volume-8-part-b-chapter-6, accessed January 10, 2023. Note that HIV was taken off this list only in 2010. On reaction to the Ebola outbreak, see "2014–2016 Ebola Outbreak in West Africa," *Centers for Disease and Control and Prevention* website, https://www.cdc.gov/vhf/ebola/history/2014–2016-outbreak/index.html; Andrew Jerell Jones, "Ebola Fears Turn into an Epidemic of Racism and Hysteria," *Intercept*, October 21, 2014, https://theintercept.com/2014/10/21/cant-ebola-become-latest-racist-national-security-issue/. On reactions to Ebola exacerbated by the stigmatization of Black people, see Kevin J. A. Thomas, *Glo-*

*bal Epidemics, Local Implications: African Immigrants and the Ebola Crisis in Dallas*
(Baltimore: Johns Hopkins University Press, 2019); and Guy-Lucien S. Whembolua,
Donaldson Conserve, and Daudet Ilunga Tshiswaka, "Socio-cultural Factors Influenc-
ing the Ebola Virus Disease–related Stigma among African Immigrants in the United
States," *Ìrìnkèrindò: A Journal of African Migration*, December 2017, https://africami
gration.com/issue/dec2017/Whembolua_Conserve_Tshiswaka_issue_9.pd.

47. Jeremiah Jacques, "The Wuhan Coronavirus and the Bible's Prophesied Disease
Pandemics," *Trumpet*, January 30, 2020, https://www.thetrumpet.com/21859-the-
wuhan-coronavirus-and-the-bibles-prophesied-disease-pandemics. Of course, just as
many articles appeared debunking these claims, demonstrating the beliefs, questions, and fears of many congregants and readers. See, for example, Geoff McMas-
ter, "Why Some People Think COVID-19 Heralds the Apocalypse," *Folio*, April 24,
2020, https://www.folio.ca/why-some-people-think-covid-19-heralds-the-apocalypse;
Travis Bohlinger, "COVID-19 and the Mark of the Beast," *Logos Academic Blog*,
May 9, 2020, https://academic.logos.com/covid-19-and-the-mark-of-the-beast; and
Jim Denison, "COVID-19 Is Not God's Judgment," *Christianity Today*, April 21,
2020, https://www.christianitytoday.com/ct/2020/april-web-only/covid-19-is-not-
gods-judgment.html. Quotation from Stephen D. Moore, "Beastly Boasts and
Apocalyptic Affects: Reading Revelation in a Time of Trump and a Time of
Plague," *Religions* 11 (2020): 2.

48. On the Trump White House downplaying the threat of COVID, see Juana Sum-
mers, "Timeline: How Trump Has Downplayed the Coronavirus Pandemic," *NPR*,
October 2, 2020, https://www.npr.org/sections/latest-updates-trump-covid-19-
results/2020/10/02/919432383/how-trump-has-downplayed-the-coronavirus-pan-
demic. Quotation from Donald J. Trump, Twitter post, May 3, 2020, 10:43 a.m.,
accessible at *Trump Twitter Archive v2*, https://www.thetrumparchive.com/, quoted
in Moore, "Beastly Boasts and Apocalyptic Affects," 1.

49. Ronald Reagan, "Farewell Address to the Nation," January 11, 1989, Ronald Reagan
Presidential Library and Museum, https://www.reaganlibrary.gov/archives/speech/
farewell-address-nation; Alan Fram and Jonathan Lemire, "Trump: Why Allow Immigrants from Shithole Countries?" *AP News*, January 12, 2018, https://apnews.com/
article/immigration-north-america-donald-trump-ap-top-news-international-
news-fdda2ffob877416c8ae1c1a77a3cc425.

50. On hate crimes, see Stop AAPI Hate, *Two Years and Thousands of Voices: What
Community-Generated Data Tells Us about Anti-AAPI Hate*, July 20, 2022, https://
stopaapihate.org/wp-content/uploads/2022/07/Stop-AAPI-Hate-Year-2-Report.pdf.
On Trump's racist language, see David Nakamura, "With 'Kung Flu,' Trump
Sparks Backlash over Racist Language—and a Rallying Cry for Supporters," *Washington Post*, June 24, 2020, https://www.washingtonpost.com/politics/with-kung-flu-
trump-sparks-backlash-over-racist-language—and-a-rallying-cry-for-
supporters/2020/06/24/485d151e-b620-11ea-aca5-ebb63d27e1ff_story.html; John

Bowden, "Use of 'China Virus' Led to Spike in Anti-Asian Bias: Study," *The Hill*, September 9, 2020, https://thehill.com/homenews/news/518806-use-of-china-virus-led-to-spike-in-anti-asian-bias-study; and Elizabeth Dwoskin, "When Trump Gets Coronavirus, Chinese Americans Pay the Price," *Washington Post*, October 9, 2020, https://www.washingtonpost.com/technology/2020/10/09/twitter-asian-americans-discrimination.

51. On travel restrictions, see Michael Corkey and Annie Karni, "Trump Administration Restricts Travel into U.S. from China," *New York Times*, January 31, 2020, https://www.nytimes.com/2020/01/31/business/china-travel-coronavirus.html. On Title 42, see 42 U.S. Code § 265—Suspension of entries and imports from designated places to prevent spread of communicable diseases (July 1, 1944, ch. 373, title III, § 362, 58 Stat. 704), accessible at Legal Information Institute, Cornell Law School, https://www.law.cornell.edu/uscode/text/42/265. Ted Cruz, "South Texas COVID Rates Are Rising Because of the Biden-Harris Border Crisis," July 14, 2021, accessible at Ted Cruz U.S. Senator for Texas, Newsroom: Press Releases, https://www.cruz.senate.gov/newsroom/press-releases/sen-cruz-south-texas-covid-rates-are-rising-because-of-the-biden-harris-border-crisis.

52. On lack of evidence linking immigrants to the COVID surge, see Tara Subramaniam and Holmes Lybrand, "Fact-Checking Claims That Migrants on the Southern Border Are to Blame for COVID Surge," *CNN*, August 10, 2021, https://www.cnn.com/2021/08/10/politics/desantis-border-covid-fact-check/index.html. On American linking of COVID with immigrants and tourists, see Liz Hamel, Lunna Lopes, Grace Sparks, et al., "Kaiser Family Foundation COVID-19 Vaccine Monitor: September 2021," *Kaiser Family Foundation*, September 28, 2021, https://www.kff.org/coronavirus-covid-19/poll-finding/kff-covid-19-vaccine-monitor-september-2021. On deportations to Colombia, see Camilo Montoya-Galvez, "U.S. Launches Deportation Operation to Colombia Using Title 42 Border Rule," *CBS News*, March 24, 2022, https://www.cbsnews.com/news/immigration-title-42-colombia-deportations-us-mexico-border.

53. See, for example, Minna Stern, "Buildings, Boundaries, and Blood," 70: "The border quarantine is significant for several reasons. It helped to solidify a boundary line that had previously been much more indistinct. In so doing, it helped to racialize inhabitants of Mexico as *Mexicans* and to demarcate northern Mexico as a distinct geographical entity, despite its topographic and climatic similarity to southern Texas."

## Chapter 5. The Book of Life and the Book of Deeds in American Immigration and Naturalization

Epigraph 2: Cotton Mather, *Unum Necessarium Awakenings for the Unregenerate* (Boston: B. H. [Benjamin Harris] for Duncan Campbell, 1693), 107–8.

1. On Revelation and phenomena of spectacle in the ancient world, see Christopher A. Frilingos, *Spectacles of Empire: Monsters, Martyrs, and the Book of Revelation* (Philadelphia: University of Pennsylvania Press, 2004). On the "Hallelujah" chorus: Handel may even have composed the chorus in what may be called apocalyptic rapture, since it is related that, "being questioned as to his ideas and feelings when composing the Hallelujah Chorus, [Handel] replied in his imperfect English, 'I did think I did see all heaven before me, and the great God himself.' " Laetitia Matilda Hawkins, *Anecdotes, Biographical Sketches and Memoirs*, vol. 1 (London: Rivington, 1822), 197.

2. While this may be a final scene of resurrection after death, other resurrections are also mentioned in Revelation, for example at 6:11 and 20:4. That does not detract from the absolute language of the passage here, which emphasizes that *all* the dead are here judged, regardless. On standing in line: if entry into America as the New Jerusalem means not only immigration into but also realization of the "American dream," then white nativist outrage among poor populations toward arriving immigrants of color can also be understood as reacting to those they understand to be "cutting in line" ahead of them, when they had been "waiting patiently for their chance at the American dream." See Philip S. Gorski and Samuel L. Perry, *The Flag and the Cross: White Christian Nationalism and the Threat to American Democracy* (Oxford: Oxford University Press, 2022), 3–4.

3. The criterion of religious worship would more accurately be termed "Jewish Christian worship" if the text of Revelation is understood strictly within the historical context of the probable time of its writing (late first century CE). Here, however, I use "Christian worship" to account for its long history of interpretation through the centuries specifically as a *Christian* text. On the imbrication of race and religion, see especially Kathryn Gin Lum, *Heathen: Religion and Race in American History* (Cambridge, MA: Harvard University Press, 2022).

4. See A. H. Carpenter, "Naturalization in England and the American Colonies," *American Historical Review* 9.2 (1904), 290–91.

5. *The Statutes of the Realm*, vol. 1 (1810; repr., London: Dawsons of Pall Mall, 1963), 310. For the different possibilities of those residing in England as citizen, alien, or denizen, see Carpenter, "Naturalization in England and the American Colonies," 290–91.

6. *The Statutes of the Realm*, vol. 4, part 2 (1819; repr., London: Dawsons of Pall Mall, 1963), 1157, text somewhat modernized for ease of reading.

7. *The Statutes of the Realm*, vol. 7 (1820; repr., London: Dawsons of Pall Mall, 1963), 590.

8. On the wave of German immigrants in 1709, see Philip Otterness, "The 1709 Palatine Migration and the Formation of German Immigrant Identity in London and New York," *Pennsylvania History: A Journal of Mid-Atlantic Studies* 66 (1999): 8–23. *The Statutes of the Realm*, vol. 9 (1822; repr., London: Dawsons of Pall Mall,

1963), 63; see Carpenter, "Naturalization in England and the American Colonies," 292–93.

9. "The Plantation Act: The British Naturalization Act of 1740," in *U.S. Immigration and Naturalization Laws and Issues: A Documentary History*, ed. Michael Lemay and Elliott Robert Barkan (Westport, CT: Greenwood, 1999), 6–9. A subsequent bill in 1753 that allowed Jews to be naturalized by Parliament in Britain without taking the Lord's Supper caused an uproar and was repealed the next year. This did not, however, affect the 1740 act in regard to naturalization in the American colonies. See Jacob H. Hollander, "The Naturalization of Jews in the American Colonies under the Act of 1740," *Publications of the American Jewish Historical Society* 5 (1897): 106–9. For more on the 1753 "Jew Bill," see Dana Rabin, "The Jew Bill of 1753: Masculinity, Virility, and the Nation," *Eighteenth-Century Studies* 39.2 (Winter 2006): 157–71. I use "Old Testament" here to mean the first portion of the Christian Bible and not the Hebrew Bible. See Charles Egan, *The Status of the Jews in England from the Time of the Normans to the Reign of Her Majesty Queen Victoria* (London: J. Mallett, 1848), 177ff. There had been, of course, a long history of conflict between Protestants and Catholics in England, so that Catholics *were* more possibly a political threat.

10. Massachusetts Colony, *Acts and Resolves, Public and Private, of the Province of Massachusetts Bay, 1692–1786*, vol. 2. (Boston: Wright & Potter, 1869–74), 2:336; Thomas Cooper, *The Statutes at Large of South Carolina*, vol. 2 (Columbia, SC: A. S. Johnston, 1837), 131, 252; Letter of Governor Fletcher to the Lords of Trade, June 10, 1696, in *Documents Relative to the Colonial History of the State of New York*, vol. 4, ed. John Romeyn Brodhead (Albany: Weed, Parsons, 1854), 159; see also Carpenter, "Naturalization in England and the American Colonies," 297–303.

11. Province laws of Massachusetts from March 12, 1700, and June 29, 1722, regarding passenger lists; and April 2, 1731, regarding the naturalization of foreign Protestants from Massachusetts Colony, in *Acts and Resolves*, 1:244–53, 2:244–45, 2:586–87, quoted in LeMay and Barkan, *U.S. Immigration and Naturalization Laws and Issues*, 2–5; the office for keeping records was "the Office of the commissioners for Trade and Plantations kept in the City of London or Westminster," from section V of the Plantation Act, quoted in *Publications of the American Jewish Historical Society* 1 (1892): 98, also quoted in Lemay and Barkan, *U.S. Immigration and Naturalization Laws and Issues*, 9.

12. On visions of the Book of Life, see Douglas L. Winiarski, *Darkness Falls on the Land of Light: Experiencing Religious Awakenings in Eighteenth-Century New England* (Chapel Hill: University of North Carolina Press, 2017), 248–66; and Douglas L. Winiarski, "Souls Filled with Ravishing Transport: Heavenly Visions and the Radical Awakening in New England," *William and Mary Quarterly* 61.1 (January 2004): 3–46. On the vision from Hebron: Hebron is the town where Eleazar Wheelock, a minister, received the account, not necessarily where the vision took place.

See Winiarski, *Darkness Falls*, 250. The text of the manuscript is transcribed with original spelling and lack of punctuation in Winiarski, "Souls Filled with Ravishing Transport," 43–46. I've modernized the spelling and added appropriate punctuation for ease of reading here.

13. E. H. Gillett, ed., "Diary of Rev. Jacob Eliot," *Historical Magazine and Notes and Queries, concerning the Antiquities, History, and Biography of America*, 2nd ser., 5 (1869): 33, quoted in Winiarski, *Darkness Falls*, 253.

14. On the debate over these visions, see Winiarski, *Darkness Falls*, 258; "Extract of a Letter from a Gentleman of Unquestionable Veracity in Hopkinton, to His Friend in This Town, dated March 1, 1742," *Boston Evening-Post*, March 14, 1743.

15. For locations of visions outside of New England, see Winiarski, "Souls Filled with Ravishing Transport," 41; Richard J. Hooker, ed., *The Carolina Backcountry on the Eve of the Revolution: The Journal and Other Writings of Charles Woodmason, Anglican Itinerant* (Chapel Hill: University of North Carolina Press, 1953), 110.

16. See Winiarski, *Darkness Falls*, 265–66. On Puritan preoccupation with the "visible" versus "invisible" church, especially in the establishment of colonial governance and church purity in Massachusetts and Connecticut, see Michael P. Winship, *Godly Republicanism: Puritans, Pilgrims, and a City on a Hill* (Cambridge, MA: Harvard University Press, 2012), 198–205, 225–26.

17. "Extract of a Letter," emphasis in the original; Solomon Williams, *The More Excellent Way; or, The Ordinary Renewing and Sanctifying Graces of the Holy Spirit That Can be Coveted or Obtained by Men* (New London, CT: T. Green, 1742), ii.

18. Winiarski, *Darkness Falls*, 266; "To the Author of the *Weekly Post-Boy*," *Boston Post-Boy*, September 28, 1741, 3, quoted in Winiarski, *Darkness Falls*, 265; Samuel Cooke to Thomas Foxcroft, May 15, 1745, Thomas Foxcroft Correspondence, 1714–1759, Connecticut Historical Society, Hartford, quoted in Winiarski, *Darkness Falls*, 266.

19. Book of Life visions were also experienced about fifty years earlier during the Salem witch trials, but these were limited to only a few individuals. See Winiarski, *Darkness Falls*, 248–50.

20. For categorizing this book as a "book of action" (and not a book of life or book of deeds) that is handed to the Lamb at its "investiture," see Leslie Baynes, *The Heavenly Book Motif in Judeo-Christian Apocalypses, 200 BCE–200 CE*, Supplements to the *Journal for the Study of Judaism* 52 (Leiden: Brill 2012), 152–54. For more on this as an "investiture," see David E. Aune, *Revelation 1–5*, Word Biblical Commentary 52A (Dallas: Word Books, 1997), 336–38.

21. Giorgio Agamben, "Angelology and Bureaucracy," in *The Kingdom and the Glory: For a Theological Economy and Government* (Stanford: Stanford University Press, 2011), 158.

22. See TV Tropes, "Celestial Bureaucracy," https://tvtropes.org/pmwiki/pmwiki.php/Main/CelestialBureaucracy, accessed March 14, 2023. Ancient examples of celestial

bureaucracy include Seneca's *Apocolocyntosis* and Lucian's *Deorum conciliuim.* For more on *mysterium* and *ministerium* and their conflation in early Christian texts (such as Jerome's) and in contemplation of the "economy of Christ" and the Trinity, see Agamben, "Angelology," 158–59.

23. Scholars agree that citizenship lists found throughout the ancient Mediterranean and Near East are a close historical parallel to Revelation's Book of Life. See Wolfram Hermann, "Das Buch des Lebens—Ein israelitisch-jüdisches Theologumenon," in *Jüdisches Glaubensfundamente,* BEATAJ 36 (Frankfurt: Peter Lang, 1994), 93–117; Hans-Georg Gradl, *Buch und Offenbarung: Medien und Medialität der Johannesapokalypse* (Freiburg: Herder, 2014), 365; Veronika Androsova, "The System of Heavenly Books in the Apocalypse of John: A Dialogue with Hans-Georg Gradl," in *New Perspectives on The Book of Revelation,* ed. Adela Yarbro Collins, Bibliotheca Ephemeridum Theologicarum Lovaniensium (Leuven: Peeters, 2017), 379–92; and Baynes, *Heavenly Book Motif,* 33. Related to citizenship lists, there is also evidence of census-taking in both biblical narratives (for example, Ex 30:11 and Luke 2:1) and other texts. Roman birth and manumission records were also kept as proof of one's citizenship, and military diplomas likewise proclaimed that one has served honorably in the Roman army and been rewarded with citizenship. For more on Roman *tabulae,* see Elizabeth A. Meyer, *Legitimacy and Law in the Roman World:* Tabulae *in Roman Belief and Practice* (Cambridge: Cambridge University Press, 2004).

24. Baynes, *Heavenly Book Motif,* 35. In ancient literary works, the Book of Life appears in several different genres, for example, in Psalm 69:28, where the psalmist wishes his enemies would be "blotted from the book of the living." The otherworldly book also appears with roughly the same characteristics as in Revelation—as a list of names of those who are righteous or who worship God faithfully—in Second Temple literature, such as *Jubilees, Joseph and Asenath,* and in the Dead Sea Scrolls. And the Book of Life appears consistently in apocalyptic literature, for example, in Daniel 12:1, which states, "But at that time [God's] people shall be delivered, everyone who is found written in the book." See Baynes, *Heavenly Book Motif,* 65–84, 137–67. For a handy list of references to heavenly books in the ancient world, see Shalom M. Paul, "Heavenly Tablets and the Book of Life," JANES 5 (1973): 345–54.

25. On Book of Deeds comparanda, see Baynes, *Heavenly Book Motif,* 58–59; for more on military diplomas as proof for citizenship, see Anna Dolganov, "Documenting Roman Citizenship," in *Roman and Local Citizenship in the Long Second Century CE,* ed. Myles Lavan and Clifford Ando (Oxford: Oxford University Press, 2022), 185–228. Aeschylus's quotation from Baynes, *Heavenly Book Motif,* 39.

26. Translation of 2 Baruch from R. H. Charles, *The Apocrypha and Pseudepigrapha of the Old Testament in English* (Oxford: Oxford University Press, 1913) 2:481–524. On the Book of Deeds in Second Temple literature, see Baynes, *Heavenly Book Motif,* 85–105.

27. On theological debate about these contradictory books, see, for example, Alexandra Pârvan, "Revelation 20:12–15: Augustine on the 'Book of Life,' and the conflicting picture of predestination in *De civitate dei* 20,14–15," *Zeitschrift für Antikes Christentum* 21.3 (2017): 472–95. Modern biblical scholars also debate the theological import of these books in terms of fate and free will. See Baynes, *Heavenly Book Motif*, 147 n. 27.

28. John Belton, ed., *The Negro Law of South Carolina* (Columbia, SC: John G. Bowman, 1848).

29. The first record of Native peoples naturalizing as U.S. citizens dates to 1831, after the Choctaw Nation signed the Treaty at Dancing Rabbit Creek, which, on the condition that they ceded their native homeland, promised citizenship to Choctaw who did not remove from the land, took a land allotment, and remained there for five years. See Ronald N. Satz, "The Mississippi Choctaw: From the Removal Treaty to the Federal Agency," in *After Removal: The Choctaw in Mississippi*, ed. Samuel J. Wells and Roseanna Tubby (Jackson: University Press of Mississippi and Choctaw Heritage, 1986), 3–32; see also chapter 7.

30. *The Fundamental Constitutions of Carolina* (1669; repr., Boston: Directors of the Old South Work, 1906), §107; emphasis in the original. For more on the Constitutions, see Vicki Hsueh, "Giving Orders: Theory and Practice in the Fundamental Constitutions of Carolina," *Journal of the History of Ideas* 63.3 (July 2002): 425–46.

31. Tisa Wenger, *Religious Freedom: The Contested History of an American Ideal* (Chapel Hill: University of North Carolina Press, 2017), 7. See also Rebecca Anne Goetz, *The Baptism of Early Virginia: How Christianity Created Race* (Baltimore: Johns Hopkins University Press, 2012).

32. The separation of religion and race, however, does not follow a straight trajectory and the relationship between them shifted with political winds. The identification of Chinese as irredeemably "heathen" is an example of recourse to race-as-religion in the late nineteenth century. See Gin Lum, *Heathen*.

33. Cotton Mather, *The Negro Christianized: An Essay to Excite and Assist That Good Work, the Instruction of Negro Servants in Christianity* (Boston: B. Green, 1706), 12; emphasis in the original.

34. Increase Mather, *A Discourse concerning the Glorious State of the Church on Earth under the New Jerusalem*, in *Increase Mather's "New Jerusalem": Millennialism in Late Seventeenth Century New England*, ed. Mason I. Lowance and David Watters (Worcester, MA: American Antiquarian Society, 1978), 389; emphasis added and spelling modernized; Mather, *A Discourse*, 390; Cotton Mather, *Unum Necessarium*, 109.

35. Cotton Mather, *The Negro Christianized*, 2.

36. See Travis Glasson, " 'Baptism doth not bestow Freedom': Missionary Anglicanism, Slavery, and the Yorke-Talbot Opinion, 1701–30," *William and Mary Quarterly* 67.2 (April 2010): 279–318.

## Chapter 6. The Book of White Life

Epigraph 2: My translation of the Greek text from Montague Rhodes James, *The Testament of Abraham: The Greek Text Now First Edited with an Introduction and Notes*, Texts and Studies (Cambridge: Cambridge University Press, 1892).

1. 1st Cong., 2nd sess., February 3, 1789, *The Debates and Proceedings in the Congress of the United States*, vol. 1 (Washington, DC: Gales & Seaton, 1834–56), 1152, 1156.

2. 1st Cong., *Debates and Proceedings*, 1149–50, 1148–49.

3. Juan Bautista Alberdi, *Escritos póstumos de J. B. Alberdi: América*, vol. 3 (Buenos Aires: Imp. Cruz Hermanos, 1899), 266; Armando García González, Raquel Álvarez Peláez, and Consuelo Naranjo Orovio, *En busca de la raza perfecta: Eugenesia e higiene en Cuba (1898–1958)* (Madrid: Consejo Superior de Investigaciones Científicas, 1999), 478; both quotations from and translated by David Scott FitzGerald and David Cook-Marín, *Culling the Masses: The Democratic Origins of Racist Immigration Policy in the Americas* (Cambridge, MA: Harvard University Press, 2014), 1. Of course, beyond shaping population, immigration policy also serves as a tool and weapon of foreign policy.

4. The Naturalization Act of 1798 extended mandatory residency to fourteen years, a move by the Federalist Party to block the naturalization of citizens who would vote against them. The act was repealed by the Naturalization Act of 1802, which returned the residency requirement to five years.

5. Anthony Marx, *Making Race and Nation: A Comparison of the United States, South Africa, and Brazil* (New York: Cambridge University Press, 1988), 5, quoted in Charles W. Mills, "Race and the Social Contract Tradition," *Social Identities* 6.4 (2000): 450.

6. Matthew Frye Jacobson, *Whiteness of a Different Color: European Immigrants and the Alchemy of Race* (Cambridge, MA: Harvard University Press, 1998), 21, 26, 42; emphasis in the original, quoted in Mills, "Race and the Social Contract," 457.

7. Mills, "Race and the Social Contract," 458; Benjamin R. Ringer, *We the People and Others: Duality and America's Treatment of Its Racial Others* (New York: Tavistock, 1983), 8.

8. For more on the 1803 ban on the "importation" of Black peoples and other related laws, see Gerald L. Neuman, "The Lost Century of American Immigration Law (1776–1875)," *Columbia Law Review* 93.8 (1993): 1869ff. On the content of citizenship as "belonging-based" or "rights-based," see Henry L. Chambers Jr., "Slavery, Free Blacks and Citizenship," *Rutgers Law Journal* 43 (2013): 488–97.

9. New Jersey changed its state constitution in 1807 so that it explicitly stated that only white men could vote. Connecticut followed suit in 1818, Pennsylvania in 1838, and many other northern states placed such restrictions on voting so that free Black people never constituted more than 1 percent of eligible voters. Jan Ellis Lewis, "Rethinking Women's Suffrage in New Jersey, 1776–1807," *Rutgers Law Review* 63.3

(2011): 1017–35; 1818 Constitution of the State of Connecticut, *CT.org*, article VIII, https://portal.ct.gov/SOTS/Register-Manual/Section-I/1818-Constitution-of-the-State-of-Connecticut; and PBS, "Raced-Based Legislation in the North (1807–1850)," *Africans in America*, https://www.pbs.org/wgbh/aia/part4/4p2957.html#:~:text=African%20Americans%20in%20the%20North,used%20to%20jus tify%20the%20institution, accessed July 1, 2023.

10. John Adams to Abigail Adams, April 14, 1776, in *Adams Family Correspondence*, ed. L. H. Butterfield (New York: Atheneum, 1963), 382–83, quoted in Lewis, "Rethinking Women's Suffrage," 1028.

11. "Legally white" could also be termed "white other," but my focus here is on the legal rights still accessible to the "white other." For more on the construction of hierarchies within the category of "white" in U.S. history, see Matthew Frye Jacobson, *Whiteness of a Different Color: European Immigrants and the Alchemy of Race* (Cambridge, MA: Harvard University Press, 1998). Other possible terms for this category include "white on arrival," used in Thomas A. Guglielmo, *White on Arrival: Italians, Race, Color, and Power in Chicago, 1890–1945* (Oxford: Oxford University Press, 2003); and "white by law," used in Ian F. Haney López, *White by Law: The Legal Construction of Race* (New York: New York University Press, 2006).

12. See, for example, the lynching of eleven Italian prisoners in New Orleans in 1891 and of a Jewish man in Atlanta in 1915, in Jacobson, *Whiteness of a Different Color*, 56–68.

13. Naturalization Act of 1795, quotation from January 29, 1795, 3rd Cong., sess. 2, chapter 20, p. 414, accessible at https://govtrackus.s3.amazonaws.com/legislink/pdf/stat/1/STATUTE-1-Pg414a.pdf. On "potentate," see David A. Gerber, *American Immigration: A Very Short History* (New York: Oxford, 2011), 21; on association of the Antichrist with the papacy, see Robert C. Fuller, *Naming the Antichrist: The History of an American Obsession* (New York: Oxford University Press, 1995), 60–67. Know Nothing quotation from *Boston Know Nothing*, May 6, 1854, quoted in Tyler Anbinder, *Nativism and Slavery: The Northern Know Nothings and the Politics of the 1850s* (New York: Oxford University Press, 1992), 110.

14. For quotations including "born again" as meaning Christian Protestant conversion in the eighteenth century (by Jonathan Edwards) and in the nineteenth (by Bennet Tyler), see David W. Kling, *A History of Christian Conversion* (New York: Oxford University Press, 2020), 378, 396, respectively. The doctrine of the "two swords" that declares powers both civic and religious belong ultimately to the pope can be traced back for centuries. See Patrick Stephen Healy, "Doctrine of the Two Swords," in *The Oxford Dictionary of the Middle Ages*, ed. Robert E. Bjork (Oxford: Oxford University Press, 2010), https://www.oxfordreference.com/view/10.1093/acref/9780198662624.001.0001/acref-9780198662624-e-5802.

15. For example, itinerant English preacher John Townsend writes in 1801, "That the papal hierarchy is *AntiChrist, the Beast, the Man of Sin* spoken of in Scriptures, has

been the standing opinion of the wisest and most celebrated Protestant divines in every age and in every country." John Townsend, *Hints on Sunday Schools, and Itinerant Preaching; in a Letter to the Bishop of Rochester* (London: n.p. 1801), 9, quoted in Andrew Robinson, "Identifying the Beast: Samuel Horsley and the Problem of Papal AntiChrist," *Journal of Ecclesiastical History* 43.4 (1992): 594. For this equation in the Middle Ages, see Stephen J. Nichols, "Prophecy Makes Strange Bedfellows: On the History of Identifying the Antichrist," *Journal of the Evangelical Theological Society* 44.1 (March 2001): 79–80.

16. Carlos Corella, oral interview with Rebecca Craver, February 5, 2003, *Bracero History Archive*, https://braceroarchive.org/items/show/37. On the gatekeepers: "Every single employee [at Rio Vista] was bilingual. The only non-bilingual personnel was the center manager, Mr. Rhodes, the assistant to the manager, Mr. Rucker, the chief of reception, Mr. Schaeffer, and the chief of contracting, Mr. McDonald, but their assistants were all Mexican American, all bilingual." From Corella, interview.

17. Amelia W. Williams and Eugene C. Barker, eds., *The Writings of Sam Houston, 1813–1863*, 8 vols. (Austin: University of Texas Press, 1938–43), 5, quoted in Paul Spickard, *Almost All Aliens: Immigration, Race, and Colonialism in American History and Identity* (New York: Routledge, 2007), 148; U.S. Congress, Senate, *The Congressional Globe*, 30th Cong., 1st sess. (1848), 98–99, quoted in Spickard, *Almost All Aliens*, 148.

18. Article XIV, Treaty of Dancing Rabbit Creek, September 27, 1830, Choctaw Nation of Oklahoma website, https://www.choctawnation.com/wp-content/uploads/2022/03/1830treaty-of-dancing-rabbit-creek.pdf.

19. Ronald N. Satz, "The Mississippi Choctaw: From Removal Treaty to the Federal Agency," in *After Removal: The Choctaw in Mississippi*, ed. Samuel J. Wells and Roseanna Tubby (Jackson: University Press of Mississippi and Choctaw Heritage, 1986), 5: "Secretary of War Eaton, who personally handled the negotiations in Mississippi, inserted several provisions in the final document not only to woo influential tribal leaders into signing away their tribal land but also to convince U.S. senators (who would be asked to ratify the treaty) and their colleagues in the House of Representatives (who would be asked to appropriate funds to execute it) that the document had not been forced upon the Choctaw and that it served the best interests of the 'beleaguered Indians' (in the phrase of some religious spokesmen and many anti-Jacksonites) as well as those of the United States."

20. On the refusal to grant citizenship to Native peoples at field offices, see Satz, "The Mississippi Choctaw," 7–13; Spickard, *Almost All Aliens*, 150–53; Molina, *How Race Is Made in America: Immigration, Citizenship, and the Historical Power of Racial Scripts* (Berkeley: University of California Press, 2014), 25–26; Manuel G. Gonzalez, *Mexicanos: A History of Mexicans in the United States* (Bloomington: Indiana University Press), 87. On the conditions by which a Native person could gain citizenship: the Dred Scott case allowed that "Indians" could naturalize if they forsook

tribal membership. The Fourteenth Amendment was ruled not to expand birth-right citizenship to Native Americans in 1870 by the Senate Judiciary Committee. The *Elk v. Wilkins* U.S. Supreme Court decision of 1884 and the Dawes Act of 1887 also restricted Native American paths to citizenship.

21. Spickard, *Almost All Aliens*, 150.

22. *In re Ricardo Rodríguez* 81 F. 337 (1897), 349, 354–55, accessible at *Case Law Access Project Harvard Law School* website https://cite.case.law/f/81/337/; Chief examiner in St. Louis, Missouri, to commissioner of immigration, on various cases, June 26, 1916; quoted in Molina, *How Race Is Made in America*, 47. For more on racialization of Mexicans in America, see Martha Menchaca, *Recovering History, Constructing Race: The Indian, Black, and White Roots of Mexican Americans* (Austin: University of Texas Press, 2002), 215–76.

23. See Mae M. Ngai, *Impossible Subjects: Illegal Aliens and the Making of Modern America* (Princeton: Princeton University Press, 2004), the magnum opus on the history of this phenomenon in U.S. immigration.

24. On the clearer definition of whiteness following the Treaty of Guadalupe Hidalgo, see Molina, *How Race Is Made in America*, 43–48. On the fifty-two lawsuits, see Ian Haney López, *White by Law: The Legal Construction of Race*, 10th ed. (New York: New York University Press, 2006), 35. On immigrant understanding of white identity as secure, see, for example, George A. Martinez, "Legal Construction of Race: Mexican-Americans and Whiteness," *Harvard Latino Law Review* 2 (1997): 321–48. On examples of continued Black disenfranchisement: this was the case regardless of the Enforcement Acts of 1870 and 1871, which were created to protect Black voters. Ku Klux Klan violence, Jim Crow laws, sundown towns, and multiple other forms of disenfranchisement abounded. See, for example, Everette Swinney, "Enforcing the Fifteenth Amendment, 1870–1877," *Journal of Southern History* 28.2 (1962): 202–18. Even in the present-day, post–civil rights era, violence and the disenfranchisement of Black people persist in similar but mutated forms. See, for one example of many, Michelle Alexander, *The New Jim Crow: Mass Incarceration in the Age of Colorblindness* (New York: New Press, 2012).

25. *Ozawa v. United States*, 260 U.S. 178 (1922), 197, 198; emphasis added.

26. *United States v. Bhagat Singh Thind*, 261 U.S. 204 (1923), 214–15.

27. *United States v. Bhagat Singh Thind*, 213–14.

28. For a history of the US Census, see Paul Schor, *Counting Americans: How the US Census Classified the Nation* (New York: Oxford University Press, 2017).

29. Ngai, *Impossible Subjects*, 26. These categories are riddled with conceptual problems; for example, the conceptualization of nationality "streams" continuing as discrete and countable from ancestor to descendants. See Ngai, *Impossible Subjects*, 27–37.

30. Joseph A. Hill, "The Problem of Determining the National Origin of the American People," address at the Social Science Conference, Hanover, NH, August 25, 1926, quoted in Ngai, *Impossible Subjects*, 26.

31. Ngai, *Impossible Subjects*, 26; emphasis added. See also 27–28 on how the National Origins Formula allotted countries in Asia (China, Japan, India, and Siam) a quota of one hundred that could be filled only by people who were otherwise eligible for citizenship, that is, by *non-Asians*. The three independent African nations (Ethiopia, Liberia, and South Africa) were allotted one hundred, and European colonial nations also received quotas, which de facto increased the quotas of European nations, particularly Belgium, France, and Great Britain.

32. On the reconceptualization of Mexicans as non-native and immigrants and, furthermore, illegal, see Molina, *How Race Is Made in America*, 53–67; and Ngai, *Impossible Subjects*, 60–61. Quotation from Ngai, *Impossible Subjects*, 71.

33. Molina, *How Race Is Made in America*, 59.

34. On the use of photographs beginning with the Page Act, see Anna Pegler-Gordon, *In Sight of America: Photography and the Development of U.S. Immigration Policy* (Berkeley: University of California Press, 2009), 24. On the fluctuation of enforcing documentation at the border, see Pegler-Gordon, *In Sight of America*, 17–18, 192–220.

35. On mass deportation during the 1930s, see Francisco E. Balderrama and Raymond Rodríguez, *Decade of Betrayal: Mexican Repatriation in the 1930s* (Albuquerque: University of New Mexico Press, 1995); Fernando Saúl Alanís Enciso, *They Should Stay There: The Story of Mexican Migration and Repatriation during the Great Depression*, trans. Russ Davidson (Chapel Hill: University of North Carolina Press, 2017); Ngai, *Impossible Subjects*, 56–90. On the rounding up of people to demand documentation, see for example, Ngai, *Impossible Subjects*, 73: "On February 26, [1931,] authorities raided *La Placita*, the plaza at the center of the Mexican *colonía* in downtown Los Angeles. Police and immigration officers raided the park at midday, lined up some four hundred people, and demanded to see passports or other evidence of legal entry and residence."

36. On the threat of deportation, see Molina, *How Race Is Made in America*, 91–111. On Operation Wetback, see Juan Ramon García, *Operation Wetback: The Mass Deportation of Mexican Undocumented Workers in 1954* (Westport, CT: Greenwood, 1980); Molina, *How Race Is Made in America*, 112–38. For more on the history of deportation, the development of deportation laws, and the network of deportation institutions linked by rail, see Daniel Kanstroom, *Deportation Nation: Outsiders in American History* (Cambridge, MA: Harvard University Press, 2007); and Ethan Blue, *The Deportation Express: A History of America through Forced Removal* (Berkeley: University of California Press, 2021), respectively.

37. On the status of Filipinos as "nationals," see Ngai, *Impossible Subjects*, 96–126. On the denial of veteran benefits to Filipino veterans, see Satoshi Nakano, "Nation, Nationalism and Citizenship in the Filipino World War II Veterans Equity Movement, 1945–1999," *Hitotsubashi Journal of Social Studies* 32.2 (2000): 33–53. On the Muslim Ban orders: the last iteration of these, Executive Order 13780 and its subsequent proclamations, was revoked by President Biden on January 20, 2021.

38. On the extreme reduction of numbers from Mexico, see Ngai, *Impossible Subjects*, 261. Quotation from Ngai, *Impossible Subjects*, 264.

39. Greg Abbott [@GregAbbott_TX], "I've announced a $50K reward for info on the criminal who killed 5 illegal immigrants Friday," Twitter, April 30, 2023, https://twitter.com/GregAbbott_TX/status/1652783731290013696; news release, "Governor Ron DeSantis Signs Strongest Anti-Illegal Immigration Legislation in the Country to Combat Biden's Border Crisis," May 10, 2023, *Ron DeSantis, 46th Governor of Florida*, https://flgov.com/2023/05/10/governor-ron-desantis-signs-strongest-anti-ille-gal-immigration-legislation-in-the-country-to-combat-bidens-border-crisis/. On the increase in ICE raids, see John Gramlich, "How Border Apprehensions, ICE Arrests and Deportations Have Changed under Trump," *Pew Research Center*, March 2, 2020, https://www.pewresearch.org/short-reads/2020/03/02/how-border-apprehen sions-ice-arrests-and-deportations-have-changed-under-trump/.

### Chapter 7. "Even Heaven Is Going to Have a Wall around It"

Epigraph 1: Thomas Bailey Aldrich, "The Unguarded Gates," *Atlantic Monthly*, July 1892, 57.

Epigraph 2: Ronald Reagan, Remarks at a White House Ceremony Celebrating the 207th Birthday of the United States Marine Corps, November 10, 1982, online at UC Santa Barbara, *The American Presidency Project*, https://www.presidency.ucsb. edu/documents/remarks-white-house-ceremony-celebrating-the-207th-birthday-the-united-states-marine-corps.

1. The border patrol really is a "brotherhood." Women make up around 5.5 percent of those uniformed in the U.S. Border Patrol. U.S. Customs and Border Patrol, "Recruitment and Retention of Women in Law Enforcement Positions," Fiscal Year 2020 Report to Congress, August 6, 2021, p. 6, on the Department of Homeland Security website, https://www.dhs.gov/sites/default/files/publications/cbp_-_recruit ment_and_retention_of_women_in_law_enforcement_positions.pdf.

2. Border Patrol Museum, "Centennial Commemorative Weapon," http://borderpa trolmuseum.com/bpcentennial/, accessed May 30, 2023. Only active, former, or retired Customs and Border Patrol agents or CBP-trained and/or CBP-employed persons can purchase the weapon. These are nicknamed the "Fearless 5%." See Erin Siegal McIntyre, "The Border Patrol's Fearless 5%," *Reveal*, a website of the Center for Investigative Reporting, May 13, 2023, https://revealnews.org/podcast/ border-patrol-sexual-misconduct/.

3. Edwin M. Reeves, interview by Robert H. Novak, June 25, 1974, Institute of Oral History, University of Texas, El Paso, quoted in Mae M. Ngai, *Impossible Subjects: Illegal Aliens and the Making of Modern America* (Princeton: Princeton University Press, 2004), 68. On the Border Patrol functioning as a criminal enforcement agency, see Ngai, *Impossible Subjects*, 69.

4. Labor Appropriations Act of 1924, Title IV, Department of Labor, accessible at Immigration History website, https://immigrationhistory.org/item/labor-appropriations-act-of-1924/. On Texas Rangers' violence against Mexicans, see Monica Muñoz Martinez, *The Injustice Never Leaves You: Anti-Mexican Violence in Texas* (Cambridge, MA: Harvard University Press, 2020).

5. On dismissed Rangers joining the Border Patrol, see Muñoz Martinez, *The Injustice Never Leaves You*, 215; Kelly Lytle Hernández, *Migra! A History of the U.S. Border Patrol* (Berkeley: University of California Press, 2010), 19–44.

6. Quotation from military journalist, brigadier general, and historian Samuel L. A. Marshall, as a young journalist in El Paso in 1922 (and not in the KKK), as quoted in Shawn Lay, *War, Revolution, and the Ku Klux Klan: A Study of Intolerance in a Border City* (El Paso: Texas Western Press of the University of Texas at El Paso, 1985), 111: "[The Klan] was in control, for instance, of the American Legion here. It was in control of the Masonic Lodge. It was in control of the National Guard. I had been an officer in the National Guard and practically every other member of the Guard was in the Klan." See also Greg Grandin, "The Border Patrol Has Been a Cult of Brutality since 1924," *Intercept*, January 12, 2019, https://theintercept.com/2019/01/12/border-patrol-history/.

7. On revenge by proxy, see Lytle Hernández, *Migra!*, 20. See also Clifford Alan Perkins, *Border Patrol: With the US Immigration Service on the Boundary, 1910–54* (El Paso: Texas Western Press of the University of Texas at El Paso, 1978), 102–3, on two border patrol officers who tied the feet of a man and repeatedly dunked him in the river until he "confessed." On charges of murder against the Border Patrol in the first six years, see U.S. Seventy-First Congress House Committee on Immigration and Naturalization, *Immigration Border Patrol: Statements of Hon. Harry E. Hull, Hon. George J. Harris January 15, 1930* (Washington, DC: United States Government Printing Office, 1930), 47. On vigilante killings, see Lytle Hernández, *Migra!* 57–65.

8. U.S. Seventy-First Congress House Committee on Immigration and Naturalization, *Immigration Border Patrol*, 28; emphasis added; excerpt of appropriation act approved March 3, 1925, H.R. 11753, in Committee on Immigration and Naturalization Report, 21.

9. Giorgio Agamben, *State of Exception*, trans. Kevin Attell (Chicago: University of Chicago Press, 2005). For the border as a space of exception, see Miguel Díaz-Barriga and Margaret E. Dorsey, *Fencing in Democracy: Border Walls, Necrocitizenship, and the Security State* (Durham, NC: Duke University Press, 2020).

10. For a summary timeline of fences and walls along the U.S.-Mexico border, see Greg Grandin, "How Not to Build a 'Great, Great, Wall': A Timeline of Border Fortification," *Truthout*, January 14, 2019, https://truthout.org/articles/how-not-to-build-a-great-great-wall-a-timeline-of-border-fortification/.

11. Cristina Beltrán, *Cruelty as Citizenship: How Migrant Suffering Sustains White Democracy* (Minneapolis: University of Minnesota Press, 2020), 3.

12. H.R. 1268, section 102, https://www.congress.gov/bill/109th-congress/house-bill/1268, accessed June 2, 2023. On the overruling of laws, see Díaz-Barriga and Dorsey, *Fencing in Democracy*, 8–11.

13. Jimmy Carter, Interview with the President, Remarks and a Question-and-Answer Session with Editors and News Directors, November 17, 1978, archived at *The American Presidency Project* website, https://www.presidency.ucsb.edu/documents/ interview-with-the-president-remarks-and-question-and-answer-session-with-editors- and-14; Richard Nixon, Remarks on Arrival at Puerto Vallarta, Mexico, August 20, 1970, archived at *The American Presidency Project* website, https://www.presidency. ucsb.edu/documents/remarks-arrival-puerto-vallarta-mexico; Franklin D. Roosevelt, Address at Dedication of International Bridge, Clayton, New York, August 18, 1938, archived at *The American Presidency Project* website, https://www.presidency.ucsb. edu/documents/address-dedication-international-bridge-clayton-new-york.

14. George W. Bush, Remarks to the Hispano Chamber of Commerce in Albu- querque, August 15, 2001, archived at *The American Presidency Project* website, https://www.presidency.ucsb.edu/documents/remarks-the-hispano-chamber-com- merce-albuquerque.

15. Maya Yang, "*Newsmax* Bans Lara Logan After QAnon-Tinged On-Air Tirade," *Guardian*, October 21, 2022, https://www.theguardian.com/media/2022/oct/21/news- max-lara-logan-qanon-conspiracy-theory.

16. Conservative Political Action Conference panel, "If Heaven Has a Gate, a Wall, and Extreme Vetting, Why Can't America?" February 25, 2017, video available on YouTube: https://www.youtube.com/watch?v=Nuc1H7Base4; Steve King [@SteveK ingIA], "Heaven has a wall, a gate and a strict immigration policy. Hell has open borders," Twitter, February 11, 2019, https://tinyurl.com/yjvzw7nh; Marjorie Taylor Greene, interview with Michael Voris at Church Militant, video available at Right Wing Watch, "Marjorie Taylor Greene Says 'Satan's Controlling the Church,'" vimeo, April 27, 2022, https://vimeo.com/703762288?embedded=true&source= vimeo_logo&owner=5657100; for Kiyan Michael's quotation, see Jim Saunders, " 'Heaven Has Borders': Florida Republicans Advance Controversial Immigration Bill," *Orlando Weekly*, May 3, 2023, https://www.orlandoweekly.com/news/heaven- has-borders-florida-republicans-advance-controversial-immigration-bill-34114012.

17. The other occurrences of "wall" (τεῖχος) of the New Testament occur in Acts 9:25 and 2 Corinthians 11:33, in which the Apostle Paul escapes through a window in the city wall; and Hebrews 11:30, in which the walls of Jericho fall (albeit in an act of conquest). In Ephesians 2:14, the word for "dividing wall" is μεσότοιχος, etymo- logically related to τεῖχος, used in Revelation 21. On the contrast between other New Testament passages and Revelation: this is not to imply that the labeling of people as unclean, dogs, "sexually immoral," idolators, or guilty of murder as a whole people is acceptable. The point is that the general ethos of forgiveness and subversive acceptance of those socially shunned in the Gospels and other books of

the New Testament (as well as in other, noncanonical early Christian texts) is definitely not that of the city of the New Jerusalem.

18. Frederick J. Turner, "The Significance of the Frontier in American History (1893)," American Historical Association website, https://www.historians.org/about-aha-and-membership/aha-history-and-archives/historical-archives/the-significance-of-the-frontier-in-american-history-(1893), concluding paragraph. For a brief account of Turner's reception, see Ann Fabian, "The Ragged Edge of History: Intellectuals and the American West," *Reviews in American History* 26.3 (1998): 575–80, and the book it reviews, Kerwin Lee Klein, *Frontiers of Historical Imagination: Narrating the European Conquest of Native America, 1890–1990* (Berkeley: University of California Press, 1997).

19. On the American frontier mentality and "gifts of free land," see Turner, "The Significance of the Frontier": "He would be a rash prophet who should assert that the expansive character of American life has now entirely ceased. Movement has been its dominant fact and, unless this training has no effect upon a people, the American energy will continually demand a wider field for its exercise. But never again will such gifts of free land offer themselves." See Greg Grandin, *The End of the Myth: From the Frontier to the Border Wall in the Mind of America* (New York: Metropolitan Books, 2019) for several pertinent discussions: on the social frontier under FDR: 175–76; on the frontier of individual freedom in the Reagan years: 217–18; on war: throughout.

20. Trump, Remarks Announcing Candidacy for President in New York City, June 16, 2015, archived at *The American Presidency Project* website, https://www.presidency.ucsb.edu/documents/remarks-announcing-candidacy-for-president-new-york-city; see discussion of Trump's statement "I will build a great, great wall" as marking the end of the pioneer myth in Grandin, *End of the Myth*, 2; quotation from Grandin, *End of the Myth*, 275.

21. Grandin, *End of the Myth*, 274.

22. "Read the Sermon Donald Trump Heard Before Becoming President," *Time*, January 20, 2023, https://time.com/4641208/donald-trump-robert-jeffress-st-john-episcopal-inauguration/.

23. For more on Nehemiah's political role as a cupbearer and possibly as a eunuch, see Edwin M. Yamauchi, "Was Nehemiah the Cupbearer a Eunuch?" *Zeitschirft für die alttestamenliche Wissenschaft* 92.1 (1980): 132–42.

24. Interview with Christian Broadcasting Network, quoted by William Cummings, " 'A WALL is a WALL!' Trump Declares. But His Definition Has Shifted a Lot over Time," *USA Today*, January 31, 2019, https://www.usatoday.com/story/news/politics/onpolitics/2019/01/08/trump-wall-concept-timeline/2503855002/; New Hampshire campaign speech, quoted in Ian Schwartz, "Trump on Border: Maybe They'll Call It 'the Trump Wall,' " *RealClear Politics*, August 19, 2015, https://www.realclearpolitics.com/video/2015/08/19/trump_on_border_maybe_theyll_call_it_the_trump_wall.html.

25. Donald Trump [@realDonaldTrump], "We are no longer silent! We are energized & ready to take our country back. Let's Make America Great Again! https://t.co/u25yI5T7E8," *Twitter*, July 14, 2015; archived at *The American Presidency Project*, https://www.presidency.ucsb.edu/documents/tweets-july-14-2015. For contextualization of the ending of the book of Nehemiah in its ancient setting, see Pieter M. Venter, "The Dissolving of Marriages in Ezra 9–10 and Nehemiah 13 Revisited," *HTS Teologiese Studies* 74.4 (2018), https://doi.org/10.4102/hts.v74i4.4854.

26. Fox News Insider, "Rev. Jeffress on Dem Rep's Border Rant: 'Bible Says Even Heaven Is Gonna Have a Wall around It,' " YouTube, December 18, 2022, https://www.youtube.com/watch?v=hRmdwPuosxY.

27. Of course Revelation's New Jerusalem draws from other Jewish apocalyptic sources, including Ezekiel 40–48, especially the measurements and outlines in 48:16, 30–35; and Isaiah 54:11–12, 60, and 65:17–18. For a comparison of Revelation 21–22 and other Jewish texts of the Second Temple period, see Florentino García Martínez, "New Jerusalem at Qumran and in the New Testament," in *The Land of Israel in Bible, History, and Theology: Studies in Honour of Ed Noort*, Vetus Testamentum Supplements, vol. 124 (Leiden: Brill, 2009), 277–89; and Scott Chase, "The New Jerusalem: A Real and Imagined City in Late Second Temple Literature" (paper presented at the Ancient Judaism Regional Seminar, Princeton University, February 23, 2023).

28. On the height of the wall: a wall fifteen hundred miles tall would extend beyond the International Space Station and reach the exosphere, the very last layer of the Earth's atmosphere before space technically begins. See *NASA Space Place*, s.v. "exosphere," https://spaceplace.nasa.gov/exosphere/en/, accessed July 2, 2023. Perhaps the height given is not necessarily that of the wall, but it is not clear what else it might be. On 144 cubits as the thickness of the wall (rather than of another wall, only 144 cubits high), see Craig R. Koester, *Revelation: A New Translation with Introduction and Commentary* (New Haven: Yale University Press, 2014), 814.

29. On ancient square cities, see Koester, *Revelation*, 815–16. On architectural rhetoric, see Cynthia Frewen Wuellner, "Towards a Rhetoric of Architecture: A Framework for Understanding Cities" (PhD diss., University of Kansas, 2008), 1: "Similar to language, the built environment serves as a context that frames our sense of reality and privileges certain forms and omits others," https://kuscholarworks.ku.edu/bitstream/handle/1808/4428/FrewenWuellner_ku_0099D_10126_DATA_1.pdf. The walls could also communicate incarceration: what would it be like to live within these walls, never going outside them? For a more positive (and also confessional) interpretation of the architectural rhetoric of Revelation's New Jerusalem, see Külli Tõniste, "Measuring the Holy City: Architectural Rhetoric in Revelation 21:9–21," *Conversations with the Biblical World* 34 (2014): 269–93.

30. On Trump's claims about the length of the wall, see Elyse Samuels, "Fact-Checking Trump's Misleading Border 'Wall' Spin," *Washington Post*, October 11, 2019, https://

www.washingtonpost.com/politics/2019/10/11/fact-checking-trumps-misleading-border-wall-spin/. On varying wall heights, see Schwartz, "Trump on Border"; and Cummings, " 'A WALL is a WALL!' "

31. Lloyd Barba, "Trump's Wall: A Monument of (Un)Civil Religion?" *MAVCOR Journal* 3.1 (2019): §9, https://mavcor.yale.edu/mavcor-journal/trump-s-wall-monument-uncivil-religion.

32. See Kevin Quealy, "A Fence, Steel Slats or 'Whatever You Want to Call It': A Detailed Timeline of Trump's Words about the Wall," *New York Times*, February 13, 2019, https://www.nytimes.com/interactive/2019/02/13/upshot/detailed-timeline-trumps-words-border-wall.html.

33. On Trump's use of the word *beautiful*, see Christina Cauterucci, "Trump Wants to Make the Word 'Beautiful' Great Again. He's the One Who Ruined It," *Slate*, October 26, 2018, https://slate.com/news-and-politics/2018/10/trump-beautiful-handsome-banned-words.html. For the "I want it to be beautiful" speech, see Schwartz, "Trump on Border." For barbed wire comment, see "Trump: 'Barbed Wire Used Properly Can Be a Beautiful Sight,' " *Washington Post*, November 3, 2018, https://www.washingtonpost.com/video/politics/trump-barbed-wire-used-properly-can-be-a-beautiful-sight/2018/11/03/a40e475c-dfa3-11e8-8bac-bfe01fcdc3a6_video.html.

34. On the building of prototypes, see "CBP Completes Construction of Border Prototypes," U.S. Customs and Border Protection website, October 26, 2017, https://www.cbp.gov/newsroom/national-media-release/cbp-completes-construction-border-wall-prototypes. On "aesthetics," see Ronald D. Vitiello, quoted in Paul Koscak, "Construction Completed for Prototype Wall Designs," U.S. Customs and Border Protection website, n.d., https://www.cbp.gov/frontline/border-wall-prototype-designs, accessed June 9, 2023. On aesthetics evaluation, see Office of Acquisition, U.S. Customs and Border Protection, "Border Wall Mock-Up and Prototype Test Final Report," February 23, 2018, Document No: ENT12-BW-14–000004 Revision A, page 166,https://www.documentcloud.org/documents/4895718-Border-Wall-Mock-up-and-Prototype-Test-Final. Also cited in Ian Volner, *The Great Great Wall: Along the Borders of History from China to Mexico* (New York: Abrams, 2019), 197–98. On preserving the prototypes, see MAGA, *Prototypes*, https://www.border wallprototypes.org/, accessed June 9, 2023. On tours of the prototypes, see MAGA, "Tours," *Prototypes*, https://www.borderwallprototypes.org/tours, accessed June 9, 2023.

35. On the historical meaning of these stones in Israelite history, see Koester, *Revelation*, 817–19. On the lavish materials and ornamentation of the New Jerusalem and their possible domestication and democratization of the décor of the Roman elite, see Candida R. Moss and Liane M. Feldman, "The New Jerusalem: Wealth, Ancient Building Projects and Revelation 21–22," *New Testament Studies* 66 (2020): 351–66. On the inscriptions of the New Jerusalem, I disagree here with Koester, *Revelation*, 829, who differentiates between Greco-Roman inscriptions of the

names of emperors, rulers, and gods on public structures as "shap[ing] a city's identity and reflect[ing] its power structures," and the names of the tribes and apostles
on the New Jerusalem as "tell[ing] a different story" because they "name the leading figures in the history of the community to which John's readers belong." This is
a false dichotomy.

36. Editorial, "A Chance to Reset the Republican Race," *New York Times*, January 30,
    2016, quoted in Volner, *The Great Great Wall*, 136.

37. Modern jasper does not have the quality of clarity like crystal. But the description
    emphasizes the preciousness of the stone by comparison to an ancient stone called
    jasper (ἰάσπιδι), and the walls' clarity with reference to crystal (κρυσταλλίζοντι).
    Crystal is also mentioned in Revelation 4:6 and 22:1 in describing the sea of glass,
    "like crystal" (ὁμοία κρυστάλλῳ), and the water of the River of Life, "bright as
    crystal" (λαμπρὸν ὡς κρύσταλλον).

38. July 12, 2017, comments to reporters on Air Force One, quoted in Jacob Pramuk,
    "Trump Explains Why He Wants to Be Able to 'See Through' His Border Wall,
    *CNBC*, July 13, 2017, https://www.cnbc.com/2017/07/13/trump-explains-why-
    he-wants-to-be-able-to-see-through-his-border-wall.html; "Transcript of Donald
    Trump Interview with the *Wall Street Journal*," *Wall Street Journal*, January 11,
    2018 (updated January 14, 2018), https://www.wsj.com/articles/transcript-of-donald-
    trump-interview-with-the-wall-street-journal-1515715481.

39. Remarks on the border during the third presidential debate with Hillary Clinton,
    October 19, 2016, accessible at CNN, "Donald Trump: We Need to Get out 'Bad
    Hombres,' " YouTube, https://www.youtube.com/watch?v=AneeacsvNwU.

40. On Light Up the Border, see Patrick McDonnell, "Tactic of Lighting Up Border
    Raises Tensions," *Los Angeles Times*, May 26, 1990, https://www.latimes.com/
    archives/la-xpm-1990–05–26-mn-262-story.html. On stadium lighting, see Seth My-
    dans, "Clampdown at Border Is Hailed as Success," *New York Times*, September 28,
    1995, https://www.nytimes.com/1995/09/28/us/clampdown-at-border-is-hailed-as-
    success.html. On surveillance technology, see Mydans, "Clampdown," for technol-
    ogy used in Operation Gatekeeper and for recent innovations at the border, see
    Shirin Ghaffary, "The 'Smarter' Wall: How Drones, Sensors, and AI Are Patrolling
    the Border," *Vox*, February 7, 2020, https://www.vox.com/recode/2019/5/16/18511583/
    smart-border-wall-drones-sensors-ai.

41. On angels as guards, see Koester, *Revelation*, 814–15, who notes that ancient texts
    describe guards posted at the city of Jerusalem's gates and temple (1 Chr 23:5; 26:1–
    9; Neh 3:29; Isa 62:6); and these guards are later understood as angels (*Exod. Rab.*
    18:5; *Mart. Asc. Isa.* 10:17); likewise, cherubim guarded the way back into Eden
    (Gen 3:23). However, Koester does not believe that the angels at the gates of Reve-
    lation 21:12 are there as sentries "since the city descends after the devil and the
    wicked have been banished and evil no longer threatens." This ignores the incoher-
    ent chronology of apocalypse as well as the mention, after the lake of fire and the

descent of the city, that "nothing unclean will enter [the city]" in 21:27 and "Outside are the dogs and sorcerers" in 22:15. On "border angels," see Grandin, *End of the Myth*, 227–28. For more on Birchers, see Matthew Dallek, *Birchers: How the John Birch Society Radicalized the American Right* (New York: Basic Books, 2022). A new group of migrant *advocates* also call themselves Border Angels: see Salvador Rivera, "Advocates Condemn Dismantling of Migrant Camp in Tijuana," *Everything Lubbock*, February 8, 2022, https://www.everythinglubbock.com/border-report/advocates-condemn-dismantling-of-migrant-camp-in-tijuana/.

42. In the ancient context, the lighting of the city may also signify the luxury of living without lamps. See Moss and Feldman, "The New Jerusalem," 352: "The city is technologically superior to ordinary spaces; it is permanently lit with the glory of God, so that there is no need for lamps or even the sun."

43. Trump referred to immigrants as such in a meeting with state and local leaders from California, May 16, 2018. See Julie Hirschfeld Davis, "Trump Calls Some Unauthorized Immigrants 'Animals' in Rant," *New York Times*, May 16, 2018, https://www.nytimes.com/2018/05/16/us/politics/trump-undocumented-immigrants-animals.html.

44. Face the Nation, "Transcript from August 23, 2015: Trump, Christie & Cruz," *CBS News*, August 23, 2015, https://www.cbsnews.com/news/face-the-nation-transcripts-august-23-2015-trump-christie-cruz/.

45. Ronald Reagan, "Farewell Address to the Nation," January 11, 1989, Ronald Reagan Library and Museum online archive, https://www.reaganlibrary.gov/archives/speech/farewell-address-nation.

46. Up until George W. Bush, post 9/11, references by U.S. presidents to walls both literal and figurative were negative, especially around figurative walls preventing trade. See, for example, Richard Nixon, Remarks at Question-and-Answer Session with a 10-Member Panel of the Economic Club of Detroit, September 23, 1971, archived at *The American Presidency Project*, https://www.presidency.ucsb.edu/documents/remarks-question-and-answer-session-with-10-member-panel-the-economic-club-detroit; Jimmy Carter, Interview with the President, Remarks and a Question-and-Answer Session with a Group of Editors and News Directors, October 14, 1977, *The American Presidency Project*, https://www.presidency.ucsb.edu/documents/interview-with-the-president-remarks-and-question-and-answer-session-with-group-editors-3; William J. Clinton, Telephone Interview with Samuel Orozco of Radio Bilingue, November 2, 1998, *The American Presidency Project*, https://www.presidency.ucsb.edu/documents/telephone-interview-with-samuel-orozco-radio-bilingue.

47. Face the Nation, "Transcript from August 23, 2015"; Tom Homan, *Defend the Border and Save Lives: Solving Our Most Important Humanitarian and Security Crisis* (New York: Center Street, 2020), 244–45.

48. On "brain drain," see, for example, Harold M. Schmeck, "Asia Biggest Source of Brain Drain to U.S.," *New York Times,* January 13, 1973, https://www.nytimes.com/1973/01/13/archives/asia-biggest-source-of-brain-drain-to-us-many-here-for-years-8-per.html. SEC. 3, Section 203 amendment (a) (3), Public Law 89–236/H.R. 2580, October 3, 1965 (Immigration and Nationality Act of 1965), 913, accessible online at https://www.govinfo.gov/content/pkg/STATUTE-79/pdf/STATUTE-79-Pg911.pdf; SEC. 8, Section 207 amendment (b) (32), Immigration and Nationality Act of 1965, 917.

49. Contra Koester, *Revelation,* who understands "glory" as "worship," citing Revelation 4:9, 11, 5:12–13, 7:12, where glory is mentioned in the context of worship (that is, singing). These instances do not exclude wealth or tribute as a meaning of "glory" in Revelation 21:24, 26, and 5:12, where "wealth" appears as poetically symmetrical with "glory": "Worthy is the Lamb who was slain | to receive power and wealth and wisdom and might | and honor and glory and blessing!" Isaiah 60, from which Revelation borrows its description of the New Jerusalem, also mentions the wealth of nations, synonymous with "glory." For example, "Your gates shall always be open; day and night they shall not be shut, so that nations shall bring you their wealth, with their kings led in procession. . . . The glory of Lebanon shall come to you, the cypress, the plane, and the pine, to beautify the place of my sanctuary" (Isa 60:11, 13).

50. It could be argued that the kings of the earth are led as captives in a triumphal procession here, as they are in Isaiah 60:11, but there is no mention of that in Revelation 21. Additionally, parallel to Revelation 21:24, "The nations will walk by its light, and the kings of the earth will bring their glory into it" is 21:26: "People will bring into it the glory and the honor of the nations." These verses do not present subjugated captives. For an overview of the debate on the possible identities of the "kings of the earth" of Revelation, see Matthew Charles Baines, "The Identity and Fate of the Kings of the Earth in the Book of Revelation," *Reformed Theological Review* 75.2 (2016): 73–88.

51. Todd Miller, *Empire of Borders: The Expansion of the US Border around the World* (New York: Verso, 2019), 167–75.

52. On drug trafficking through sanctioned ports of entry, see Gustavo Solis, "Drug Smuggling, and the Endless Battle to Stop It," part of "The Wall" project, *USA Today,* 2021, https://www.usatoday.com/border-wall/story/drug-trafficking-smuggling-cartels-tunnels/559814001/. On the effectiveness of the border wall to prevent drug trafficking, see Nick Miroff, Scott Higham, Steven Rich, et al., "Cause of Death: Washington Faltered as Fentanyl Gripped America," *Washington Post,* December 12, 2022, https://www.washingtonpost.com/investigations/interactive/2022/dea-fentanyl-failure/; and Brian Mann, "Politicians Say They'll Stop Fentanyl Smugglers. Experts Say New Drug War Won't Work," WAMU.org, National Public Radio, February 2021, https://wamu.org/story/23/02/21/politicians-say-theyll-stop-fentanyl-

smugglers-experts-say-new-drug-war-wont-work/. David Shaw quotation from Solis, "Drug Smuggling." On the role of prescription opioids in the fentanyl crisis, see Richard J. Bonnie, Morgan A. Ford, and Jonathan K. Phillips, eds., *Pain Management and the Opioid Epidemic: Balancing Societal and Individual Benefits and Risks of Prescription Opioid Use*, A Consensus Study Report of the National Academies of Sciences, Engineering, Medicine (Washington, DC: National Academies Press, 2017), https://nap.nationalacademies.org/catalog/24781/pain-management-and-the-opioid-epidemic-balancing-societal-and-individual. On the percentage of smugglers who are U.S. citizens, see U.S. Sentencing Commission, "Quick Facts: Fentanyl Trafficking Offenses," USSC.gov, 2022, https://www.ussc.gov/sites/default/files/pdf/research-and-publications/quick-facts/Fentanyl_FY21.pdf; granular data available online at U.S. Sentencing Commission, "Commission Datafiles," USSC.gov, https://www.ussc.gov/research/datafiles/commission-datafiles#individual, accessed June 15, 2023.

53. On human trafficking victims and demand as coming from the United States, see Polaris, "Myths, Facts, and Statistics," *Polaris Project*, https://polarisproject.org/myths-facts-and-statistics/, accessed June 15, 2023. See also, for example, Kristina Davis, "Will a Border Wall Prevent Human Trafficking?" *San Diego Tribune*, February 17, 2019, https://www.sandiegouniontribune.com/news/public-safety/sd-me-human-trafficking-truth-20190217-story.html. On a case of human smuggling, see, for example, Dave Harmon and Uriel J. García, "U.S. Charges Driver and 3 Others in Deaths of 53 Migrants Found in Tractor-Trailer," *Texas Tribune*, June 29, 2022, https://www.texastribune.org/2022/06/29/san-antonio-migrant-smuggling-trailer/. On the actions of Governors DeSantis and Abbott, see Camilo Montoya-Galvez, "GOP Govs. Ron DeSantis, Greg Abbott Send Migrants to Martha's Vineyard and Vice President's Residence," *CBS News*, September 16, 2022, https://www.cbsnews.com/news/ron-de-santis-flies-texas-florida-migrants-marthas-vineyard-kamala-harris-residence/; Andrew Atterbury and Gary Fineout, "DeSantis Readies More Migrant Flights as He Intensifies Fight with Biden," *Politico*, May 10, 2023, https://www.politico.com/news/2023/05/10/desantis-migrant-flights-00096216; see also Rebecca Falconer and Yacob Reyes, "Newsom Threatens DeSantis with Kidnapping Charges over Migrant Flights," *Axios*, June 6, 2023, https://www.axios.com/2023/06/06/california-florida-migrants-sacramento-newsom-desantis.

54. On the breaching of the wall, see Nick Miroff, "Trump's Border Wall Has Been Breached More Than 3,000 Times by Smugglers, CBP Records Show," *Washington Post*, March 2, 2022, https://www.washingtonpost.com/national-security/2022/03/02/trump-border-wall-breached/. On enforcing national borders without physical barriers, see Miller, *Empire of Borders*. Quotation from Greg Grandin, comment on Miller, *Empire of Borders*, back cover. On the proliferation of physical walls around the globe, see Díaz-Barriga and Dorsey, *Fencing in Democracy*, 7–8, listing over thirty different border walls that have been built since 1989.

55. See Abram Van Engen, *City on a Hill: A History of American Exceptionalism* (New Haven: Yale University Press, 2020), 284–85, on Trump's America First rhetoric as diametrically opposed to Reagan's American exceptionalism with regards to immigration.

56. On the recycling of rhetoric and materials, Harsha Walia, *Border and Rule: Global Migration, Capitalism, and the Rise of Racist Nationalism* (Chicago: Haymarket, 2021), 36–37, makes a related point about the recycling of these materials from different moments of American imperialism. On the recycled chain-link fencing, see Rachel St. John, *Line in the Sand: A History of the Western U.S.-Mexico Border* (Princeton: Princeton University Press, 2011), 204. On the severing of fingers, see Greg Grandin, "The Militarization of the Southern Border Is a Long-Standing American Tradition," *NACLA*, January 17, 2019, https://nacla.org/blog/2019/01/17/militarization-southern-border-long-standing-american-tradition. See also Randall H. McGuire, "Walls and Picket Fences: Rematerializing the US-Mexico Border in Ambos Nogales," *American Anthropologist* 115.3 (2013): 466–80.

## Conclusion

1. On continued construction of the wall under the Biden administration, see Colleen Long, "Biden Says He Had to Use Trump-Era Funds for the Border Wall," *Associated Press*, October 6, 2023, https://apnews.com/article/biden-us-mexico-border-wall-immigration-texas-f99fd10257292a898618236df3613979. Congresswoman Alexandra Ocasio-Cortez issued a statement regarding the environmental laws waived for construction. See "Rep. Ocasio-Cortez Urges Biden Administration to Reverse Decision on Border Wall," *Alexandria Ocasio-Cortez Representing New York's 14th District*, October 5, 2023, https://ocasio-cortez.house.gov/media/press-releases/rep-ocasio-cortez-urges-biden-administration-reverse-decision-border-wall. On a floating barrier, see Juliana Kim, "Texas Plans a Floating Barrier in the Rio Grande," *NPR*, June 9, 2023, https://www.npr.org/2023/06/09/1181244928/texas-floating-barrier-rio-grande.

2. On gradual slowing rate of increase in immigration, see, for example, Nicole Ward and Jeanne Batalova, "Frequently Requested Statistics on Immigrants and Immigration in the United States," *Online Journal of the Migration Policy Institute*, March 14, 2023, https://www.migrationpolicy.org/article/frequently-requested-statistics-immigrants-and-immigration-united-states; Anthony Knapp and Tiangeng Lu, "Net International Migration Return to Pre-COVID-19 Levels," US Census Bureau, December 22, 2022, https://www.census.gov/library/stories/2022/12/net-international-migration-returns-to-pre-pandemic-levels.html.

3. On immigration at the border after the lifting of Title 42, see Luke Barr, "Unlawful Southern Border Entries Down 70% from Record Highs since End of Title 42," *ABC News*, June 6, 2023, https://abcnews.go.com/Politics/unlawful-

southern-border-entries-70-record-highs-end/story?id=99868336; Elliot Spaga, "Fewer Venezuelan Arrivals Lead to Drop in Illegal Entries to US After Pandemic Asylum Limits," *AP News*, May 17, 2023, https://apnews.com/article/biden-title-42-immigration-asylum-mexico-47613011abce05267954a5c243b9a5fc.On low number of refugees, see Nicole Ward and Jeanne Batalova, "Refugees and Asylees in the United States," *Online Journal of the Migration Policy Institute*, June 15, 2023, https://www.migrationpolicy.org/article/refugees-and-asylees-united-states#refugee-admission-ceiling; and "U.S. Annual Refugee Resettlement Ceilings and Number of Refugees Admitted, 1980–Present," *Migration Policy Institute*, https://www.migrationpolicy.org/programs/data-hub/charts/us-refugee-resettlement, accessed June 20, 2023.

4. "Florida's Tough New Immigration Law Could Lead to Labor Shortage," *CBS News Miami*, June 6, 2023, https://www.cbsnews.com/miami/news/florida-tough-new-immigration-law-labor-shortage/; Vanessa Romo, "Why Florida's New Immigration Law Is Troubling Businesses and Workers Alike," *NPR*, May 30, 2023, https://www.npr.org/2023/05/30/1177657218/florida-anti-immigration-law-1718-desantis; Bill Conerly, "Drop in U.S. Immigration Further Tightens Labor Market," *Forbes*, April 28, 2022, https://www.forbes.com/sites/billconerly/2022/04/28/immigration-very-low-despite-border-controversy-contributing-to-tight-labor-market/?sh=2f45c1392e30.

5. On slowing population growth, see Ward and Batalova, "Frequently Requested Statistics": "The slowing growth of the immigrant population over the past few years is mirrored by the slowing growth of the overall U.S. population since 2015." On Americans wishing to leave the country, see Julie Ray and Neli Esipova, "Record Numbers of Americans Want to Leave the U.S.," *Gallup*, January 4, 2019, https://news.gallup.com/poll/245789/record-numbers-americans-leave.aspx; Andrew Van Dam, "Why Have Millions of Americans Moved to These Countries Instead?" *Washington Post*, December 23, 2022, https://www.washingtonpost.com/business/2022/12/23/american-emigrants/.

6. William H. Frey, "New Census Estimates Show a Tepid Rise in U.S. Population Growth, Buoyed by Immigration," *Brookings*, January 4, 2023, https://www.brookings.edu/research/new-census-estimates-show-a-tepid-rise-in-u-s-population-growth-buoyed-by-immigration/; Kai McNamee, "Migration Could Prevent a Looming Population Crisis. But There Are Catches," *NPR*, January 27, 2023, https://www.npr.org/2023/01/27/1151734308/immigration-economy-birth-rate-population; Matthew Yglesias, "Too Much of America Is Emptying Out. More Immigration Can Help," *Washington Post*, April 2, 2023, https://www.washingtonpost.com/business/2023/04/02/too-much-of-america-is-emptying-out-more-immigration-can-help/cdcf77b6-d150-11ed-ac8b-cd7da05168e9_story.html; Jerusalem Demsas, "The Economic Case for Letting in as Many Refugees as Possible," *Vox.com*, August 23, 2021, https://www.vox.com/22634047/afghanistan-refugees-tucker-carlson-housing-economy.

7. Greg Abbott [@GregAbbott_TX], "The Texas National Guard continues to build mile after mile of razor wire barrier, backed up by soldiers and law-enforcement, to prevent illegal immigrants from entering Texas. They have one goal—deny illegal entry into Texas," June 11, 2023, https://twitter.com/GregAbbott_TX/status/1667966483454885891. On numbers under Biden, see Julia Ainsley, "Biden Administration Says New Immigration Policy Has Slashed the Number of Migrants Who Can Claim Asylum at the Border," *NBC News*, June 20, 2023, https://www.nbcnews.com/politics/immigration/biden-admin-says-new-immigration-policy-slashed-number-migrants-rcna90261.

8. Office of Management and Budget press release, "Fact Sheet: President Biden's Budget Strengthens Border Security, Enhances Legal Pathways, and Provides Resources to Enforce Our Immigration Laws," The White House, March 9, 2023, https://www.whitehouse.gov/omb/briefing-room/2023/03/09/fact-sheet-president-bidens-budget-strengthens-border-security-enhances-legal-pathways-and-provides-resources-to-enforce-our-immigration-laws/.

9. "Why Don't Immigrants Apply for Citizenship? There Is No Line for Many Undocumented Immigrants," American Immigration Council, October 7, 2021, https://www.americanimmigrationcouncil.org/research/why-don%E2%80%99t-they-just-get-line; Miranda Dixon-Luinenburg, "America Has an Innovation Problem. The H-1B Visa Backlog Is Making It Worse," *Vox*, July 13, 2022, https://www.vox.com/future-perfect/23177446/immigrants-tech-companies-united-states-innovation-h1b-visas-immigration; Forrest Brown, "What Travel Warnings Do Other Nations Give Their Citizens about US Violence?" *CNN*, January 25, 2023, https://www.cnn.com/travel/article/travel-warnings-other-countries-us-violence/index.html. Furthermore, the NAACP has issued a travel advisory warning Black people, people of color, and LGBTQ+ people against travel to the state of Florida; see Press Statement, "NAACP Issues Travel Advisory in Florida," NAACP, May 20, 2023, https://naacp.org/articles/naacp-issues-travel-advisory-florida. Stephanie Ferguson, "Understanding America's Labor Shortage," US *Chamber of Commerce*, October 16, 2023, https://www.uschamber.com/workforce/understanding-americas-labor-shortage.

10. On the policies of family separation and subsequent events, see "Family Separation—A Timeline," Southern Poverty Law Center, March 23, 2022, https://www.splcenter.org/news/2022/03/23/family-separation-timeline. On the story behind the photograph, see Avi Selk, " 'I Wanted to Stop Her Crying': The Image of a Migrant Child That Broke a Photographer's Heart," *Washington Post*, June 18, 2018, https://www.washingtonpost.com/news/post-nation/wp/2018/06/18/i-wanted-to-stop-her-crying-the-image-of-a-migrant-child-that-broke-a-photographers-heart. On the effects of the photograph, see Laura M. Holson and Sandra E. Garcia, "She Became a Face of Family Separation at the Border. But She's Still with Her Mother," *New York Times*, June 22, 2018, https://www.nytimes.

com/2018/06/22/us/immigration-toddler-trump-media.html. Although the little girl was not separated from her mother—they were detained together—the emotions displayed across her face was certainly the same as those of thousands of children separated from their parents at the border.

11. On the chasing of Haitian migrants, see Bill Chappell, "U.S. Border Agents Chased Migrants on Horseback. A Photographer Explains What He Saw," *NPR*, September 21, 2021, https://www.npr.org/2021/09/21/1039230310/u-s-border-agents-haiti-migrants-horses-photographer-del-rio. On the challenge coins, see Jaclyn Diaz, "EBay Seller Says Coins Depicting Haitian Migrant Incident at Border May Be Sold Again," *NPR*, June 17, 2022, https://www.npr.org/2022/06/17/1105901312/ebay-seller-challenge-coins-border-patrol-horseback-haiti-migrants-mexico. See also Hamed Aleaziz, "Coins Depicting Border Patrol Agent Grabbing Haitian Migrant Trigger Investigation," *Los Angeles Times*, June 16, 2022, https://www.latimes.com/world-nation/story/2022-06-16/coins-border-patrol-haitian-immigrants. For a recent example of CBP violence, see Julia Ainsley, " 'What Happened to Ray?' Family of Native American Man Killed by Border Patrol in Arizona Wants to Know Why He Was Shot," *NBC News*, June 1, 2023, https://www.nbcnews.com/news/us-news/family-wants-know-why-border-patrol-agents-shot-ray-mattia-rcna87113.

12. Priscilla Alvarez, "US Customs and Border Protection Investigating an Unofficial Challenge Coin Depicting Haitian Migrant Incident," *CNN*, June 17, 2022, https://www.cnn.com/2022/06/16/politics/unofficial-challenge-coin-haitian-migrant-incident-investigation-cbp/index.html. For more on the CBP, see chapter 7.

13. Cristina Beltrán, *Cruelty as Citizenship: How Migrant Suffering Sustains White Democracy* (Minneapolis: University of Minneapolis, 2020), 23; emphasis added. See also, on the spectacle of punishment, Michel Foucault, *The Spectacle of the Scaffold* (London: Penguin, 2008).

14. Beltrán, *Cruelty as Citizenship*, 19.

15. On early Christian texts with hell tours, see Meghan R. Henning, *Hell Hath No Fury: Gender, Disability, and the Invention of Damned Bodies in Early Christian Literature* (New Haven: Yale University Press, 2021), 1–22. On theological debate over seeing suffering sinners from heaven, see Trevor C. Johnson, "Seeing Hell: Do the Saints in Heaven Behold the Sufferings of the Damned (And How Do They Respond)" (MA thesis, Reformed Theological Seminary, 2004).

16. Jonathan Edwards, "The Eternity of Hell Torments," in *The Wrath of Almighty God* (Morgan, PA: Soli Deo Gloria, 1996), 356–57, quoted in Johnson, "Seeing Hell," 13; on this as the reason for transparent walls, see Johnson, "Seeing Hell," 18.

17. On gun death rates, see Mike Stobbe, "Study: U.S. Gun Death Rates Hit Highest Levels in Decades," *AP News*, November 29, 2022, https://apnews.com/article/gun-violence-science-health-covid-mental-20f5e2cb5fb50ff747fe316fdc4db5c4. On increase in gun purchases, see Edward Helmore, "Gun Purchases Accelerated in the

US from 2020 to 2021, Study Reveals," *Guardian*, December 20, 2021, https://www.theguardian.com/us-news/2021/dec/20/us-gun-purchases-2020–2021-study.

18. On xenophobia and gun deaths: deaths here include suicide by guns, also linked to race, economics and, recently, the COVID pandemic, which is discussed below. See John Gramlich, "What the Data Says about Gun Deaths in the U.S.," *Pew Research Center*, April 26, 2023, https://www.pewresearch.org/short-reads/2023/04/26/what-the-data-says-about-gun-deaths-in-the-u-s/. On gun ownership tied to numbers of enslaved people, see Nicholas Buttrick and Jessica Mazen, "Historical Prevalence of Slavery Predicts Contemporary American Gun Ownership," *PNAS Nexus* 1.3 (2022), https://academic.oup.com/pnasnexus/article/1/3/pgac117/6656154. On racism and gun ownership, see Kerry O'Brien et al., "Racism, Gun Ownership and Gun Control: Biased Attitudes in US Whites May Influence Policy Decisions," *PLoS One* 8.10 (2013), https://www.ncbi.nlm.nih.gov/pmc/articles/PMC3815007/. On Black and Asian gun ownership for protection, see Curtis Bunn, "Why More Black People Are Looking for Safety in Gun Ownership," *NBC News*, June 14, 2022, https://www.nbcnews.com/news/nbcblk/black-people-are-looking-safety-gun-ownership-rcna32150; Tsu-Yin Wu, Hsing-Fang Hsieh, Chong Man Chow, et al., "Examining Racism and Firearm-Related Risks among Asian Americans in the United States during the COVID-19 Pandemic," *Preventative Medicine Reports*, June 2022, https://www.ncbi.nlm.nih.gov/pmc/articles/PMC9152798/.

19. Massachusetts Colony, *The Acts and Resolves, Public and Private, of the Province of Massachusetts Bay*, 2 vols. (Boston: Wright & Potter, 1869–74), 1:452; on blaming foreigners to the detriment of public health, see Michelle Falkenbach and Scott L. Greer, "Denial and Distraction: How the Populist Radical Right Responds to COVID-19," *International Journal of Health Management* 10.9 (2021): 578–80, https://www.ncbi.nlm.nih.gov/pmc/articles/PMC9278382/; Jill Colvin and Zeke Miller, "White House Eyes Travel from Mexico as Source of Virus Spike," *AP News*, June 11, 2020, https://apnews.com/article/virus-outbreak-latin-america-understanding-the-outbreak-politics-129cbe9e6320cd16ce3e845f29deocac; Zachary Cohen, Jennifer Hansler, Kylie Atwood, et al., "Trump Administration Begins Formal Withdrawal from World Health Organization," *CNN*, July 8, 2020, https://www.cnn.com/2020/07/07/politics/us-withdrawing-world-health-organization/index.html; Lawrence O. Gostin, Harold Hongju Koh, Michelle Williams, et al., "US Withdrawal from WHO Is Unlawful and Threatens Global and US Health and Security," *Lancet*, 396.10247 (2020): 239–95; Joel Rose, "Some Republicans Blame Migrants for COVID-19 Surges. Doctors Say They're Scapegoating," *NPR*, August 10, 2021, https://www.npr.org/2021/08/10/1026178171/republicans-migrants-covid-19-surges.

20. Todd Miller with Nick Buxton and Mark Akkerman, *Global Climate Wall: How the World's Wealthiest Nations Prioritise Borders over Climate Action* (Amsterdam: Transnational Institute, 2021), https://www.tni.org/files/publication-downloads/

global-climate-wall-report-tni-web-resolution.pdf. The seven countries are the United States, Canada, the United Kingdom, Germany, France, Australia, and Japan.

21. Donald J. Trump [@realDonaldTrump], *Truth Social*, June 12, 2023, https://truthso cial.com/@realDonaldTrump/posts/110531998908318312; see also Aleks Phillips, "The One Word Used by Donald Trump That Has Sparked Conspiracy Theories," *Newsweek*, June 13, 2023, https://www.newsweek.com/donald-trump-truth-social-book-revelation-indictment-theory-1806208.

22. On crossing from Juárez into El Paso, from author's personal communication with local guide Rich Wright, El Paso and Ciudad Juárez border, May 30, 2023 (used with permission). On passports, see National Archives, "Passport Applications, 1795–1925," *National Archives and Records Administration*, online at https://www.archives.gov/files/research/naturalization/400-passports.pdf, accessed June 23, 2023. On first documents required: the Geary Act of 1892 required Chinese immigrants entering the country to register to obtain a document proving their legal entry. On the construction of the illegal alien, see Mae Ngai, *Impossible Subjects: Illegal Aliens and the Making of Modern America* (Princeton: Princeton University Press, 2004), 6: "Illegal alienage is not a natural or fixed condition but the product of positive law; it is contingent and at times unstable," and 10: "The concept of inalienable individual rights, central to European political philosophy, was shown to inhere not in human personage after all, but in the *citizen*, as rights were only meaningful as they were recognized and guaranteed by the nation-state."

# INDEX

Note: Page numbers in italics refer to figures.